RECIPES AND STORIES FROM SOUTHERN KITCHENS

EDITED BY

Johnathon Scott Barrett

FOREWORD BY MARY KAY ANDREWS

MERCER UNIVERSITY PRESS
MACON, GEORGIA

2017

Praise for *Cook & Tell*

Chef, raconteur, and old-school bon vivant Johnathon Scott Barrett celebrates the most glorious aspects of Southern life in his new book, *Cook & Tell*. Alongside poignant, hilarious tales of his own family table are guest authors with pet recipes, both heirloom and newbie; city and farm-fresh. The effect is like sitting on the porch of an old hotel and getting into a cornbread discussion that widens to a smoked mullet, pork belly, best-iced-tea debate, won not only on the merit of the recipe but the quality of the story-telling.

—Janis Owens
author of *American Ghost* and *The Cracker Kitchen*

Get a fabulous taste of food-driven life down South from a man who can cook and write. Here's a "mess" of a good read that's as sweet as a fried peach pie.

—Tom Poland
author of *Georgialina: A Southland as We Knew It* and
Solid Ground, a play for Georgia's Swamp Gravy Folk Theater

Johnathon Scott Barrett writes books for cooks, not for people who went to culinary school or command a kitchen. They are for the people who love to cook for friends and family, and understand the emotional connection we all have with food. Barrett understands how food can be memory and warmth and love. This book is filled with great recipes, but it's also full of life and humor and kindness, just like Grandma's kitchen.

—Celeste Headlee
host/executive producer of "On Second Thought," Georgia Public Broadcasting

What's the higher compliment—being called a great Southern writer or a great Southern cook? Johnathon Scott Barrett is both, which is upsetting to those of us who are only one of those things. *Cook & Tell* is a high-calorie romp through the kitchen of memory. I ate it up. You will, too.

—Harrison Scott Key
author of *The World's Largest Man* and recipient of the 2016 Thurber Prize for American Humor

Recalling a summertime shelling of black-eyed peas in a porch swing. Getting to the top of a 10-foot ladder to reach Brown Turkey Figs to make preserves. Mulling down a pot of just-caught catfish with potatoes, tomatoes, and onions for two hours. Frying pies stuffed with Georgia peaches in a black-iron skillet. These are some of the scenes from *Cook & Tell*, Johnathon Scott Barrett's endearing collection of food-centered stories and recipes from around the South. With a bowl of curried cocktail pecans on your kitchen counter, you'll be frying corn in bacon grease and topping banana pudding with meringue just like the best cooks in the South, no matter where you grew up.

—Fred W. Sauceman
author of *The Proffitts of Ridgewood* and editor of the book series *Food and the American South*

I'll bet you a hot ham biscuit with redeye gravy that Johnathon Scott Barrett's fabulous collection of tales and tables will soon be joining your shelf of well-worn favorites!

—Cassandra King, author of *The Sunday Wife*

A certified Southern gentleman and an engaging storyteller, Johnathon Scott Barrett has woven together a wonderful collection of not only recipes, but the stories behind them. *Cook and Tell* is more than a cookbook: it is a collection of heart-warming and funny essays. Just like the wonderful food featured in this anthology, the stories are to be savored from one chapter to the next.

—Michael Morris
award-winning author of *Slow Way Home, Man in the Blue Moon,* and *Wiregrass*

Join Johnathon Scott Barrett on this virtual front porch, as his friends drop by to share their stories and recipes with you. You'll laugh, you'll cry, and you'll feel cathartically nostalgic. Make a tall pitcher of iced tea, indulge your palate with the recipes in this book, and feed your soul with these stories from the heart.

—Sandra A. Gutierrez
award-winning author of *Empanadas: The Hand-Held Pies of Latin America* and
The New Southern-Latino Table

Johnathon Scott Barrett captures the subtle essence of outstanding Southern cultural cooking. Readers will enjoy these recipes along with his sensitive narratives on life in the South. He is a charming storyteller who combines the distinctive Southern cadence of memories and stories of home and loved ones swapped across the dinner table with delicious Southern recipes. You get generous servings of each and both are delicious.

—Pat Branning
editor-in-chief of *Shrimp, Collards & Grits: Lifestyle of the Coastal South*

Cook & Tell brings together those two things that are irresistible to Southerners —home cooking and storytelling. Johnathon Scott Barrett's work is a cookbook you can read, and a collection of stories you can cook from.

—Nicki Pendleton Wood
author of *Southern Cooking for Company, All-New Square Foot Gardening Cookbook,* and
Seductive Tables for Two

Cook & Tell is exactly as it sounds—a sharing of family and food history from Johnathon Scott Barrett, an exceptional author and son of the South, whose love of his land shows through every word he writes. If you want to know Southern foodways from real family stories, this is the book to read.

—Linda Rogers Weiss
author of *Memories from Home* and *Seasoned in the Kitchen,* and
former food editor at *South Carolina Home & Garden*

Cook & Tell is a collection of time-honored Southern recipes and stories curated and collected by native Georgian Johnathon Scott Barrett. Not only will you find delectable recipes for everything from Caramel Cake to Pimento Cheese, BBQ to Biscuits, but also a veritable slew of tantalizing tidbits and tales from a wide variety of Southern writers and authors.

—Virginia Willis
James Beard award-winning cookbook author and chef

MERCER UNIVERSITY PRESS

Endowed by

TOM WATSON BROWN
and
THE WATSON-BROWN FOUNDATION, INC.

MUP/ H938

© 2017 by Mercer University Press
Published by Mercer University Press
1501 Mercer University Drive
Macon, Georgia 31207
All rights reserved

First Edition

9 8 7 6 5 4 3 2 1

Books published by Mercer University Press are printed
on acid-free paper that meets the requirements of the
American National Standard for Information Sciences—
Permanence of Paper for Printed Library Materials.

Book design by Burt&Burt

ISBN 978-0-88146-622-5

Cataloging-in-Publication Data is available from the Library of Congress

With Amy, Myrtle Beach, 1998

Cook & Tell is dedicated in loving memory
to Amy Allyn Swann (1963–2016).
That girl could cook up a storm and straight tell a story.
And while she was from the small town of Claxton, Georgia,
it seemed as if the whole world loved her.
She was a once-in-a-lifetime friend.

This series explores the central and profound role that food and foodways play in understanding the South's past, its present, and its future. Through a broad variety of academic disciplines, the series examines the region's culinary history, celebrates the glories of the Southern table, and analyzes the many influences that come together to define Southern food.

—Fred W. Sauceman, Series Editor

In the Series

The Proffitts of Ridgewood: An Appalachian Family's Life in Barbecue
Fred W. Sauceman

Cook & Tell: Recipes and Stories from Southern Kitchens
Johnathon Scott Barrett, Editor

When my first book, *Rise & Shine! A Southern Son's Treasury of Food, Family, and Friends* was published (Mercer University Press, September 2015) an extensive promotional tour was in order. During the course of that eight-state, forty-plus city tour, countless folks across the South at literary festivals, libraries, and lectures shared with me their thoughts; without fail, two recurrent themes were always brought into those conversations at each stop along the way.

The first was the commonalities readers found with my family and friends who populate *Rise & Shine!* Time and again people said that my recollections were so similar to their own memories of growing up in the South—such as a morning out picking peas or family picnics eaten while fishing along a creek bank. And countless folks shared that they'd only need to change out the names in the book for it to become their own memoir. Those bonds are both humbling and flattering.

The second thing that people continuously shared was how my recipes brought back memories and stories that they had not thought about in years. At one function, a lady hugged me and said "Johnathon, I have not tasted a lemon meringue pie like your Aunt Lil's since my Mama died more than thirty years ago. Thank you so much, honey, for sharing that recipe." She then went on to tell me about her mother, how she cooked, and what it was like to have dinner at her house on a Sunday. At another event, a man in his late eighties, crouched over a walker, regaled me with all sorts of stories about the food his

Helping my father blow out his birthday candles, August, 1968

family cooked on the homestead in the mountains of Virginia, including a hilarious aside about false teeth and fishing.

What was realized from the tour, and from the voluminous correspondence received since, is that *everyone* has warm and special memories tied to the food they love. I had known from an early age that any dish worth repeating has some interesting tidbit or tale that goes along with it. These readers reaffirmed this knowledge, and gave me a "calling" to write about it. Thus *Cook & Tell: Recipes and Stories from Southern Kitchens* was born. Hopefully you will enjoy reading this warm and delicious collection as much as I enjoyed putting it together.

Cheers, JSB

As he demonstrated with his first culinary memoir, *Rise & Shine*, Johnathon Barrett has a refined palate, a hunger for the next great Southern recipe, and a nose to discern the story behind family favorite recipes. This time around, with *Cook & Tell*, John has cast a wider net, drawing in disparate recipes and reminiscences from old friends and new acquaintances, whose most important common denominator is their love and appreciation for the dishes of their Southern hearts and homes. *Cook & Tell* will earn a treasured spot on bookshelves everywhere because, once again, John has proven his talent for tapping into our deeply rooted longing for one more taste of the beloved and familiar.

*Mary Kay at my home with a first edition
of her book, **Savannah Blues**.*

COOKING, TALKING, & ENJOYING LIFE IN DIXIE

Southerners are famous for many things: gracious manners, our sense of decorum, having a nose for good bourbon, persevering in the face of odds (think Reconstruction), raising the best hunting dogs in the US of A, providing some of the nation's most talented musicians (Ray Charles, Johnny Cash, Jessye Norman, Elvis, and Loretta Lynn to name just a handful), catching our trophy-sized bass found in cypress-rimmed lakes, and speaking with our soft, lulling, melodious accents. The list could go on and on, making people all over God's green earth envious of our culture and way of life. This attraction to the American South is such that folks, particularly from colder climes, flock here to live. We have more Yankees in Georgia now than when Sherman occupied Savannah, and this migration can be seen across Dixie from the Shenandoah down through the Sunshine State and over to the Texas Hill Country.

Yes, people love what we have in the land of magnolias and mint juleps, and while the attributes that make us desirable company are extensive, we are known universally for two main reasons: our ability to tell a good story, and the delicious and incredible food that is lovingly prepared in our own kitchens.

In oral histories, short stories, and novels, the American South holds a distinctive and unparalleled niche in our country's culture. With its emphasis on family and relationships, history and community, the Southern voice has such a strong sense of place that it is recognized across the globe. While I am not a historian and cannot explain why our region has produced so many acclaimed writers, I do know for a fact that people from the South—regardless of race or class—like to talk. And when we talk, we absolutely love to make our stories colorful, adventuresome, and interesting. We use adjectives to emphasize other adjectives, if necessary, just so the point we're trying to make can be as florid and descriptive as possible. From great storytellers come great writers, maybe?

I admit my own compulsion to "go on and on" about something when talking or writing, and this attribute was one of my biggest challenges when I started blogging. Experts told me that I should keep each blog to fewer than 500 words. Excuse me? I could not even tell you how to make a proper pitcher of iced tea in that short length of time. And take for example *Gone with the Wind*, which, when you really look at it, is a short story: a beautiful, pampered, and strong-willed Southern girl grows up to face adversity and learns a valuable life lesson. Margaret Mitchell, drawing on her generations of Dixie heritage, was able to embellish and enrich Scarlett O'Hara's tale until it reached a massive 1,037 pages—and then received a Pulitzer Prize for her innate penchant of descriptive narrative.

Further emphasizing my train of thought here is John Berendt, the famed best-selling author of *Midnight in the Garden of Good and Evil*. He made this observation about Southern writers at the Savannah Book Festival, and I paraphrase: "Most authors would write, 'Susan went to the closet to get her coat.' However, those from the South would relate, 'Susan walked through the impressive, oak-paneled entrance hall of her Tuxedo Road manse to the coat closet, where she retrieved a full-length black mink, a present from her third husband, Chandler Prescott Madison, on their tenth wedding anniversary.'"

Midnight, which the book is popularly called, was Mr. Berendt's first novel; published in 1994, it debuted as a *New York Times* bestseller and stayed on that iconic list for 216 weeks, the longest-standing bestseller on record for the newspaper. And while Mr. Berendt is a native New Yorker, he was recently quoted in an article for *Connect Savannah* as saying, "I have actually been referred to as a Southern writer. It's the highest form of compliment I could receive." There you go.

And Southern food, just like Southern writing, is without a doubt the most famous of any regional fare found in our great country. Not that New England isn't known for lobster rolls and maple syrup, or that TexMex isn't lauded to an extent. And I'll give you that you can't beat a piece of roasted, wild-caught salmon from the Pacific Northwest. But nowhere in the States is a cuisine so thoroughly defined, studied, and celebrated than "down South."

Starting at our most northern limits, the border states of Kentucky, with its vast array of bourbons, and Maryland, with its seafood and crab cakes, and then traveling into the Deep South and over to west of the Mississippi, you'll find an array of tastes and styles that have captured the attention of the food world for decades. There are even sub-categories that have evolved, such as the Gullah dishes of the South Carolina and Georgia Low Country, the Cajun and Creole traditions that exist in Louisiana, along with the pinto beans, apples, and cabbage found in Appalachia. Our food is, like our writing, expansive and detailed, colorful but maybe at times heavy, often sweet with sentiment, and then again something that can give a shudder in your gullet like a straight shot of stump liquor or a Big-Daddy sized helping of cayenne hot sauce.

Again, speaking as a layman and not an expert, I will put forth that this extensive palate of tastes comes about because of the vast melting pot that is the American South. We created fusion cuisine before there was a term for it. Here in our land of plenty, we first had the Native Americans, who were farming long before European settlers arrived. Their intercropping of corn, beans, and squash, called "The Three Sisters"—where the beans ran up the corn stalks to grow, and the squash gave shade on the garden floor, helping retain moisture and hinder weeds—provided a solid base for Southern food that is still used today. Just think of all the food we have on our tables from corn: cornbread, whiskey, hush puppies, and succotash, for example.

Then came Señor DeSoto from Spain, making his long foray into North America in the 1500s and dropping off pigs along his way through the Southeast. Where would we be today without bacon? To me it is almost a food group unto itself. The hog not only played a huge role in the culinary development of our part of the country but was also how Southerners literally survived in terms of protein and other nutrients. People, particularly through the hard times of Reconstruction and the Great Depression, would eat every bit of a pig, from the ears to the tail and from the brains to the feet; nothing was left to waste. The expression "eating high on the hog," which means that someone is living well, alludes to the fact that the best cuts of meat, such as the loin and chops, are found on a pig above the belly.

Then we had the Scotch-Irish, along with the Germans, who traversed the Great Wagon Road and settled throughout Appalachia, bringing their own food traditions, as did the English who poured into our coastal cities, and of course the French,

Even up North folks appreciate the food and stories from Dixie. This sign was posted in front of Mable's Restaurant, Brooklyn, NY, winter 2016

who were instrumental in the creation of Cajun and Creole cooking. Other ethnicities helped form our taste and palate as well, but arguably one of the most influential groups of people who shaped what was cooked in our kitchens were the Africans. These folks from such faraway places as present-day Senegal, Ivory Coast, Angola, and Ghana introduced a whole new array of delicious fare, including rice, okra, yams, and a variety of peas. And their influence did not stop at what have become household staples in the South. The African cooks went on to create a variety of dishes and traditions that helped firmly shape what is now known as Southern Cuisine.

In *Cook & Tell*, my wish is to showcase the intersection of the wonderful food created in our kitchens and the engaging stories that are then told in the dining rooms, paneled libraries, and front porches throughout the South. If you take a moment to speak to a Southern cook, he or she will inevitably have an aside that goes along with any particular dish or recipe. It might be a funny tidbit about Aunt Merriweather's penchant for drinking more sherry than she pours into her trifle, or maybe a sentimental piece about how a beloved son asked to have his Mama's fried pork chops each and every day before he left on his deployment overseas.

In these pages you'll find stories and dishes that have been a large part of my life, but you will also discover numerous chapters with recipes and related tales from cooks from across the South. Some of the people I have the privilege to highlight and share with you are well-known authors or chefs; others could be your best friends from down the street or your cousin who lives down in Fairhope. I do hope that, when you finish reading this cookbook, you'll feel like you've met a bevy of new friends, all good cooks and wonderful souls: folks who make up what is the wonderful, flavorful, and colorful place we call home. The South.

CHAPTER 1

HOW TO IRON
A SANDWICH

and

A GRANDMOTHER'S
GIFT OF FOOD

by Fred W. Sauceman

O ne of the most well-respected authorities on the history and art of Appalachian cooking is Fred Sauceman, a Senior Writer and Associate Professor at East Tennessee State University. He has been featured in countless magazine articles, newspaper columns, radio, and documentary films celebrating the people and foods that have been born, and continue to thrive, in this special part of the South. He has also written a number of books on the subject, four from this publisher, Mercer University Press. The dust jacket of his work *Buttermilk & Bible Burgers* tells us that "In his latest collection of writings about the foodways of the Appalachian region, Fred W. Sauceman guides readers through country kitchens and church fellowship halls, across pasture fields and into smokehouses, down rows of vegetable gardens at the peak of season, and alongside ponds resonant with the sounds of a summer night." Who wouldn't want to make one of those journeys with him?

I particularly enjoy Fred's authentic voice in telling about Southern food, and how he dispels those perceptions that we fry everything we eat and dispense lard like candy. In an article he wrote for the Smithsonian-hosted website *What It Means to Be an American*, titled "What Exactly Is Appalachian Cuisine?" (March 13, 2015), he shares,

> Appalachian food has been sustainable and organic for generations. We've been offering "farm-to-table" fare forever, without ever having to say so. Sit down to many farmhouse tables in the summertime and you might conclude that the family has embraced a vegetarian diet. Sliced tomatoes still warm from the sun, corn on the cob boiled and then bathed in butter, cucumber slices bobbing in ice water, and a "mess" of green beans consti-tute a common meal in my part of America.

Fred is also one of the nicest authors I've encountered since starting my venture into writing. Having never met me, he still agreed to review my first book, saying, "*Rise & Shine* is a family memoir, a culinary travelogue, and a rich collection of inherited and invented recipes." He is always quick to give praise and is known for his generosity of spirit.

The generosity is evident here, as Fred shares with us two stories from home. One is about the Southern, 1960s version of a panini—which is made with a unique "press"—and the other a warm and moving memory about "Grandmother food." After reading them, I imagine you will soon be heading to your local bookstore for more of Fred's magic in the printed word.

How to Iron a Sandwich

It was the pre-panini era. A time long before George Foreman started making grease-draining grills.

When I was growing up in the 1960s, my mother, Wanda Sauceman, made "iron" sandwiches. She said she got the idea either from a televi-sion program or out of the paper. This was long before our newspaper, **The Greeneville Sun**, *started carrying the "Rookie Cookie" recipes for children. They were, in actuality, simple cheese sandwiches, but calling them "iron" sandwiches carried more elementary school playground* cachet. Perhaps the practice has its beginnings in pioneer cookery, when flatirons were heated in a fireplace.

At our house, "iron" sandwiches began around the time of Permanent Press. My mother recalled the sandwiches ending up "flat as a flitter and not greasy at all."

I suppose you could take a highbrow approach with a French baguette, artisanal cheddar cheese, and homemade mayonnaise. But those elements would be at odds with the working-class profile of the sandwich. Wonder Bread, singles of Kraft American pasteurized prepared cheese product, and Miracle Whip make more sense.

"Have the iron on pretty high," my mother instructed. On our thirty-year-old GE, the "cotton" setting produces the right amount of heat.

Coat the insides of the bread with Miracle Whip and place one slice of cheese between the bread. Butter the outside if you want. I daub salted butter in five spots, like the pattern on a die.

"Use as little foil as possible," my mother advised. In other words, one layer only. If your foil is 12 inches wide, roll out 12 inches to make a square. Fold the ends over the sandwich just until they meet, then roll up the other ends to make handles to keep you from burning your fingers.

Place the hot iron on top of the sandwich and listen and smell. On our "cotton" setting, two minutes per side and the bread is browned.

"Heat it until it suits you," my mother said. "Check it, and if it's not brown enough, put the iron back on."

Is the memory better than the sandwich? Well, when I tested the recipe, I hadn't eaten an "iron" sandwich in probably forty years. I ate three.

—Fred W. Sauceman

A Grandmother's Gift of Food

Milk so cold it was crunchy with ice crystals. The interplay of popcorn and roasted peanuts. An angel food cake cooling in its pan and mounted on a Coke bottle, like a crown.

Fred's grandparent's, Edith Ethel Koontz Royall and William F. Royall

They are flavors from a lost world. Grandmother food. Of my maternal grandmother's kitchen handiwork, I remember only a few sit-down-at-the-table dishes.

What stands out more clearly is the little-boy food, the between-meal creations intended not so much to satisfy hunger as to please a grandson. My grandmother, Edith Ethel Koontz Royall, knew exactly the right temperature to ice the milk without freezing it. She knew just when to remove the popcorn popper from the heat so the peanuts were pleasantly parched, not scorched. She knew how to add just enough bread to stretch her hamburger meat into a pleasant, peppery softness.

Kitchen technique wasn't the only thing she mastered in her lifetime. Born on March 6, 1894, in Afton, Tennessee, she learned to drive a car in an era when not many rural women in her part of the country had the chance to pick up that skill. She worked outside the home as a telephone switchboard operator while her husband was protecting the Town of Greeneville as Night Chief of Police.

Despite their odd, sometimes out-of-synch schedules, they raised three children. My grandmother and my grandfather, William Franklin Royall, were night-and-day different. When it came to food, she had no hang-ups.

But he had a phobia of egg whites. Shaped by the Depression as she was, my grandmother turned his dislike into a sort of cottage industry. With my grandfather eating only the yolks of his eggs, she would collect the whites, bake angel food cakes, and sell them for a dollar each on the streets of their neighborhood in Greeneville in the 1930s.

Otherwise calm and quiet, my grandmother was a torrent in the kitchen. She was known for her monumental messes. She prepared the meals. She expected others to deal with the aftermath.

In her final years, her labors ended by strokes and a failing heart, kinfolks brought the food to her. March 6 meant coconut cake and boiled custard and the Wesley Blessing, its words etched into a family heirloom teapot.

Even though her own kitchen duty ended some six years before her death in 1971, my grandmother never lost interest in cooking. She was a faithful fan of Mary Starr, host of the Homemakers' Show on WATE-TV, channel 6, in Knoxville. In fact, when my grandmother recalled, verbatim, a Mary Starr potato soup recipe from the television show, we knew she had overcome her stroke.

To celebrate my grandmother's life, we stuff peppers. The ingredients hearken back to a Greene County farm from long ago: tomatoes, onions, whole-hog sausage, and leftover biscuits. The method reveals my grand-mother's wisdom and frugality. For its nutrients and flavor, she insisted, the water you boil the green peppers in must be saved. Despite the intervening years, it's a lesson in character and in cooking that I've never forgotten.

—Fred W. Sauceman

Grandmother Royall's Stuffed Peppers

INGREDIENTS

6 medium-sized green bell peppers

1, 14-ounce package stuffing mix or the equivalent amount of toasted left-over biscuits or cornbread

3 ears fresh corn, removed from the cob (or about 1½ cups frozen kernels)

2 tomatoes, chopped (about 2 cups)

1 onion, chopped (about 1 cup)

Season to taste with any combination of oregano, sage, chili powder, salt, and pepper

1 pound bulk sausage, fried, crumbled, and drained of grease

12 slices cheddar cheese

INSTRUCTIONS

1. Preheat oven to 350 degrees.

2. Slice off the top third of each pepper. Remove the seeds and trim the membranes; discard the seeds and white membranes.

3. Place hollowed-out peppers in a large pot of boiling water and parboil briefly, about 1 minute. Remove and drain well. Save the pepper water.

4. Mix stuffing or bread with corn, tomatoes, onion, seasonings, and sausage. Add enough pepper water to make a moist mixture.

5. Grease a large baking dish and pour a little pepper water in the bottom to cover about ¼ inch.

6. Stuff the peppers with the sausage filling and cover each with a slice of cheddar cheese. Tent the dish with foil and bake for about 35 minutes. Uncover and cook another 10 minutes so the cheese can brown slightly. Allow to cool for about 5 minutes before serving.

Serves 6

CHAPTER 2

THE MAGIC IN MARTHA'S KITCHEN

by Elizabeth Tornow Skeadas

f you look at a map of the South, you'll see that each state is dotted with small towns and rural communities, many of them only connected to their nearest neighbor by a state highway or county road. Many of these "stops in the road" have produced a number of famous chefs and cookbook authors—such as Craig Claiborne, born in the delta town of Sunflower, Mississippi; Janis Owens, who says that she "is of an ancient line (of Crackers) born in rural Florida when Destin was a shallow, nameless bay"; and John T. Edge, who grew up in the lower piedmont of Georgia in the tiny town of Clinton. But for every well-known chef who has emerged from these hamlets and agrarian centers and made our cuisine famous, there are countless other excellent cooks who tended only to their own kitchens back home. Elizabeth Skeadas tells of one such home chef, her mother, Mrs. Winston (Martha) Tornow, who performed her magic in the little sandhill town of Laurinburg, North Carolina.

Elizabeth married a Savannah boy and has now made the Hostess City of the South her home for the last several years. She brought with her Mrs. Tornow's incredible culinary skills and gracious ways, and has garnered her own reputation for being a magnificent cook. She is, by the way, a member of the Girls on the Grill Supper Club, the group that provided the catalyst for my first book, *Rise & Shine!* Elizabeth was actually present in my home the night I hosted their group, and she heard what were to be the first chapters of the food memoir. I'll always appreciate her encouragement and kind words while the book was coming to fruition.

In 2001, when Mrs. Tornow turned eighty-three, Elizabeth put together a spiral-bound collection of all the best of her Mom's recipes that their family had enjoyed over the decades. The recipes and stories therein tell, in true Southern tradition, how food and love are so interrelated within our lives. And in her words below, you'll hear again about the close relationship we Southerners have with farm-to-table food. So pour yourself a spot of wine or a glass of iced tea, sit back, and savor this wonderful story and the recipes that follow.

Looking back over the decades, I see that food has always had a significant place in the life of our family. We all have fond memories of divine homemade birthday cakes, holiday feasts at the dining table at 315 Prince Street, boxes full of fresh cookies sent to us while at college, Southern cooking at Colin McArthur's—our favorite Laurinburg restaurant—picnics on July 4th at Sam Snowden's pond, churns full of peach ice cream in the hot Carolina summers, and so many more.

This important role that food has played in our lives for so many years can be attributed to Mom's awesome skills in the kitchen. She was a great Southern cook, and we always had a made-from-scratch meal on the table every night for dinner: a meat, sometimes a congealed salad, a vegetable or two, starch, bread, and dessert. There was at least one, and often two or more, homemade sweets in our kitchen, whether it was a peach pie, beautifully iced sugar cookies, or meringues left over from bridge parties. I was in college before I ever tasted a cake made from a box!

And living in the Sandhills of North Carolina, an area with lots of local farmers, each summer we had produce of every kind available. Mom made sure we enjoyed them all—from bushels of black-eyed peas to butterbeans to peaches to tomatoes and so much more. As a child, I spent many an evening with a big bowl of purple hull, crowder, or black-eyed peas in my lap, shelling them, as we all watched TV together. And the vegetables were always prepared with a large piece of ham hock and a pinch of sugar, and cooked forever over a low, simmering stove. My mom would also freeze a lot of the summer produce so that we could enjoy it year-round, and peach pies were one thing that were always in her extra freezer in the garage. And of course, those pies were much better if you topped them with homemade ice cream, just out of the churn.

And while Mama was known for all of her foods, we especially enjoyed her congealed salads; they were made in every flavor and color imaginable, and I loved every one of them! At Thanksgiving and Christmas, she made cranberry salad in individual molds, and my brother Mac and I each got two, topping them with dollops of creamy mayonnaise. To this day, Mac, who is now seventy, and I call each other on these two holidays and talk about that cranberry salad, and how good it was.

I could go on and on, and I have had such a great time going down memory lane. I hope you all enjoy Mama's recipes as much as my family has, and that they'll bring back memories for you, too, when you prepare them in your own home.

—Elizabeth Tornow Skeadas

★　★　★　★　★

I'm betting that so many readers, particularly those from the South and of our era, can visualize sitting with Elizabeth, bowl of black-eyes in hand, either watching TV or sitting in the front porch swing. We can see her mama putting the finishing touches on one of her incredible fresh, peach pies or feel the anticipation of waiting for that first bite of the favored cranberry salad on Christmas Day, while big, opaque colored lights glowed on a decorated cedar tree in the next room. Just change the names of the players, and so many of our warm stories read the same from across our region.

Our friend from Laurinburg has provided four of her mother's best recipes here. The first is the aforementioned peach pie. It's not a cobbler, mind you, or one of those deep-dish creations where you mix together butter, milk, flour, and sugar and scatter the fruit on top (not that I don't enjoy eating those desserts, Lord no). But a peach pie, a real one that is loaded with fruit and has a light crust, is simply one of the best dishes that has ever come out of the South. Enjoy!

Martha's Peach Pie

You could look in Mom's freezer any time of year, and you'd be guaranteed to find at least one peach pie that she made in the summertime with fresh, local peaches. Serve this pie with plenty of vanilla ice cream, preferably homemade. —ETS

INGREDIENTS

3-3½ cups fresh peaches, peeled and sliced
    1 inch thick

¾ cup sugar

Pinch of salt

A couple pinches of cinnamon

1½ tablespoons cornstarch

1 teaspoon all-purpose flour

2 unbaked piecrusts

¼ stick of unsalted cold butter, cut into thin slivers

Vanilla ice cream or fresh whipped cream for topping

INSTRUCTIONS

1. Preheat oven to 400 degrees.

2. Place peaches in a mixing bowl. In a separate small bowl, mix together the sugar, salt, cinnamon, and cornstarch with a fork. Sprinkle the dry ingredients over the peaches, and gently mix with a spatula.

3. Roll out the prepared piecrust and dust the bottom of one crust with the flour. Place the crust flour-side down in a non-stick pie pan (skip this step if you are using crusts already in a commercial aluminum pan).

4. Pour the peach mixture into the first shell, and gently spread evenly. Place the slivers of butter at intervals across the peaches.

5. Lay the other crust on top of the peaches and crimp the edges together to seal. Cut 4 or 5, 1-inch slits in the top crust.

6. Place the pie on a cookie sheet and bake for 40 minutes or until the crust is a golden brown. Remove from oven, and allow to cool 20 minutes before serving. Serve with a dollop of ice cream or whipped cream.

Serves 6-8

Of course, after reading about Elizabeth and Mac's favorite congealed salad, we had to be able to sample it for ourselves. Elizabeth asked me in correspondence the reflective question, "I guess people just don't make these congealed salads much anymore, do they?" Maybe not nearly as often, I thought, but these dishes sure do make my taste buds smile, and memories light up when I'm served one at Christmas, Thanksgiving, or Easter.

Cranberry Salad

Thanksgiving and Christmas feasts at our house would not be complete without this wonderful salad. For Mac, my brother, it's always two salads on lettuce, heavy on the Hellman's mayonnaise! —ETS

INGREDIENTS
Vegetable oil
2 envelopes unflavored gelatin
⅓ cup cold water
3 small boxes cherry-flavored Jell-O
3 cups boiling water
3 cups sugar
pinch of salt
1, 18-ounce can crushed pineapple, drained (don't be tempted to use fresh, the salad won't congeal)
1 cup orange juice
Juice of 1 lemon
3 cups chopped pecans
2 cups chopped celery
3 cups fresh cranberries, coarsely chopped
Iceberg lettuce leave and mayonnaise, for garnish

INSTRUCTIONS
1. Lightly oil a large, 2-quart mold or 10 individual half-cup molds. Set aside.
2. In a large mixing bowl, mix the gelatin with the cold water.

3. Add to the bowl the cherry Jell-O, and pour boiling water over the gelatins. Add in the sugar and salt, and stir until the gelatin/Jell-O is dissolved. Place in the refrigerator, and allow to chill for about 30 minutes.

4. When the chilling Jell-O starts to set, add the pineapple, juices, pecans, celery, and cranberries. Stir well. Refrigerate again for 15-20 minutes.

5. When the mixture starts to set again, pour into one large mold or the smaller individual molds. Chill 4-6 hours, or overnight, until firm.

6. To serve, unmold onto lettuce leaves and serve each slice or mold with a dollop of mayonnaise.

Serves 8-10

★ ★ ★ ★ ★

These last two recipes, the oh-so-classic-Southern Tomato Aspic and the Chicken Salad, were favorites of Mrs. Tornow's to serve for a ladies' luncheon or bridge club repast. Her fame for the aspic was such that the *Laurinburg Exchange* featured a photo of her making the dish in an article from the 1950s. Titled "My Favorite Recipe," it includes the caption "Mrs. Winston Tornow was caught by 'The Exchange' photographer in the attractive kitchen of her Prince Street home as she was making one of her favorite recipes which is for tomato aspic. This is a grand, cool summer salad."

Mrs. Tornow and her aspic featured in
The Laurinburg Exchange, 1955

Tomato Aspic

INGREDIENTS

Vegetable oil

2 envelopes plain gelatin

½ cup cold water

3 cups tomato or V-8 juice

Dash cayenne pepper

2 stalks of celery, chopped into thick slices

1 bay leaf

2 tablespoons fresh lemon juice

2 tablespoons finely grated onion or 1 tablespoon onion juice

Salt to taste

Iceberg lettuce leaves, lemon slices, fresh parsley, mayonnaise
   to garnish

INSTRUCTIONS

1. Lightly oil a 1-quart salad mold or 6 half-cup individual molds. Set
   aside.

2. In a small bowl, mix together the gelatin and cold water. Set aside.

3. In a medium-sized, heavy-bottom pot, mix the tomato juice,
   cayenne, celery, and bay leaf; bring to a boil. Allow it to cook at a
   gentle boil for 10 minutes, stirring occasionally. Remove from heat.

4. Add the gelatin to the hot liquid, and stir until dissolved.

5. Add the lemon juice and onion, stir to mix, and strain into a large
   bowl. Discard the celery and bay leaf. Allow the mixture to cool
   slightly. Taste and add in salt if needed.

6. Pour into one large mold or individual molds. Refrigerate 6-8 hours
   or overnight.

7. To serve, unmold the aspic, and serve each slice or individual mold
   on a leaf of iceberg lettuce. Decorate with a slice of lemon, sprig of
   parsley, and a teaspoon or so of mayonnaise.

Serves 6

Chicken Salad

This is Mom's "old" chicken salad recipe that she made for decades. It is also one of my husband's favorite dishes. —ETS

INGREDIENTS

1, 4-4½ pound fryer chicken

2-3 quarts water

3 tablespoons salt

4 large or 6 medium-sized hard-boiled eggs, shelled and chopped finely

½ cup finely diced celery

¼ cup diced sweet pickle

1 cup (less or more) real mayonnaise

¼ teaspoon salt

¼ teaspoon finely ground black pepper

¼ cup chopped pecans

INSTRUCTIONS

1. Wash the chicken. Place it in a large pot, cover with water and salt, and bring to a boil. Allow it to simmer for 1 hour, until done. Remove from heat and place the chicken on a platter to cool.

2. When cool enough to handle (about an hour later), skin the chicken and discard skin. Remove the chicken from the bones, dice the meat into small pieces, and place into a large mixing bowl.

3. Add the remaining ingredients, mix thoroughly, and place in covered, airtight container. Refrigerate 4-6 hours, or overnight. Serve on a bed of lettuce for a luncheon entrée, with crackers for a cocktail party hors' d'oeuvre, or as filler for a fantastic sandwich.

Serves 6-8

CHAPTER 3

THINKING OF MAMA & DADDY, AND PICKING FIGS

by JSB

Summertime when I was a child meant waking up before dawn on Saturdays to my father singing "She'll be Comin' Round the Mountain" or "This Train Is Bound for Glory"—his signal that it was time to pile in the truck and head to the country. There were vegetables and fruit to be gathered, and he wanted us pullin' and pickin' before the Georgia heat became unbearable. I hated those mornings and, if put to an oath, would have to admit to some very un-Christian thoughts about Papa rolling around in my head on those outings. Besides being a typical teenager, I also suffered from a malfunctioning internal temperature gauge that stayed stuck on "HIGH HEAT" most of the time; seriously, I can still break a sweat just walking out onto the porch. Daddy would have us all dressed in full-length trousers (in case of snakes) and long-sleeved shirts (to help keep the okra or peach fuzz off our skin). I would be soaking wet before pulling the first ear of corn off a stalk and it wouldn't even be 7 a.m. By mid-morning when we were finished, you could literally wring water out of my shirt and underclothes.

But that was decades ago, and during that lapse of time, I can't go to a farmers' market or see a picture of fresh vegetables without thinking about Mama and Daddy, and how I'd gladly give up a Saturday or any other hot, summer morning to have the chance to be in the middle of a tomato patch with the two of them, sweating away. Interesting how things in life, particularly loss, can change your views and outlook.

One of our summer staples was the brown turkey fig. Daddy dearly loved Mama's homemade biscuits and a bowl of her incredible fig preserves. She cooked her figs whole, poaching them slowly in a big boiler until a thick, sweet-tea colored syrup was made. We would pick them at my cousin Joyce's place down in Dooly County; she had fig trees so tall you needed a 10-foot stepladder to reach the upper limbs.

Until recently, I had not picked any figs in years; the ones I used for cooking usually came from Davis Produce or the grocery store. Through a random conversation with a gentleman at the Piggly Wiggly, I received an invitation to drive out to his place in the little town of Faulkville and "pick all the figs you want." So on a late-July Saturday I retrieved two half-bushel peach baskets, a damp washcloth for cleaning my hands—figs can be sticky—and a towel to mop the sweat off my head, and headed to west Chatham County.

I drove up to find a comfortable-looking older home, complete with a tin roof, a screened-in porch, and a big, magnificent fig tree full of ripe brown fruit. Even though it was the middle of a humid afternoon in July, with the temperature well into the 90s, I took my sweet time with my chore. I stood inside the low-reaching limbs of the tree, admiring the big, sage-green colored leaves covered in their hair-like fuzz, and carefully picked each brown, plump fig within reach. And with each one placed in the baskets, I thought about my Mama and Daddy and summers back home. What a wonderful gift, those memories.

Picking away, lost in yesterdays, my mind wandered to my nephew, Jason, and I thought how pleased my parents would be of him. My sister's only child had inherited his grandparents' love of the land and fresh farm-to-table food, and even outdid me when it came to gardening and his commitment to tilling our Georgia soil.

Oh what a sweet child he was growing up, with dimples so big he could've held a plump blackberry in each cheek, and enormous blue eyes that danced when he was happy. He's all of forty-four now, with an elegant and chic French wife (I tease him that he married way up the ladder) and two beautiful children of his own, each with their own set of those sparkling eyes. I stopped by his house the other day and watched him in his backyard garden. Sporting a wide-brimmed straw hat, he was working on a raised bed of vegetables that sat next to a big, fine fig tree. Some of the first things he planted when he bought his property were brown turkey fig trees. He loves fig preserves as much as the rest of the Barrett clan.

Jason has also taken to making jellies, preserves, and jams, excelling at it as did his Grandmama Barrett, whom he called "Ninnie." Mama's mama was also referred to as Ninnie, and her mother before her, a Nipper tradition. Mama was a prize champ in the condiment competition at the National Fair the first few years it came into existence in Perry, and she took home numerous blue ribbons for her pear preserves, fig preserves, peach jam, scuppernong jelly, and a host of others. Many a day I watched her in the kitchen doing her canning, and years later, when her arthritis got the best of her, I would slice the hard Georgia pears she needed for her preserves, or peel the bushels of peaches for the jam. I've kept all of her recipes and make those items myself, and Jason has continued on as well. You'll find dozens of jars of such delicacies in his pantry, including a few of his own that he's created, such as Vanilla Peach Butter.

Jason with Ninnie in his Grandparents' front yard, Perry, Georgia, 1974

Late last summer he called me up one Saturday afternoon and told me he'd just returned with a truckload of pears. Seems he was out exploring on a rural, South Georgia road (another family tradition, which we called "ridin' in the country") with his son, Tommy. They'd come upon a huge pear tree on an old abandoned homestead, full of ripe fruit. Tommy shimmied up the tree and, hanging on with his left arm, picked and then pitched the baseball-sized fruit down to his Pops in the Ford truck bed. Jason said the pears were now laid out on towels in the cool of his kitchen floor—just like Mama would do—so that they would not spoil until he had time to cook them all. He had plans for making Ninnie's prized pear preserves and doing a couple of cookings of spicy pear relish. Tommy said he was going to help. Maybe he'll catch the cooking and gardening bug like his great-grandparents, his daddy, and his Great-uncle John; that would make us all proud.

Here I've included a collection of recipes that all hold memories like I've described in the previous paragraphs. Some were a part of my first cook-book, *Rise & Shine!* while the others are from Jason's repertoire of dishes, such as his Vanilla Peach Butter and an outstanding Fig Preserve Cake.

Mama's Whole Fig Preserves

Mama's recipe was very general, like many that are handed down from the generations before us. Hers read only the ingredients, with no steps whatsoever. Fortunately, I had watched her cook dozens of batches of these specialties and could remember that they cooked for several hours over a low flame. I consulted several Southern cookbooks, too, to try and discern the steps and sequences, and have perfected it here for you.

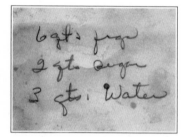

Mama's much-used recipe card for fig preserves

Most folks make their preserves like a jam, where the fruit is cooked down and spreadable. Mama, though, kept her fruit whole, leaving just a bit of stem on the end so that each fig stayed intact through the cooking process. These are delicious served with hot, buttered biscuits or toasted English muffins. Or, if you'd like to go the Southern haute cuisine route, serve some alongside a flavorful wedge of Stilton cheese and crackers for a cocktail party.

INGREDIENTS

6 quarts brown, firm figs

2 quarts water

3 quarts sugar

INSTRUCTIONS

1. Place all ingredients in a 3-gallon stockpot or other large pan.
2. Over medium-high heat, bring to a gentle boil. Reduce heat to a steady simmer.
3. Continue cooking for 2½ to 3 hours, stirring very gently during the process, being careful not to break the figs.
4. The preserves are ready when the syrup is thick, the color of iced tea, and coats a spoon.
5. Remove from heat, and immediately ladle into sterilized jars and seal with sterilized bands and lids.

Makes 12 half pints or 6 pint jars

Note on jar sterilization: Mama never did a boiling process to sterilize her jars. Instead, she washed them well in hot, soapy water and then placed them in a 250-degree oven for half an hour. Next, she removed the heated jars from the oven with tongs and immediately ladled in the hot preserves. Then she sealed the jars with lids and bands that came right out of a simmering pot of water on the stove. She must have canned thousands of jars this way in her lifetime, and there was never an instance of spoilage. However, I bow to the suggestions of the USDA and advise you to use the conventional boiling method per manufacturer directions. (Although mine still come out of an oven.)

Glazed Fig Preserve Cake

This recipe is one that my nephew adapted; it is now a family favorite at Thanksgiving and Christmas. The richness of the figs and the autumn-flavored spices makes the cake perfect for those holidays.

INGREDIENTS

1½ cups sugar
2 cups all-purpose flour
1 teaspoon baking soda
½ teaspoon salt

1 teaspoon nutmeg

1½ teaspoons cinnamon

½ teaspoon allspice

1 cup vegetable oil

3 large eggs, lightly beaten

1 cup whole milk buttermilk

2 teaspoons vanilla extract

1 cup fig preserves

½ cup chopped pecans

Buttermilk Glaze (recipe follows)

INSTRUCTIONS

1. Preheat oven to 350 degrees.

2. In a large mixing bowl, add the sugar, flour, baking soda, salt, nutmeg, cinnamon, and allspice. Stir together with a fork until just mixed.

3. Add the oil and eggs to the bowl, and on medium speed beat well with an electric mixer until just incorporated.

4. While continuing to beat, add the buttermilk and vanilla. When thoroughly mixed, stir in the preserves and pecans.

5. Grease and flour a 10-inch tube or Bundt pan. Add the batter and bake in the preheated oven for 1 hour.

6. When done, place the cake on a rack and allow to cool for 15-20 minutes. When ready, invert the cake onto a cake platter or serving tray. Pour the glaze over the cake.

7. When completely cooled, cover and refrigerate overnight before serving.

Serves 10-12

Buttermilk Glaze

INGREDIENTS

1 tablespoon unsalted butter

¼ cup whole milk buttermilk

1½ cups confectioner's sugar

1 teaspoon vanilla extract

INSTRUCTIONS

1. Melt the butter over medium-low heat.
2. Add the whole milk buttermilk and sugar, and gently stir until the sugar is dissolved and the mixture creamy.
3. Stir in the vanilla, and stir until mixed well. Remove from heat and allow to cool 2-3 minutes before spreading over the cake.

Vanilla Peach Butter

A whole vanilla bean split and added to a pot of simmering peaches makes for a very flavorful spread. This recipe was inspired by Jason's wife, Caroline Grimaldi, lately of Bordeaux and now living in Milledgeville, Georgia. This peach butter is perfect on a slice of toasted brioche or baguette, or on a flaky croissant. If you don't have any of those breads available, make it Southern and spoon some on a piece of toasted Sunbeam white bread. That tastes quite good, too.

Jason relates that he generally followed the recipe for Peach Butter on the Ball jar instructions, but in his words, "Okay, I don't really prepare them the way they do. They blanch the peaches, and throw in another useless step. Here is what I do, though." His version is excellent, and I'm always perusing his cupboard for a stray jar.

INGREDIENTS

18 medium-sized peaches, peeled and pitted
3½ cups sugar
One whole vanilla bean, split

INSTRUCTIONS

1. Cut the peaches into small chunks, about 1 inch square. Make sure you save the juices and any pulp from the peaches as you cut.
2. Place the peaches, juice and fruit, sugar, and vanilla bean in a large pot or Dutch oven. Bring to a low simmer, and stir often.
3. After the fruit has been simmering for 5-6 minutes and the peaches soften, use a potato masher to mash the fruit until there are no longer any large chunks. You could also use a hand-held submersion mixer for this task. (Don't mash or crush the bean, though!)

4. When the fruit can round up on a spoon, it is ready.

5. Remove bean and discard.

6. Ladle the butter into sterilized jars, seal, and process.

Makes 4-5 pints

My mom would also make a dozen or more jars of pear relish each year; the recipe she used was from my Aunt Ida Pauline "Polly" Barrett, who was a tremendous cook and baker. Aunt Polly left us in 2016 at the astounding age of 110. Can you imagine all that she experienced in her lifetime? She went from using a wood-burning stove to a microwave oven, sending telegraphs to tapping out texts, and riding in a horse-drawn buggy to cruising around in a Toyota Prius. She was like a second grandmother to me, and I adored her. One of my best memories of us together was harvesting pears. She'd don a large straw hat and gardening gloves, and then take a long wooden pole to knock the fruit out of her trees. My job was to pick up the rock-hard pears as they dropped to the ground, being careful not to get hit in the head—they'd leave a big goose-egg on your noggin.

Important note here: both for the relish and the following preserves, you have to use the very hard, Keiffer variety of Southern pears. These varieties are not commonly found in stores, but mostly on old family farms, alongside a country road, or, if you're lucky, at your local farmers' market. These hard pears ensure that your relish doesn't turn mushy, and the slices of your preserves remain whole and don't disintegrate into pear sauce. Using the softer, sweeter types of pears, such as Bartlett and Anjou, will not work properly.

*   *   *   *   *

Pear Relish

Daddy's family was from North Georgia, and a lot of food on their tables had an Appalachian influence. The recipe here is similar to ones made from that area, including those in such books as *The Foxfire Book of Appalachian Cookery*. Other preparations, using the pear and vinegar base, are in Mrs. R. S. Dull's *Southern Cooking* and Mildred Evans Warren's *The Art of Southern Cooking*. This condiment is very similar to chow-chow and is perfect spooned atop a bowl of pinto beans, Hoppin' John, or dried butterbeans. Make sure you have a slice of hot cornbread on the side.

INGREDIENTS

2 gallons (1 peck) hard pears, peeled and cored, cut into 2-inch cubes

6 large onions, chopped

4 red bell peppers, seeded and chopped

4 green bell peppers, seeded and chopped

3 stalks celery, chopped

1 medium-sized jalapeno, seeded and chopped

5 cups white vinegar

1 tablespoon allspice berries, crushed

1 tablespoon salt

3½ cups sugar

1 tablespoon turmeric (for color)

INSTRUCTIONS

1. Grind the pears, onions, bell peppers, and celery in batches. Ladle each batch into a large pot or Dutch oven. Add the jalapeno to the last batch. Stir to mix.

2. Add the vinegar, allspice berries, salt, sugar, and turmeric to the vegetable mix. Place in the refrigerator and allow to sit overnight.

3. The next day, bring the mixture to a boil, reduce heat to medium, and cook for 30 minutes.

4. Ladle into sterilized jars, seal, and process.

Makes 9-10 pints

Pear Preserves

My mother's recipe here creates some of the finest preserves you'll ever taste. It also makes a beautiful presentation, as the pears are surrounded in a thick, amber-colored syrup. I remember rows of them sitting on our pantry shelves, many destined as Christmas or birthday presents for friends and family.

You may find it interesting that there isn't any water added to this recipe. None is needed, as you'll see once you start the process. After the pears chill overnight in the refrigerator, moisture is released and the sugar melts, resulting in a poaching liquid in which the pears will cook.

INGREDIENTS

6 quarts Southern hard pears

2½ pounds of sugar

INSTRUCTIONS

1. Rinse the pears, peel and core. Cut them into large slices, about 3 inches long and 1 inch thick.

2. In a 3-gallon stockpot or pan, layer the pears and sugar, starting at the bottom with the pears. Make each pear layer 3 to 4 inches thick, and top with sugar. End with sugar as the top layer.

3. Cover and store in a refrigerator overnight. The pears will release a great deal of juice during this time, which will melt the sugar.

4. Over medium-high heat, bring the pot to a slight boil, then reduce to a medium simmer.

5. Cook for 2½ to 3 hours, stirring occasionally and being careful not to break the pears, and at the same time not allowing the syrup or pears to stick to the bottom of the pan. When finished, the syrup should coat a spoon.

6. Remove from heat and immediately ladle into hot, sterilized jars and seal with hot, sterilized bands and lids.

Makes 4 pints or 8 half pint jars

CHAPTER 4

GRITS: A PILLAR OF SOUTHERN CUISINE

by James T. Farmer III

James T. Farmer is well known to many readers, particularly those who enjoy Southern cooking, traditions, and style. With several beautifully written and photographed books under his name, including the popular *A Time to Cook*, this *Southern Living* editor-at-large is seen regularly as a guest on national TV and is a highly sought-after speaker. And while we both lay claim to the lovely Middle Georgia hamlet of Perry as our hometown, we did not meet in person until recently. I knew of the Farmer family, but with James being a good twenty years younger, I was grown and off to college by the time he graced Houston County.

Our introduction happened at the 2015 Southern Independent Booksellers Association (SIBA) in Raleigh, where we shared in making two presentations. One was on a panel about Southern food with a couple of incredible cooks and authors, Bridgette Lacy and Sandra Gutierrez. The other slot was part of the "Authors in the Round" luncheon event, where visiting writers go from table to table to sit and hopefully charm the booksellers in attendance. The authors followed each other in order throughout the program, and I was immediately behind James. At three separate stops along the way, people remarked about our similar voices. One lady even said, "You and James Farmer sound so much alike you could be brothers." What a compliment. I know that James's family has been in the Middle

James (far left) and his family at the Red Lion Inn, Stockbridge, Massachusetts, 1993

Georgia area for generations, and on my Mom's side, the Nippers and Mus-selwhites have been in residence since 1830. I'm proud that we've inherited and kept alive those soft, almost melodic accents of our forbearers.

Here James, in his remarkable writing style, brings us a lesson in the Southern staple of grits. His recipe for Rosemary Shrimp and Garlic Grits could easily become a signature dish for your dining room, whether it is served just after the cock crows or right as the sun sets. Note: This story and recipe is by James T. Farmer III from his book *A Time to Cook*, reprinted by permission of Gibbs Smith.

Grits—a pillar of Southern cuisine. No matter your rank below the Mason-Dixon Line, you shall eat grits. They are a "first" food, sweetened with fruit and served to our children as soon as they can eat solids. They may be baked in a casserole dish or ladled from a pot. They may be break-fast or supper; served at the finest restaurants known to man and from a fast-food drive-thru. They are what they are—a vehicle, a transport, a conveyer, conductor, and deliverer of flavor from the plate to the palate.

Mama and Daddy took the three of us kids to Stockbridge, Massa-chusetts, one Thanksgiving to stay at the Red Lion Inn and have a truly

Norman Rockwell Thanksgiving in the famed artist's hometown. Our first morning there, we children were shocked when the wait staff could not fulfill our grits order but rather thought a supplement of cream of wheat would suffice. No ma'am. No sir. The former and the latter are not one in the same. Of course, though, being recent attendees of cotillion classes and manners courses, we three were as reverently polite and grateful as three disappointed Southerners can be!

There are two types of grits that I love to use when making shrimp and grits: Nora Mills Granary, Inc.'s "Georgia Ice Cream" white speckled grits and Logan Turnpike Mill's old-fashioned speckled white grits. These are true grits—corn that is milled and ground the old-fashioned way and full of texture. To prepare this dish, you make the grits and shrimp separately, and then put them together when you're ready to serve. Leftover grits or even grits made ahead of time can be cut and baked into grit cakes and the shrimp served over these.

—James T. Farmer III

Rosemary Shrimp & Garlic Grits

Note: As it takes the grits a while to cook, and the shrimp are done in short time, you'll want to prepare your grits in advance.

INGREDIENTS

1 cup grits

4 cups water

1 generous tablespoon salt

1 tablespoon butter

1 tablespoon garlic powder

INSTRUCTIONS

1. Pour grits into a heavy saucepan and cover with the water.

2. Add the salt, butter, and garlic powder and stir. Remove or skim any large pieces of bran and discard.

3. Bring the pot to a boil. Turn down the heat and simmer uncovered, stirring often to prevent sticking. Cook about 30 minutes, until grits are soft, adding more liquid if necessary.

Tip from JTF: The liquid can also be chicken stock, which makes a flavorful pot of grits! I use milk to thin the grits if need be, as an extra splash of milk (or cream) adds a luscious layer of flavor. Remember this: use a 1 to 4 grits to liquid ration, stir frequently, and always flavor while boiling, not after.

Rosemary Shrimp

INGREDIENTS

½ cup olive oil

2 bay leaves

3 drops Tabasco sauce

1 tablespoon minced fresh rosemary

6 garlic cloves, chopped

½ teaspoon salt

½ teaspoon freshly ground black pepper

1 cup dry white wine

2 pounds raw shrimp, peeled and heads removed

INSTRUCTIONS

1. Combine oil, bay leaves, Tabasco, rosemary, and garlic in a heavy skillet over medium-low, and heat slowly for 10 minutes. Stir occasionally.

2. Add the salt, pepper, wine, and shrimp. Increase heat and bring to a simmer.

3. Simmer slowly until the shrimp are no longer translucent but pink and in the shape of Cs—usually 3 to 5 minutes. Stir and turn shrimp often.

4. Remove shrimp and keep warm.

5. Reduce sauce to thicken.

6. To serve, place a helping of grits into a serving bowl or on a plate. Ladle portions of the shrimp and sauce over the grits.

Serves 6-8

CHAPTER 5

AUNT NORA
ON A TRACTOR

by JSB

n the previous chapter, James Farmer says that Nora Mills is one of his
favorite purveyors of grits. And mine, too. I've been visiting this Georgia
landmark, which is located just outside the little town of Helen in North
Georgia, since old enough to walk. My father's family is from that area,
and we're kin to many, many folks up there, including the Trotters, Alli-
sons, Turners, Etrises, and Wests. You can ride through downtown Cleve-
land and see Barrett Funeral Home atop a hill; it's owned by a third cousin.
And my great-grandfather was the sheriff in White County for years.

As an adult, I love Nora Mill's products, and frequently cook with
their grits and cornmeal, which are ground on 1,500-pound French Burr
Mill stones. You can easily spend an hour wandering around the store,
admiring the Southern gourmet food items that are set alongside the enormous water wheel and cast iron machinery.

But as a child, I was enamored with the mill first because it is located
right on the banks of the Chattahoochee River, and just below the building,
pouring off the dam, is a deep pool of clear mountain water filled with
dozens of enormous trout. Throwing food pellets off the porch and seeing
the trout break the water in a big swirl of feeding was a huge thrill for this
fish-loving boy. My other fascination with the mill growing up was that I
was convinced it was named after my father's aunt, Nora Barrett. She would
often accompany us to the store when we were in town, and some of my

Mama, Daddy, cousin Ruth Barrett Davidson, and Aunt Nora, Clarkesville, Georgia, 1996

first memories of watching those trout flipping about in the Chattahoochee have her by my side. I learned later that the mill was indeed named after someone named Nora, but this lady was the sister of the mill's owner, Dr. Lamartine G. Harding, Governor of Georgia from 1927–1931.

Aunt Nora was a wonderful and interesting soul. When she was a teenager, she married my father's uncle Lee, who died not too many years later. A mountain woman through and through, she took over the reins of the farm, literally, and worked it until the day she passed away. A gentle soul, she was nonetheless strong as an ox: her forearms were roped with veins and muscles from the labor she loved. It was rather fitting that the good Lord took her while she was mowing one of her fields—the sweet but strong lady had a heart attack and fell off her tractor at the age of seventy-eight. I loved her dearly and miss her to this day. She was one of a kind, even if there wasn't a gristmill named for her after all.

Now continuing this traipse down memory lane, I recall that Aunt Nora loved her cornbread, whether served with a pot of pinto beans or a bowl of beef stew. And some of the best cornmeal in the US of A comes from the mill that carries the name of the other Nora. So it is only fitting to include a recipe for that Southern staple. This version comes from my dear friend Janis Owens, the award-winning and highly praised author from "Old Florida," whom you'll read more about in a later chapter. Her cookbook, *A Cracker Kitchen*, is a go-to for me. If you don't have a copy, treat yourself and buy one for your library. It is an excellent guide for Southern food, and also reads like a novel. The secret in her cornbread? A little bit of bacon fat—it makes all the difference in the world in the taste. And for those of you who are health conscious, come on…make just a pan or two a year and leave regret behind.

Florida Cracker Cornbread

INGREDIENTS

1½ cups plain cornmeal

½ cup self-rising flour

1 teaspoon baking powder

Pinch of salt

1½ cups whole buttermilk

2 tablespoons bacon drippings or vegetable oil

INSTRUCTIONS

1. Preheat oven to 350 degrees.

2. Combine the dry ingredients in a large bowl, and then add in the buttermilk and fat. Mix well.

3. Pour the batter into a greased baking dish or a greased muffin pan.

4. Bake until golden brown, about 15 minutes.

5. Remove from heat and allow to cool slightly before serving.

Makes one large pan of cornbread or 12 to 16 muffins

* * * * *

And I guess if we're going to make the cornbread, we ought to have some beans to go with it. These hearty and flavorful legumes are extremely popular in Appalachia, and I love to sit down to a big bowl of them during the winter. One of my favorite spots to sample these is the Moose Café located at the state farmers' market in Asheville. They serve the beans with a side of chopped onion and chow-chow, and it is what we in the South call "good eatin.'" The Moose Café also has on hand at every table a container of their apple butter to spread on your cornbread or biscuits.

So here are my recipes for Pinto Beans and also for my homemade Apple Butter; this way, you can prepare the entire meal inspired by my tractor-driving aunt. Serve your pintos with Mama's Pear Relish (recipe found on page 23), or buy yourself a jar of chow-chow at the grocer's. This is a great, comfort-food supper for a casual evening with friends who would enjoy our traditional flavors of the Blue Ridge.

JB's Pinto Beans

INGREDIENTS

1 pound dried pinto beans (I prefer Camellia brand.)

Water

¼ pound salt pork, side meat, bacon, or ham

1 teaspoon salt

INSTRUCTIONS

1. Rinse the beans in a colander. Remove any shells or pieces of bean and discard.

2. Place the beans in a large, heavy pot, cover with water about 2 inches above the beans, and bring to a boil. Stir, cover with a lid, and remove from heat. Allow to sit for an hour.

3. Drain the water from the beans.

4. Add the meat and salt and enough fresh water to again cover the beans by about two inches.

5. Place the pot back onto the stove, and bring the beans to a boil. Reduce the heat to medium-low, and simmer for 2 or more hours until very tender. Make sure to stir periodically. If the water gets too low, add a little along the way.

6. To serve, ladle into large bowls and top with chopped onion, pear relish, or chow-chow. Enjoy with cornbread.

Serves 6-8

Apple Butter

In the Appalachian Mountains, where apples grow so abundantly, apple butter has been a staple since the settling of those lands by the Europeans. My recipe here produces a spread that is the color of burnt umber and has a smooth consistency. While it contains some spices, you can very much taste the deliciousness of the apples.

INGREDIENTS

12 cups peeled and cored tart apples, cut into 1-inch chunks

3 cups unfiltered, organic apple cider (not apple cider vinegar)

2 cups dark brown sugar, or more to taste

1 teaspoon cinnamon

½ teaspoon ground nutmeg

½ teaspoon ground allspice

INSTRUCTIONS

1. In a 3-gallon stockpot, add the apples and the cider. Bring to a boil.

2. Reduce heat to a steady simmer, cooking uncovered for an about 45 minutes, until the apples are very tender, stirring occasionally.

3. With a hand immersion blender, puree the apples in the pot. (If you do not have a hand-held blender, you can puree the apples in your food processor, but be cautious when handling the hot mixture.)

4. Add the sugar, then stir and mix well.

5. Continue cooking another half-hour or so, stirring frequently so that the mixture does not stick to the bottom of the pan.

6. The butter is ready when you can place a dollop of it on a glass plate and no circle of moisture forms around the butter (it stands dry).

7. Add spices and stir to mix.

8. Remove from heat and immediately ladle into hot, sterilized jars and seal with hot, sterilized bands and lids.

Makes 4 pint jars or 8 half pints

CHAPTER 6

CRACKER KIN

by Janis Owens

hen the Savannah Book Festival was created, I served on its board of directors for several years and planned the first authors' reception. Being in the Hostess City of the South, we wanted to make the event unique from other festivals, and made all efforts to roll out the red carpet for our visiting writers and their guests. That inaugural party started with cocktails and hors' d'oeuvres at my home, and I was thrilled to see so many of my literary idols, such as Thomas Malone and Cassandra King, milling about my house and library. Next stop was a neighbor's house for a buffet supper, and the entire group of fifty-plus folks then strolled across the street to the sprawling Belford abode for dessert and cordials. People still talk about that night all these years later.

One of the highlights of being on the board was to be paired with an author and his or her guest for the weekend, acting as their contact, scheduling manager, and sometimes tour guide. When our slate of speakers was announced for 2009, I immediately volunteered to escort Janis Owens. I had read Janis's wonderful novels, including *My Brother Michael*, *The Schooling of Claybird Catts*, and *Myra Sims*, and was a devoted fan of the first order. Besides her natural ability to spin a heartfelt yarn, what captured me about Janis was her to-the-bone pride in her North Florida "Cracker" heritage, and her love of family. About the time of the festival, she posted a photo on Facebook of her maternal grandmother, circa 1964 or so, holding

JSB and Janis during the Tour of Homes, Highlands, North Carolina, 2015

a cane pole with a hand-sized perch on the line, smiling like there was no tomorrow. I fell in love with the photo, which reminded me so much of my own mom, and have since fallen in love with my newest "cousin," Janis.

At this year's festival, Janis was presenting her newest endeavor, a cookbook memoir called *The Cracker Kitchen*. I picked up a copy and became so enthralled that I read it in one sitting, getting up only to refresh my libation upon occasion. In it, Janis tells story after story about her family's life in North Florida, and introduces you to the nuances and uniqueness of growing up as a proud Cracker. Anyone with any interest at all in Southern foodways and culture should buy a copy of this marvelous book. It is a rare gem.

As the weekend of the festival progressed, Janis and I developed a wonderful bond that has since bloomed into a great friendship. We stay in constant touch and visit when we can between our busy schedules. Janis was also my mentor, helping me when I wrote *Rise & Shine!* It was through her coaching and encouragement that the book came to fruition and was so nicely received by food lovers across the South.

And we do refer to one another as "cousins." There is no doubt that we are probably related. We both hail from the Deep South going back many, many generations, and I wouldn't be at all surprised if one of my Mama's

*Eula Roberts Rice,
Janis' maternal grandmother*

Nipper or Musselwhite kin had hitched up to a Johnson in a generational line that branched out and eventually produced the two of us. We also share the same temperament, one of inherent good humor, which is balanced with a slightly skeptical and wary outlook on life, particularly when it comes to people who think too much of themselves. (I mean, we're Crackers—we question showy people's motives.) Too, our family traditions and "ways" are so similar that if I were to stop by one of Janis's family reunions and plop myself down next to any number of her folks, they'd just assume I was a part of the clan from up Georgia way.

Here cousin Janis gives us a story of that Cracker generosity, family togetherness, and ingenuity in the garden and the kitchen. Reading it makes me wish for a visit to Old Florida: maybe a late summer day meandering down a dirt road, following pastures filled with palmettos and moss-draped oaks, and cooling off in a crystal-blue freshwater spring. In this picture is also a picnic basket with fried chicken, potato salad, and a jar of homemade pickled squash.

The great advantage of living in the country is that even in the years I don't labor over a garden of my own, I have farmer friends who pass along the fruit of their own labors. When I lived in town, my next-door neighbor's son was the manager of a cantaloupe-picking crew and would bring home the melons too ripe to ship. He'd leave them in a cardboard box on his mom's front porch, available to anyone who came along. If you happened to catch him in the yard he'd holler for you to come get some melons. He didn't have to ask twice, as all good country girls know the ones too ripe to ship are the sweetest, most delicious melons of all. (Incidentally, the same rule applies to men.)

So I've been spoiled for many years, and when I had a luncheon this week, right around Memorial Day, for three of my oldest friends, two of them brought fresh produce cooked in delicious dishes. Shari went out and dug up some small red potatoes so incredible that they required nothing more than boiling, draining, adding a little cream, butter, salt, pepper, and sprinkling of thyme, and then stirring with a heavy spoon enough to squash them a little. I don't peel, don't do anything else, and trust me, they are so incredible I wouldn't think of weighing them down with gravy. Some of nature's creations are too fabulous to cover in gravy. Not many, but there are a few.

Shari's niece by marriage, Suzy, brought the Pickled Squash below using vegetables she'd harvested the week before from the Holder family's communal garden. Suzy is actually two years younger than Shari, but both married into the enormous Holder clan, which is one of those sprawling Cracker families with enough children that generations get a little intermarried and confusing. Technically, Shari's husband is Suzy's husband's uncle. They are all neighbors and live on the original Holder land northwest of tiny Newberry, Florida. The family farms line an oak-shaded graded road for seven twisting miles, through soul-satisfying glimpses of Old Florida. The different brothers, sisters, cousins, and kin raise crops, livestock, and a heritage herd of Cracker horses and cows. They have always shared and shared alike, and have lately joined forces to create a large communal garden. Every brother contributes something: one pays for the fuel, one plows it; another provides irrigation, another seed. I'm not sure which poor soul has to weed it; I have never thought to ask. In any case, it is a wonderful idea, and in the Holder's case, it's not a trendy return to self-sufficiency but a continuation of what they've been doing since their great-great-grandfather and his brothers bought the land the century before last.

Florida Crackers are the most generous human beings on earth, and since they're also the cheapest, they have a true horror of waste. The Holder Family Garden has had a surplus of yellow squash this year— so many that they were in danger of rotting in the field. Suzy remedied the problem with a spin on the usual canned squash: a simple and tangy recipe for Pickled Squash that she put up in decorative small jars, making them perfect for gift-giving. They add a tangy side to any feast and are ready to eat immediately, though they will keep for up to a year.

—Janis Owens

Suzy's Pickled Squash

INGREDIENTS

2 pounds yellow squash, thinly sliced

2 medium-sized red bell peppers, chopped

1 onion, thinly sliced

2 tablespoons kosher salt

3 cups sugar

2½ cups apple cider vinegar

2 teaspoons mustard seeds

2 teaspoons celery seeds

INSTRUCTIONS

1. Sprinkle the squash, bell peppers, and onions with the salt in a large bowl; toss well and let it sit for an hour.

2. Gently toss the salted vegetables again, and pack them tightly into four 1-pint sterilized jars.

3. Combine the rest of the ingredients in a heavy-bottomed pot and heat to boiling, stirring, till the sugar dissolves.

4. Pour the hot liquid over the packed vegetables leaving ½ inch at the top.

5. Seal and process.

Makes 4, 1-pint jars

CHAPTER 7

A LIST OF LOVE

by Michael Morris

W hen the novel *A Place Called Wiregrass* by Michael Morris was first published, I bought a copy for a trip to the beach. After closing the last page, I thought to myself, "That was beautiful." Then along came *Slow Way Home*, and I knew I had found another "favorite" author that I would always seek out. And no wonder: his works have been compared to Harper Lee's and Flannery O'Connor's, and Pat Conroy even remarked that Michael Morris's most recent work, *Man in the Blue Moon*, was "One of the best portraits of a small Southern town I've ever encountered."

After starting my new venture into writing about Southern foodways, a mutual friend of mine and Michael's, the magnificent Southern novelist Janis Owens (she of the previous chapter), shared that he and I had much in common. Two similarities were our age and the fact that we were both, in her words, "Cracker Princes of Renown"—Michael is a fifth-generation native of Perry, Florida, while I am a seventh-generation fellow hailing from Perry, Georgia. The two towns could be interchangeable when we were growing up; with a few thousand citizens in each, and just 180 miles apart, the roots of the two small towns rested in the agrarian traditions of the Deep South. Another interesting note is that Michael worked for US Senator Bob Graham, and I had the privilege of serving The Honorable Sam Nunn as an intern in DC. Too, as aspiring young sports in our early twenties, we both flashed around town in Chevy Camaros: his fire-engine red and mine a pale yellow with tan-colored racing flames down the side. The list could go on and on.

So when we were both invited to present at the prestigious Authors in Apalach Festival in the Florida panhandle, I was excited about the opportunity to meet the other Prince of the other Perry. We "hit it off" as we Southerners say, and spent an afternoon sharing stories, laughter, and family tales over some Clyde May's Alabama Style Whiskey and a platter or two of fresh Apalachicola oysters.

Michael and his grandparents, Audrey and Curtis Whitfield, riding the train at Petticoat Junction in Panama City Beach, Florida, 1972.

During our long, rambling, whiskey-infused talk about family, life in the rural South, and all those traditions that somehow have stayed with us, Michael told me about an angel, his maternal grandmother, Audrey Whitfield. Part of his reflections was about her fried chicken, and how special and full of memories that dish was for him. I was fascinated, and the way he described her made me wish I could have been a boy sitting at her kitchen table back in Florida. I'm sure we could have been great buddies even at the age of seven or eight, and I know Miss Audrey would have treated me like another grandson.

His story here is written as beautifully as one of his novels. In it he tells with incredible affection the bond he had with Miss Audrey, and how she helped him grow into the talented and caring man he is today. She was indeed an angel.

First, full disclosure. I am not a cook. Preparing Kraft Macarconi and Cheese is an accomplishment. However, I appreciate those who have a talent for preparing food. And I certainly enjoy eating it. People say that music has memory. We can be anywhere at any given time and hear a certain song that transports us to another place in our lives. For me, food has the same effect.

Any time I smell chicken frying or the rare instances I taste chicken that has been cooked a perfectly golden brown, I return to my grandparents' house. My grandmother was called Mother because she declared she was too young to be called anything else when her first grandchild was born. Mother was absolutely the best cook on the planet, or at least in North Florida where I grew up. And I know others claim the same thing about their grandmothers but mine was the best. And that's just all there is to it.

My favorite meal was not only Mother's fried chicken but also a creamed corn she'd cook on the stove and then, right before it was done, she'd place the skillet briefly in the oven. Because it had a crispy top layer, I called the dish "fried corn." All these years later, I can still picture that plate of chicken, the skillet of corn, and a platter of freshly sliced tomatoes sprinkled with just the right amount of salt. The food was displayed like gallery art on a kitchen table ordered from a Sears and Roebuck catalogue.

Mother's enjoyment was watching family consume her food. I always said that she cooked with love as her main ingredient. My uncle once remarked that she could make the best meal out of just a few staples in the kitchen. And that was part of the joy of eating at Mother's table. Every day at noon, anyone in the family would stop by and enjoy the biggest meal of the day. We'd catch up on the latest happenings in each other's immediate family or pass along town gossip. It was exciting because I never knew who would show up or what stories they might bring along. Mother called these lunchtime meals "dinner." Decades later, while watching Downton Abbey no doubt, I came to understand that the term derives from the dining schedule of British servants.

Mother certainly served her family, especially me. I came to live next door to my grandparents at five years of age. My mama and I fled my abusive biological father and took refuge in a trailer that sat in my grandparents' side yard. While my mama went to work as a clerk for the Florida Department of Transportation so she could support us, Mother went to work on me. With one hand propped on her hip, she used the other hand to gingerly poke a fork at chicken frying in a black skillet. The blue flame on the oven was always low and the crackling sound soft. When I was little, I'd watch her and list out the people in my life who loved me. It was a ritual of sorts. Knowing I was emotionally wounded from abuse, she always told me, "You know, you're so loved. Why don't you list out all the people in this family who love you?" If a cousin or great-aunt were forgotten, she'd remind me, and each day that list grew longer. Even though she had an eighth grade education, she remains the wisest person I've ever known. Without knowing it, Mother was my psychologist. A healthcare professional with a string of degrees once told me Mother saved my sanity. All I know is she loved me unconditionally.

When I was in high school, Mother would plan her weekly menu around my schedule. During a short lunch break, I'd rush over to my grandparents' cinder-block home and open the screen door. The sweet smell of chicken frying and the closing theme song from The Price Is Right greeted me. It was the one television show she never missed. She always put the last touch on her meals when Bob Barker reminded everyone to spay and neuter their pets. Four decades later, when I pass a bank of televisions in Best Buy where The Price Is Right happens to be playing, my mouth waters and my soul aches.

The nurse who worked for our family physician told me that right before I came home from college my freshman year, Mother described the special meal she was planning for my homecoming: fried chicken and "fried corn." By then, disease had stolen her energy. Cooking began earlier in the day, before The Price Is Right. She'd still lightly flour the chicken, keep her heat low, and slowly let it fry. But now she often did the cooking while sitting on a wooden stool.

Mother's cooking technique was akin to her personality. She never made a show of herself. Unlike my granddaddy, Papa, who held court and told mesmerizing stories, Mother measured her words the same way she did her cooking ingredients. Wisdom and encouragement were served in equal measure. Even today as a middle-aged man facing obstacles, I can still hear her whisper, "You do your part and the Lord will do His." And I picture her soft smile and twinkling green eyes as she watched me eat the food she prepared. Food was her gift.

Little did I know that the first meal to kick off the summer of 1986 would also be my last at Mother's table. Weeks later she would have open heart surgery and never leave the hospital. Thirty years on, her parting

words linger. As I reached down to hug her before surgery, she squeezed my arm. And, looking as intently as she'd ever looked at me, she said, "You'll never know how much I love you." Being loved by her remains the greatest gift of my life. Mother lived as she cooked, with a light touch, a modest amount of seasoning and a desire to please her family.
—Michael Morris

* * * * *

When I asked Michael to be a part of *Cook & Tell*, he told me up front, as he did in the beginning of his story here, that he is not a cook. No problem, I said, I can provide the fried chicken recipe. Easy breezy—I mean, there is only one way to fry a chicken, isn't there? Well, maybe there is just one way, but there are dozens and dozens of variations on that "way" that gets the pullet to the platter.

Even within my own family, the ladies did things a bit different. Mama soaked the pieces of meat in buttermilk before cooking, but Aunt Bea did not. Mama used Lawry's seasoning, too, on each piece and in the flour, while Aunt Lil only used black pepper and salt. One cousin didn't even flour her pieces while everyone else I can remember did. Some folks covered their chicken for part of the frying process, and others left their skillets open....

I think most Southern cooks will agree on a few key steps that have to be followed. Other than that, you are free to add your own special touch to this dish. First, use a small fryer chicken; if you get one too large it can be tough. Second, use solid vegetable shortening—like your good old can of Crisco—for the grease. Third, make sure you don't overcrowd the pan with the chicken; if you put in too many pieces at one time, the chicken won't brown properly, and your crust will be soggy instead of crispy. And third, only turn your chicken over once while cooking—no back and forth.

That said, here is my way of cooking a hen. According to Michael's recollection, it is a mirror of how Mother Audrey prepared hers.

JB's Fried Chicken

INGREDIENTS

1, 3-pound fryer chicken, cut into 8 pieces

2 teaspoons salt, divided

1 teaspoon black pepper, divided

1½ cups all-purpose flour

2+ cups Crisco or other solid shortening

INSTRUCTIONS

1. Rinse the chicken and shake off excess water. Place the pieces on a large platter or cookie sheet. Sprinkle the pieces liberally on all sides with half of the salt and half of the black pepper.

2. In a large bowl, place the flour and the remaining salt and black pepper. Stir with a fork to mix.

3. Meanwhile, heat a large, deep frying pan (I prefer cast iron) over medium-high. Add the Crisco. When melted, you should have enough to cover about 2 inches of the bottom of the pan.

4. Dredge the thighs and legs in the flour, coating them well. Shake off the excess flour. Gently add the pieces, one at a time, to the hot grease.

5. If there is room in the pan, go ahead and dredge the breasts and then the wings and add them to the pan one at a time. *You do not want to overcrowd the pan; the pieces should absolutely not touch one another.* Leave a good inch and a half of space between each piece. If there is not enough room in your pan, you will need to cook two batches.

6. When the pan is full, cover it with a lid and allow to cook for 5-6 minutes. Uncover and continue cooking until the underside is a deep, golden brown.

7. Turn the chicken, and cover again. Cook another 5-6 minutes, and then remove the top.

8. Decrease the heat to medium low and cook another 10 minutes or so for the wings (the smallest pieces) and another 15 minutes or so for the larger pieces.

9. Remove the chicken from the pan with tongs and place on a large platter in a single layer. Serve immediately.

Serves 4-6

* * * * *

Often my Mom would make gravy after frying chicken. Thick, brown, and flavorful, it was wonderful served over rice or mashed potatoes. I thought I'd share her recipe with you here.

Fried Chicken Gravy

INGREDIENTS

3-4 tablespoons fat from the pan where you fried
   your chicken

2 tablespoons finely chopped onion

3 tablespoons flour left over from when you dredged the chicken

2 cups low-sodium chicken stock

Salt and pepper to taste, if needed

INSTRUCTIONS

1. Pour off all but 3 to 4 tablespoons of the fat from the fried chicken. Be sure to leave any of the browned bits and browned flour left in the pan.

2. Place the pan back over medium heat, and add the onions. Stir for one to two minutes until they are soft.

3. Whisk the flour into the pan, and cook for 3-4 minutes until the flour is a golden brown color.

4. Pour in the stock, and gently whisk for a few minutes until the gravy is thick. Taste, and add salt or black pepper if needed. Serve over rice, mashed potatoes, or a hot biscuit.

Makes 2 cups

* * * * *

Michael also tells us that Mother Audrey would make "fried" corn to go along with her fried chicken (an excellent pairing if I do say so myself). It is interesting how many folks in the South refer to this dish as "fried corn" instead of the more popular title of "creamed corn." Frank Stitt, the venerable chef and one of my personal culinary favorites, calls his dish "creamed," and Nathalie Dupree in *Southern Memories* lists the dish as "Creamed or Fried Corn." But then Lee Bailey calls it "fried," as does Mildred Evans Warren in her classic, *The Art of Southern Cooking*. In our household it was always "fried corn." Looking over a long list of recipes, it appears that the techniques were basically the same for creamed or fried, and, regardless of the name, each included some butter, bacon drippings, flour, milk, and black pepper.

The recipe I have here is my Mom's. I'm including, though, an additional step from Michael's grandmother. Michael relayed to me that Miss Audrey would cook her fried corn on top of the stove and then place the dish into a "slow" oven, allowing it to continue cooking until a slight crust appeared on top. So in her honor, I've added it here, and it does cook up beautifully.

Cheers to Miss Audrey for her delicious food as well as for the incredible love she gave to her grandson.

Fried Corn, Mother Audrey Style

Note: Make sure to use a very well-seasoned skillet or Dutch oven for this dish. Otherwise, the corn will stick to the bottom while baking.

INGREDIENTS

8 ears fresh, tender corn on the cob, shucked and silked

2-3 tablespoons bacon fat drippings *(If bacon drippings are not available, substitute 2-3 tablespoons of additional butter.)*

2 tablespoons unsalted butter

1½ tablespoons all-purpose flour

1 cup whole milk (or heavy cream if you'd like)

Salt and ground black pepper to taste

INSTRUCTIONS

1. Into a large bowl, cut the corn kernels from the outer edge of the cob (be careful not to cut the cob itself). After cutting the kernels off, scrape each cob with a back of a knife, releasing the juice into the bowl.

2. In a large, well-seasoned cast-iron skillet or Dutch oven, heat the bacon fat and butter over medium heat until melted. Add the corn kernels and juice to the skillet and stir to combine.

3. Whisk in the flour for 3-4 minutes until the corn and flour are heated all the way through.

4. Add the milk or cream, salt, and pepper. Stir and allow to come to a gentle simmer. Cook for about 10 minutes until thickened. Stir occasionally throughout so that the corn does not stick to the bottom of the pan.

5. Meanwhile, preheat your oven to 300.

6. Place the pan in the preheated oven. Bake for about 30 minutes until the top begins to form a light crust. Do not stir during the baking process.

7. Remove from the oven and serve at once.

Serves 6-8

CHAPTER 8

CAKES, CARS, & PURPLE BROCCOLI

by Alphus Christopher Spears

My best friend since seventh grade is Alphus, who I call Chris. We have shared wonderful times across the decades and also helped each other through crises of the heart and soul. There's only been one real disagreement in our years of friendship, but neither of us can remember why it came about. We can finish one another's sentences, and we don't even have to speak to understand what the other is thinking. He is, as the saying goes, like a brother to me; I literally don't know what I'd do without the old fool. And through all these years, food has always played a large part in what we do together, and some of our most memorable experiences are centered on eating.

One such episode happened at a family fish fry in our early teens. We feasted (or, as Mama would say, "made pigs of ourselves") so much—shamelessly consuming countless platters of fried fish, coleslaw, hush puppies, and French fries—that we went outside, flopped down on the back lawn, unsnapped our pants, and just wallowed there, burping and grunting and expelling other nonaromatic breezes for what seemed like an eternity. What we learned was that a tonnage of food cooked in grease, slathered in cups of tartar sauce, and accompanied by a mound of cabbage can really work your system.

Another time was just after college graduation. Chris was visiting with me in Savannah, and one of my former professors had invited us for dinner.

Her family home was an impressive manse on oak-lined Washington Avenue, and the meal was as rich as the setting; course after splendid course was served, ending with dessert featuring a magnificent Hummingbird Cake. A dense, moist confection filled with sweet bananas, crushed pineapple, and toasted pecans, it is frosted with a luscious cream cheese icing. Our plates were cleaned with nary a crumb left in sight, and we were kindly offered seconds. Having matured (some) since the fish fry overfill, we politely declined another helping. Sensing we were holding back, Dr. Lockwood insisted on wrapping up the remainder of the cake for us to take home.

Chris (Alphus) on our college graduation trip to Cancun, 1986. The Hummingbird Cake incident happened just before departure.

After our effusive thanks upon departure, we climbed into my car and watched until the door to the house closed. Giving me a knowing look and without uttering a single word, Chris quickly and deftly undid the foil, and we plunged into the large wedge of cake with our bare hands. The opposable thumb and fingers worked well to form improvised ladles, and we made fast work out of that three-layered wonder. It tasted as good or maybe even better eaten over the console of the Camaro—we did not have to worry about restraint. We gracefully stopped just short of licking the Reynolds Wrap clean.

Now, I know what you're thinking, just like Mama—but don't judge us. We were still growing boys and needed our nourishment.

To this day I can't read the words "Hummingbird Cake" or see one in a baker's window without being transported back thirty years as my mind sits me in the black leather seats of a Chevy with icing on my fingers and in the company of my bestest buddy. Here is my Mom's recipe for this fabulous cake. Bake one, slice off a piece, and sit yourself down at the kitchen table, or behind the wheel of your SUV, and see that—regardless of where you are—this cake is some sort of good.

Hummingbird Cake

This cake is great for dinner parties, Sunday buffets, potluck suppers, or any occasion where you need to provide a knockout dish. The secret to the moist denseness of the cake is not over-stirring the batter; you want to just mix the ingredients together and then bake. Also, use bananas that are good and ripe; those that are still partially green won't be as sweet, and you'll be able to taste the difference in the cake.

INGREDIENTS

3 cups all-purpose flour

2 cups sugar

1 teaspoon salt

1 teaspoon baking soda

1 teaspoon cinnamon

3 eggs, beaten

1½ cup vegetable oil

1½ teaspoons vanilla extract

1, 8-ounce can of crushed pineapple, drained

1 cup chopped pecans

2 cups bananas, mashed

Cream Cheese Frosting (recipe follows)

INSTRUCTIONS

1. Preheat oven to 350 degrees.

2. In a large mixing bowl, add together the flour, sugar, salt, baking soda, and cinnamon. Stir gently with a fork.

3. In another bowl, lightly beat together the eggs and oil; pour this into the flour mixture and stir gently until just mixed.

4. To the batter, add the vanilla, drained pineapple, pecans, and bananas. Stir until just mixed; again, do not beat.

5. Spoon the batter into three 9-inch or two 8-inch, well-greased and floured cake pans.

6. Bake for 20-25 minutes for 9-inch pans, 25-30 for 8-inch pans; the cakes should be browning and pulling slightly away from the edges of the pans when done.

7. Allow to cool at least 30 minutes before frosting. Spread the icing between the layers and on the tops and sides of the cake. Sprinkle the top with chopped pecans.

Serves 10-12

Cream Cheese Frosting

INGREDIENTS

1, 8-ounce block of cream cheese, at room temperature

½ cup unsalted butter, at room temperature

1, 16-ounce box of confectioner's sugar

½ teaspoon vanilla extract

1 cup chopped pecans (for topping the cake)

INSTRUCTIONS

1. Place the cream cheese and butter in a mixing bowl; beat together until smooth.

2. Add the sugar, 1 cup at a time, mixing until incorporated.

3. Add the vanilla and continue to beat until fully mixed.

4. Frost the cake when the layers are completely cooled to room temperature, and sprinkle the top with the chopped pecans.

*   *   *   *   *

And while Chris and I were close growing up, our mothers were friends as well, and our families socialized and visited together often. The Barretts and Spears had a great deal in common, as did so many of the folks in the small, agrarian communities of Middle and South Georgia. Agriculture was then, as it still is now, the largest industry in the state (though Atlanta thinks she is the biggest commodity, she is not). In the summertime our lives centered on farming, gardening, and the harvest and production of our food. Stories abound from all over the South, as you read in a number of these chapters, about growing crops, shelling peas, and "puttin' up" a bushel of corn. It was literally life as we knew it, and every family member had some role in how the fig preserves got sealed in those Ball jars. Here is Chris's reflection back to those days, which gives incredible insight to the commonality and prevalence of Southern farm-to-table food in our homes.

Growing our own, going to the farmers' markets, picking them at local farms—we really were a family that had farm-to-table vegetables. As a child, I dreaded those long, hot, sweaty summer days of picking, shelling, canning, and freezing. I hated bean days the most; those blasted butterbean hulls, particularly the young tight ones, could really swell up a boy's small, tender thumbs. But when it came time to enjoy the results of those days, we had fresh field corn, all sorts of beans and peas, okra, yellow crooked-necked squash, fat and juicy homegrown tomatoes, collards, turnips, watermelon, peaches, berries—basically any and everything that would grow well in the climate of Middle Georgia. We rarely bought fruits or vegetables at the grocery store, and when we did, it was generally iceberg lettuce, apples, oranges, or bananas.

An episode that happened when I was six years old really shows how close we all were in those days to the land and farming. My mother received a call from my first grade teacher, a lady who had just moved to our neck of the woods from somewhere outside the South. She told Mom that she wanted to see her as soon as possible because she was concerned that I had a problem with my vision. Worried, Mom went promptly to the school to meet with Miss Ott, who said, "Mrs. Spears, I administered a test this morning, and I fear sweet Chris is color blind. Please take a look at this." And with that she showed her a piece of paper with the out-

lines of fruits and vegetables I had colored. Being a pretty good student, and food being always an interest, I had taken right away to the assignment that morning. I jumped on coloring the corn and banana yellow, the tomato and apple red, and the cucumber and beans green. An orange got easily matched with orange. And then there was this thing on the page . . . it looked kind of like a flower but was too thick to be a flower. Then I thought maybe it was a bone . . . but no, that wasn't it either. I had no idea. I looked at it again. I looked at my colors. Not knowing what to do, I decided to use a crayon I had not used. What color had I not used? Purple. I colored it purple, thinking it a rich fine color. So purple it was. That's why Mama got the call.

"See," Mrs. Ott said, pointing to the purple-colored mystery, "he cannot distinguish colors. I believe you need to take him to the optometrist." Looking at the paper, Mom knew the real problem right away. She let out a relieved chuckle and told my well-meaning teacher, "Ma'am, Chris has no idea at all what broccoli looks like. It's too hot here in Georgia to raise broccoli, and since we don't grow it, you wouldn't see it on our dining table. I don't think the child's ever set eyes on any before."

After Mama and Miss Ott had a nice laugh over the incident, Miss Ott decided to help expand our rural Georgia vegetable horizons and took our entire class on a field trip to the local Piggly Wiggly grocery store! There we went through the vegetable department and frozen foods, learning about different vegetables and fruits to which we might not have been exposed. Of course she made a point of showing me the broccoli. While I wasn't really interested in these new foods, I was grateful for the trip to the grocery because it was air-conditioned, unlike rural public schools back then. The cool store was a treat in itself.

And while my mama was a good cook, she unfortunately decided to prepare some broccoli for us to eat. She was not much more exposed to it than we children had been, having grown up on the same food that her forebears for generations in Middle Georgia had served. She bought a "mess" (which means a large portion for you folks not from the South) of this newfound produce, proclaimed it a "green" like collards, and prepared it as such. She put two big crowns of broccoli in the pressure cooker with some fatback and cooked it "down." I will let you imagine how wrong that was! It would be years before I had broccoli that was not mush, and what a revelation it was when I first encountered it raw.

So it never fails: if someone mentions broccoli, I see a big, purple stalk—not a flower and not a bone—and remember a hot classroom and a kindly Yankee teacher.

The recipe I have here is great for holiday buffets or at covered dish suppers. I do use fresh broccoli, but it cooks enough so that even my dear sweet mama will eat it (like many of her generation of folks from "down South," she is not fond of crunchy veggies).

—Alphus Christopher Spears

Baked Broccoli & Rice

Buttermilk gives the casserole a smooth yet tart taste that is complemented by the sweet Vidalia onions. And the short-grain rice, like Valencia, provides a lovely soft texture. Please use only fresh broccoli; if you choose frozen, the vegetable will turn out mushy and lose its green coloring.
—ACS

INGREDIENTS

2 tablespoons sweet, unsalted butter, softened to room temperature

1 cup Mahatma Valencia rice, cooked to the package directions *(or other short-grain rice)*

1 cup chopped Vidalia onion

1 cup shredded cheddar, Swiss, or Monterey Jack cheese

1 can cream of mushroom soup

1 cup whole milk buttermilk

3 cups fresh broccoli florets, cut into 1½ to 2-inch sections *(do NOT use frozen broccoli)*

Salt to taste *(Note: I find no salt is needed, as the soup and cheese have plenty of sodium already)*

INSTRUCTIONS

1. Butter a 9"x 13" baking dish and set aside.

2. Preheat oven to 350 degrees.

3. In a large mixing bowl, add the cooked rice, onion, cheese, soup, and buttermilk. Mix well until thoroughly incorporated.

4. Fold in the broccoli, being careful not to break the florets. Stir the mixture into the buttered baking pan.

5. Bake for 35-40 minutes or until the casserole is heated through. Serve immediately.

Serves 6-8

CHAPTER 9

FRIED PIES!

by JSB, Alphus Christopher Spears, and Nancy Fullbright

W hen starting this book and asking people about potential stories, it seemed that *everyone* absolutely loves those wonderful, Southern-made, hot-out-of-the-skillet, fruit-filled confections—fried pies. Peach seems to be the favorite of folks in the Deep South, while apple takes the crown in Appalachia. Being a product of both regions, I will happily take either/or. Many Southerners out there remember standing by the stove, anxiously watching Grandmama as she ladled up those golden-crusted half-moons and placed them on a waiting platter to cool.

So many notes and calls were received about the pies that I probably could have written another whole book just on these delicacies. Here in *Cook & Tell*, though, I've limited it to three stories. Starting us off is my buddy, Chris, whom you read about in the previous chapter, and then I have to add my two cents' worth. Finishing this section is a loving tribute from a granddaughter down in Savannah who recreated her grandmother's recipe just for us.

Now, Chris is full of stories from back home, and some of his fondest memories and recollections are of his Paw-Paw and namesake, Mr. Alphus G. Moody. Unfortunately for young Alphus Christopher and the rest of the Moody clan, they lost Mr. Moody when Chris was just a child. But in their nine years together, the two Alphuses created a bond that hasn't faded over the last four decades. My buddy still talks about Paw-Paw to this day,

Mr. & Mrs. Moody's 50th wedding anniversary. Pawpaw is standing in the middle with the buotonniere, and young Alphus is in the front, far right, Manchester, Georgia, 1969

sometimes not just with a little glistening in his eyes but with full-on tears. How wonderful to have known someone you loved so much.

Here Chris shares with us his touching memory of fried fruit pies (which he called "this-aways and that-aways"), his Paw-Paw, and saying good-bye.

This-aways and That-aways

by Alphus Christopher Spears

I first remember Granny making "this-aways and that-aways" when I was a little kid, using dried fruit. Then they were fried in the black skillet. I also remember Mama making them. I gave them their name because of the way Granny and Mama used to flip them back and forth in their hands—this-away and then that-away—to pat them out. I was probably four when I started calling them that. When Paw-Paw was in the nursing home in his last month before cancer took him in 1974, he asked Mama to make him some. She had to sneak them into the nursing home because

they weren't on his diet. I remember thinking then as a nine-year-old, "That's the dumbest thing in the world. What do they think is going to happen? He's already dying." Every time I have one now, I think about Paw-Paw eating the ones that Mama lovingly made for him.
—Alphus Christopher Spears

⋆ ⋆ ⋆ ⋆ ⋆

As I've said before, the bond between people and food in the South goes beyond simple sustenance; it is such that you can easily recall the foods your loved ones enjoyed and favored just as easily as you can recall the sound of their voice or the color of their hair. And Chris's story here beautifully sums up the knowing, culinary nostalgia that is such a large part of our life here in the land of Dixie.

The Etiquette and Intricacies
of When to Eat a Fried Pie at a Wake
by JSB

Speaking of fried pies, I'd like to share a little anecdote of my own here. As a child growing up, I often saw these treats "on the back of the stove" at our house throughout the year. Mama would make the most fabulous-tasting tarts, even in the wintertime when the fruit was out of season. Our freezer was always full of homegrown peaches, crabapples, and pears, or she'd use dried fruit purchased at the store. But fried pies are rather labor intensive: rolling out the dough, mixing the fillings, and then standing over a big, cast-iron skillet filled with hot grease. As I got older, and Mom made them less often, the pies became more of a rarity. So when an opportunity came along for one of those treats, I would not let it pass me by. Even at a funeral.

Such an occasion arose several years ago, and while it happened at the wake of a dear friend, I believe she would be happy to know she had such a delicious send-off. Lougenia (Lou) Gillis Gabard was gracious, kind, well read, and extensively well traveled, and it had been a real privilege to be in her company. Her obituary saluted her with these wonderful and telling words: "Lou leaves a legacy for her hospitality, etiquette, and generosity. Her grace as a hostess honored many guests with her delectable meals . . . she remained active and independent, living each day to its fullest. It is no irony that Lou had a stroke while exercising on the elliptical machine at the YMCA."

A skillet of peach pies frying

At Lou's death at the age of ninety, my friend Lisa White and I headed west on I-16 for the funeral and visitation. Lou was a member of the highly respected Gillis family; her brother Hugh was actually the longest-serving member of the state assembly, serving fifty-four years under the Gold Dome in Atlanta.

After the internment in the family cemetery, which sits surrounded by towering pines and ancient live oaks in rural Treutlen County, we made our way with the crowd back to the Gillis homestead just down the winding country road. As Lisa and I climbed the steps leading up to the Victorian house, we were joined by our friend Mary Morrison. The three of us chatted quietly, murmuring fond remembrances, and made our way through the double doors inside. A couple of yards into the wide hallway, we spied a large sideboard laden with all sorts of Southern delicacies, including tomato sandwiches, fried chicken, deviled eggs, and cheese straws. Just as we were about to walk past the buffet, though, a waiter approached. In his hands was an ornate silver platter that held a dozen or so delicate, palm-sized, golden wedges that wafted the scents of sugar and peaches.

Lisa, Mary, and I all swooned, and in a scene worthy of the Three Stooges, we did a triple take, looking first in amazement at the platter, then to one another, then back at the platter, and finally exclaiming in total unison, "FRIED PIES!"

A few mourners turned their heads to glance over, but we paid no attention at all. Our intentions had been to make way first into the parlor and pay respects to Lou's family, and then come back for a repast at the sideboard. But the arrival of fried pies was a total game-changer.

Looking around the house and then at each other again, we realized we were in a quandary. Southern manners dictated that our first duty was to console the bereaved loved ones; food should be second. But in this case I left Emily Post and Mama's teachings outside under one of the Gillises' ancient boxwoods.

"Don't know about you all, but I have *got* to have one of those pies before someone else comes along and eats them all up. They'll be gone by the time we make our way through that line," I said in a loud whisper, gesturing toward the parlor.

Mary added wistfully, shaking her head, "Oh my! I don't know *when* I last had a fried peach pie."

Lisa, with her barrister-trained reasoning, sealed the deal with a practical outlook: "Best we take our time and don't crowd the family; we can't get in the other room right now anyway, it's so full of people."

That said, we each took a napkin and, with as much restraint as we could muster, casually lifted our pies off the doily-covered platter, and then "oohed" and "ahhed" with every mouthful. Midway through our bliss, the waiter was back with another tray of some other sort of sumptuousness. While Mary and Lisa looked away to see what he was doing, I deftly lifted another pie, placed it in a napkin, and slipped it in the right-hand pocket of my suit jacket. I knew I'd probably get a grease stain on the lining but thought, "What the hell. Twelve bucks to get it cleaned is worth another one of these pies."

After we paid our respects to the Gillis family and made the rounds visiting with friends, it was time to go, but not before I stuck my head in the kitchen to tell the ladies who were preparing the food how much I loved those pies. In return, I got two big hugs from the cooks along with a paper bag filled with four more pies for me to take home. Just goes to show that good Southern manners pay off! And thanks, Lougenia, for the great friendship and for all that you brought to Georgia. Whenever I get the chance to have one of these delicacies, you know I'll be saying a prayer for you and hoping that you and Bill are enjoying some wonderful holiday trips up in the heavens. —JSB

* * * * *

Our third fried pie story, along with the featured stellar recipe, comes from Georgia native Nancy Fullbright. Nancy grew up in Macon, just a hop, skip, and a jump from my home of Perry. It's no wonder that we've become fast friends over the years. She describes herself as someone who "enjoys traveling—Asheville, North Carolina, and 30-A on the Florida panhandle are two favorite spots—nice dinners out, live music, time spent with friends over cocktails and conversation, and reading." We're now neighbors in our new hometown of Savannah, and our revels together about our common roots from back home often include talking about food and classic country music.

Nancy called me the other day to say she had perfected her grandmother's fried peach pie recipe—one that I'd asked for—and invited me by to try one. I grabbed a jar of my homemade fig preserves to take along (you all know we Southerners can't arrive at someone's house empty-handed) and scooted down the street. Nancy and I, along with her husband Peter and basset hound Sadie, sat in the living room for the next hour, savoring the pies and remembering times back home. Listening all along, British-born Peter observed at one point in the conversation, "The stories you all tell in the South are like Tolkien novels: they all seem to take you on a journey that goes 'round the world before you can make your way home." Truer words were never spoken!

In the following passage, Nancy tells us of the beautiful memories she has of her strong and feisty grandmother, Earline. And as you'll hear, while Aunt Margie made the best sour cream pound cake in the family, the number-one-rated fried pies came out of Grandmother Earline's kitchen.

Thank you, Nancy, for recreating this Southern classic recipe for us and for giving us a glimpse of life in the colorful and interesting world of the Phillips family.

Grandma Earline's Number One Rating

by Nancy Fullbright

I'm standing in my kitchen crying. It's July in Savannah, and I may as well be standing on the surface of the sun frying pies on a sweltering Sunday afternoon. But that's not why I'm crying. It's the memories that these pies bring up that call forth the tears.

I am overcome while rolling out the dough rounds, each push of the pin mixing remembrance with loss. It occurs to me that I've never actually made my Grandma's peach tarts, and my heart twinges. Were it not for JB asking me for a recipe, I may never have attempted to make them. My sister Rebecca should have been the one to carry on Grandma's tradition. She was the Johnson & Wales student. She was the one with the gift. But she's been gone nearly three years now.

I am a pitiful substitute. I had to purchase a rolling pin at Publix this morning just to make the recipe, for crying out loud. But I will gladly pick up this mantle for Rebecca and Grandma.

I ache for my short-statured but feisty Grandma, gone nearly twenty years. My mind tumbles down the rabbit hole, across all the family stories I've been told, to 1922. That's when Earline Phillips Land, my maternal grandmother, was born to Mamie Tudor Phillips and Charlie Lee Phillips in the old family homeplace in McDuffie County, Georgia. She was the seventh child out of twelve born to Mamie, although my great-grandfather had sired four of her half-siblings before his first wife died in childbirth. Grandma used to joke that although they didn't have telephones back in those days, they "sure knew how to reach out and touch someone!"

Margie, my grandmother's last surviving sibling, remembers Grandma as "fiery" and "real bossy" as a young woman, saying she was a natural choice to be put in charge of her brothers and sisters in the field when they had to harvest the sweet potato crop (a task that drew jeers of "Tater digger!" from children riding past on the school bus, until Aunt Betty told those kids they could go straight to hell). After finishing eighth grade, young Earline quit school to help her father collect payments on his rental properties, driving him from tenant to tenant in a horse-drawn buggy.

Spending so much time around her daddy must have influenced her head for business because Aunt Margie said that while Grandma didn't finish school, she had a good education and knew how to make money. As kids, they picked cotton, earning 50 cents for every 100 pounds collected. When a half-sibling's spouse tried to offer her 45 cents for the same weight picked, Grandma let him know in a hurry they would not be back, instead going where their work was properly compensated. Later, as the proprietress of a country store, she would sell barbecue on Saturdays to make extra money and was known all over the county for her hot sauce. She would also shell pecans to sell for a little spending money, and I remember being allowed to use a mechanical nut gatherer to help Grandma pick pecans, the '80s version of Pokemon Go!

Grandma Earline picking flowers at her home

Now, with all those children—and only two boys in the lot—it stands to reason there was some serious competition among the Phillips girls. Although she is quick to point out she made the best sour cream pound cake, Aunt Margie concedes that no other sibling's cooking could compare to Earline's, and she was a jack-of-all-trades in the kitchen, whether it was baking sweet potato pies and pecan pies, cooking barbecue, or frying fish.

I vividly remember her four-vegetable soup and flour hoecake, her chicken and dumplings, her biscuits (patted on top with buttermilk to ensure that crusty, golden crown), and, yes, even the water she kept chilled ice cold in "the Frigidaire," which we eagerly drank out of tin measuring cups in the summer. But if I had to pick one recipe that sums up my Grandma, it would be her peach tarts, more commonly known to some folks as a fried pie.

Unfortunately, she never wrote down the recipe. And I suppose, foolishly, we thought she would always be around to keep frying up those golden pastries. After she passed away in 1997, my mother and aunt were trying to recreate her recipe, and Aunt Myrtle piped in with, "You know, Earline always used a quarter cup of cornstarch in her peach tarts." We all looked at each other knowingly, understanding that Grandma would do anything to retain her title of "best cook," including telling a little white lie to a sister.

This recipe, while not hers exactly, is the closest we have been able to approximate. The hallmark of these peach tarts is the dough—not sprinkled with sugar or too heavy—and the peach filling, made with dried peaches, a splash of white vinegar, and barely sweetened. To me, they're even better the day after they're made, after they've "set up" on a bed of paper towels, room temperature with a cup of coffee. Enjoy.

—Nancy Fullbright

Earline's Fried Peach Pies

You can make the filling and the dough in advance and refrigerate before assembling the tarts and frying.

INGREDIENTS

FOR FILLING

6 to 7 ounces dried peaches

2 cups water

¾ cup sugar

Pat of butter ("no bigger than an acorn," as Earline would say)

1 teaspoon white vinegar

FOR DOUGH

2 cups all-purpose flour

1 teaspoon salt

½ cup Crisco or other shortening

½ cup whole milk, plus more if needed

Vegetable oil

INSTRUCTIONS

1. Place the fruit in a large saucepan and add the water and sugar. Bring to a boil over medium-high heat, then reduce the heat to a simmer and cook until fruit is tender and sugar is dissolved (at least 30 minutes, or until you're easily able to mash the fruit mixture).

2. Remove from heat and add the butter and vinegar. Mash the peaches with a potato masher or fork. Make sure the fruit is blended well, without any big chunks. Set aside and allow to cool to room temperature while you prepare the dough.

3. To make the dough, combine the flour and salt in a medium bowl. Cut in the shortening with a long-tined fork until blended; it should look like small pieces of gravel.

4. Add the milk and stir until the dough just sticks together. (You want to be able to easily roll the dough into a ball; it should not be too dry or too sticky.)

5. With a spatula, form a ball with the dough and scrape it onto a floured surface. Gently knead the flour once or twice.

6. Divide the dough into ten equal portions. With a floured rolling pin, roll each portion into a 5 to 6-inch circle.

7. Place 2 tablespoons of filling in each round. Wet the edges of the dough with milk and fold over, crimping with a fork.

8. In a large skillet, pour the vegetable oil to a depth of ¼ inch and heat over medium high to about 350 degrees.

9. Cook the tarts in batches of three or four at a time, being careful not to crowd the pan. Place each tart carefully into the hot oil and fry until browned on both sides, 3-4 minutes, turning only once. Remove and drain on a paper towel-lined plate. Can be served immediately or stored in an airtight container at room temperature for 2-3 days.

Serves 10

CHAPTER 10

WHAT I REALLY LEARNED FROM BAKING A CAKE

by Celeste Headlee

Celeste Headlee is one of the more recognized names in Public Radio. Her résumé includes award-winning stints as the Midwest Correspondent for NPR as well as being the co-host of Public Radio International's *The Takeaway*. Currently she is at the helm of the highly acclaimed and popular *On Second Thought*, Georgia Public Broadcasting's one-hour show that focuses on news and stories from around the state and the South.

Besides having an impressive career in the news world, Celeste is also a classically trained soprano. She graduated with honors from the Idyllwild Arts Academy and earned a Master's in Vocal Performance from the University of Michigan. Music comes somewhat naturally to her, as she is the granddaughter of the renowned William Grant Still, known as "The Dean of African American Composers." Celeste frequently performs his work at concerts and recitals throughout the country.

This California native—she of the great speaking and singing voice—has been widely embraced by the folks of her new home state. People tune in from the four corners of Georgia each weekday morning at 9:00 to hear about a multitude of topics of interest; items range from hard news stories that are meant to inform to enlightening topics that entertain. When she asked me to be a guest, I jumped at the chance. Not everyone gets to share the airwaves with such a respected talent, and I gave up a little prayer of thanks for such an opportunity.

That said, I admit being more than a bit anxious about the venture. While possessing a good speaking voice myself, and can banter back and forth with the best of the best, this was LIVE radio, and I was going to be questioned by one of the nation's top interviewers. And since I had to arrive "bright-eyed and bushy-tailed" at 8:15, there wasn't a chance for a quick shot of Jack Daniel's to calm my nerves.

Upon my arrival that morning, with a tin each of Icebox Cookies and Chocolate Macaroons made from my Aunt Ida Pauline's recipes, Celeste proved to be as warm

Celeste and her pup, Simba

and gracious as she is talented. I felt right at home on the set while she breezed me through the interview with nary a hiccup on my end.

During the course of that quick twenty minutes—while we were talking back and forth—my hostess mentioned that she had made a Lane cake over the past weekend. I hope I wasn't too obvious as I did a double take looking at her—not just anyone can stride into the kitchen and make one of these legendary Southern desserts. There's the multiple layers, the bourbon-raisin-coconut-pecan filling, and the beaten frosting that go into this labor of love. Impressive! Not only could the lady sing an opera and the next morning burn up the airwaves of national radio, but she could also cook. And cook Southern.

The whole experience was wonderful, and besides making some new friends at GPB (the staff loved the cookies and macaroons), my book sales also soared that day and over the course of the next week. Friends called from all across the state saying how much they enjoyed the segment, and numerous e-mails arrived from people I had never met saying that they were getting a copy of *Rise & Shine!* as soon as possible. One lady relayed that her sister called right after the show and said, "I just ordered two copies of this new food memoir from a Georgia boy. One for me and the other for you!" Another person, a friend of a friend, wrote that her husband heard the broadcast while driving, and promptly pulled over to call their local bookstore and reserve a copy for her birthday. I was totally thrilled, and grateful to Celeste and GPB for the experience.

When starting this project, I wanted to include Celeste in one of the chapters, both as a "thank you" and since she appreciates good Southern food. The recipe she submitted is very simple, and very touching in the story behind it. And while it doesn't present a sentimental remembrance of home, the story demonstrates that many valuable lessons can be found in cooking, such as a sense of pride and self-reliance. The dessert here is delicious, and I urge you to try it for yourself. And when taking a bite, I hope you'll give a toast to strong women: those who can bake a delicious cake and then set out to conquer the world.

The power of food is in its ability to create memories and bonds of affection between people. When we tell stories about cooking with our mothers, we're really talking about them, about our love for them and their love for us. Sometimes we'll use our grandmother's recipe for pumpkin pie over and over, even if the one from America's Test Kitchen is better. Breaking the eggs and pouring the vanilla exactly as she did for years strengthens the bond with our past and our loved ones.

But I don't have any stories like that. My childhood home wasn't warm or loving, and I don't have any fond memories of cooking with my mother. So I bring you a different kind of family recipe. This cake is the only recipe my mother ever taught me how to make, and it was her go-to dish when we were going to casual parties like picnics and potlucks. I learned it when I was eleven or twelve, mostly because I think she was sick of making something for me to take to class parties.

As a dessert, it couldn't be simpler or more delicious. But this recipe, like so many others, represents much more than the list of ingredients. This was the first recipe I knew by heart, the first dish I could make without looking at a printed recipe. And there's a real power in that. I still remember, thirty years later, pulling that first cake out of the oven and thinking, *"I made this without any help and I could do it again in any kitchen, anywhere in the world."*

While my mother wasn't particularly nurturing, she did value independence highly, and she taught her children to be self-sufficient. This recipe represents my first step toward independence and capability in the kitchen. And I guess, in the end, that's a fond memory.
—Celeste Headlee

Pineapple Upside-down Cake

You'll notice that no liquid is in this recipe.

INGREDIENTS

5 ounces sliced almonds

32 ounces crushed pineapple, drained

One package yellow cake mix

16 tablespoons (2 sticks) unsalted butter, sliced into ¼-inch squares

Whipped cream for topping

INSTRUCTIONS

1. Preheat oven to 350 degrees.

2. Grease a 13" x 9" cake pan.

3. Sprinkle the sliced almonds evenly across the bottom of the pan, then follow in the same manner with the crushed pineapple.

4. Pour the dry cake mix on top of pineapple and smooth it out with a spatula or the back of a spoon so it's as flat as you can get it.

5. Place the sliced butter on top so you nearly cover the cake. This works out to about 5 squares across and 8 squares up the side.

6. Bake for 28-33 minutes, until the top is gold brown and slightly crispy. Remove from the oven and set aside. Allow to cool to room temperature and invert onto a cake plate.

7. Serve with freshly whipped cream.

Serves 8

CHAPTER 11

LOADED WITH SHINNY

by JSB

A s I am prone to do, I find that one story leads to another—so when writing about Celeste making a Lane cake, my mind went straight back to the first time I read *To Kill a Mockingbird*. As I've said, Southerners love to talk, and to talk about food, and Harper Lee humorously weaves this Dixie-made creation into her famous plot.

In the small town of Maycomb, Alabama, where the novel takes place, lives one of those storied women who is famous for making cakes. In this case, Miss Maudie Atkinson is known by everyone for her particular magic with a Lane cake. And apparently she is fond of adding in more than a fair share of bourbon, as Scout Finch, the novel's six-year-old narrator, proclaims, "Miss Maudie Atkinson baked a Lane cake so loaded with shinny it made me tight." (Note to those readers unfamiliar with Southern slang: "shinny" is a term for liquor, and "tight" means tipsy.) Ms. Lee goes on to add another delightfully entertaining aside in the novel involving the renowned Miss Atkinson, who has to move in temporarily with a rival cake baker. Miss Atkinson says,

Mr. Avery will be in bed for a week—he's right stove up. He's too old to do things like that and I told him so. Soon as I can get my hands clean and when Stephanie Crawford's not looking, I'll make him a Lane cake. That Stephanie's been after my recipe for thirty years, and if she thinks I'll give it to her just because I'm staying with her she's got another think coming.

Lord, how many times have I heard my own mother or any number of her friends or sisters make that ultimate and determined statement, "They got another think coming!" Meaning, of course, that whatever that third party is wanting to happen, well, it just ain't gonna transpire. And wouldn't you have loved to know Miss Atkinson and to have one of her prized cakes on your Christmas dinner table?

So in the roundabout way of typical Southern porch chit-chat and gossip, and taking a bend in the road of a tale, I decided to include the recipe here for a classic Lane cake, even though it only had a small part in Celeste's story. In for a penny, in for a pound, right?

In the lore of the cuisine of our country, the Lane cake holds a special place on Southern sideboards and buffets, especially during the holidays. It was created by Mrs. Emma Rylander Lane of Clayton, Alabama, who entered it into the county fair in nearby Columbus, Georgia. This multi-layered delight brought home the first prize, and since then it has been referred to as not only a Lane cake or Alabama Lane Cake but also a "Prize" cake. In 1898, the talented Mrs. Lane shared the recipe in her self-published cookbook, *A Few Good Things to Eat*, and soon a Lane cake was a must for the lady of the house throughout the Deep South. Its popularity has since spread, and if you've never sampled one, you'll see why it is so revered when you read the list of ingredients.

However, let me say that making this cake is not for a novice baker; it takes a good deal of time and a patient hand. The recipe requires the sifting of dry ingredients twice along with the careful beating and folding of egg whites, the filling has several steps that need careful attention, and the final touch is the classic but challenging 7-Minute Frosting that has to be orchestrated in a double boiler. The end product is absolutely worth it, but plan on an entire afternoon in the kitchen. My mom, who was a great cook, wouldn't even attempt one. She paid a local baker so that we would have one on our holiday table.

The recipe here is adapted from a Perry favorite, Mildred Evans Warren. Her popular book, *The Art of Southern Cooking*, was issued by Doubleday & Company, Inc. in 1967 to critical acclaim. It has been reprinted several times, and whenever I come across a copy, I buy it and save it to give as a present. I grew up just down the street from Miss Mildred; she was a wonderful and lovely lady.

Note here: Mrs. Warren and a number of other cooks did not include the frosting in their recipes. Instead, many bakers used the filling to spread between the layers as well as on the top and sides of the cake. While I don't like the challenge of making the frosting, it makes the Lane cake that much more special and attractive, so I've included the recipe and steps herein.

One big secret for the Lane cake (and this is the one part that isn't difficult!) is that it needs to "sit" and allow the flavors to develop and marry over the course of at least two days before you slice and serve it. The bourbon filling will seep into the cake, making it more delicious the longer it sits.

Lane Cake

INGREDIENTS
3½ cups cake flour

2 teaspoons baking powder

¼ teaspoon salt

1 cup unsalted butter, at room temperature

2 cups sugar

1 cup whole milk, at room temperature

2 teaspoons vanilla extract

8 large egg whites (save the yolks for the filling recipe that follows)

Filling (recipe follows)

7-Minute Frosting (recipe follows)

INSTRUCTIONS
1. Preheat oven to 350 degrees.
2. Lightly grease three 9-inch cake pans and line them with parchment paper. Grease the paper as well, and then dust the paper and the pans with flour; shake out the excess flour. Set aside.
3. Sift the flour, baking powder, and salt together into a bowl. Sift again.

4. In a separate large bowl, cream the butter for 1 minute until thoroughly softened. Add the sugar and beat on medium speed until light and thoroughly mixed, scraping the sides of the bowl periodically.

5. Add the milk and vanilla together in a measuring cup.

6. To the creamed butter and sugar, add the sifted ingredients and milk/vanilla mixture alternately in three batches, mixing over low speed, starting with the flour mixture. Beat until smooth and set aside.

7. Rinse the beaters and wipe dry. In another bowl, beat the egg whites over medium-high speed until soft peaks form. Fold the beaten egg whites gently into the batter with a wide spatula until thoroughly but gently mixed.

8. Pour the batter into the prepared cake pans, and smooth out the tops. Bake about 25 minutes until just beginning to brown. When done, an inserted toothpick will come out clean with just a few crumbs attached.

9. Allow the layers to cool in the pans for about 10-15 minutes. Invert the cakes on a wire rack and remove the paper if still attached. Allow to come to room temperature before spreading with the filling and icing the cake.

Serves 10-12

Lane Cake Filling

INGREDIENTS

2 cups sugar

8 large egg yolks

½ cup unsalted butter, melted

1 cup raisins, finely chopped

1 cup pecans, finely chopped

1 cup shredded coconut

½ cup bourbon

1 teaspoon vanilla extract

Pinch of salt

INSTRUCTIONS

1. Place the sugar and egg yolks in a large saucepan and beat until smooth.

2. Add the melted butter and cook over medium heat, stirring often and well, until the mixture is thick, smooth, and can coat the back of a spoon, about 10 minutes or more. Do not let the mixture come to a boil.

3. Stir in the raisins, pecans, and coconut, and continue to cook for 1 more minute.

4. Remove from heat and stir in the bourbon, vanilla extract, and salt. Set aside and allow to cool to lukewarm, or room temperature.

5. When cooled, spread evenly between the layers of the cake.

7-Minute Frosting

INGREDIENTS

2¼ cup sugar

3 egg whites

⅜ cup cold water

1½ tablespoons white Karo Syrup

⅜ teaspoon cream of tartar

1 teaspoon vanilla extract

INSTRUCTIONS

1. In the bottom of a double boiler, bring about 3 inches of water to a steady simmer over medium-high heat.

2. In the top of the double boiler, beat together the sugar, egg whites, water, syrup, and cream of tartar for 1 minute, until well incorporated.

3. Place the frosting base onto the simmering water, and beat at high speed for 7 minutes. Remove from heat, and add vanilla. Continue to beat until the icing is thick and forms firm peaks. This may take an additional several minutes.

4. Ice the sides and top of the cake with the frosting (the filling will be between the layers).

CHAPTER 12

YOU CAN TAKE THE GIRL OUT OF THE GARDEN, BUT…

by Teri Bell

R ecently while reading *The Savannah Morning News* I came across a column from one of my favorite of the paper's contributors, Teri Bell, aka "Miss Sophie." I always enjoy reading her stories and hearing about the delicious, down-home recipes she provides. This particular article was about her paternal grandmother and the delicious pots of chicken and rice she would create. I promptly put down the paper, googled the restaurant's phone number, and gave Teri a call. And while we had never met before, we had so much in common that our conversation was like that of two cousins sitting on a porch swing, sipping iced tea, and catching up with one another after a summer apart.

When we started talking it thrilled me to no end, too, that her husband had mentioned *Rise & Shine!* to Teri some months beforehand. He had heard my interview on Celeste Headlee's Georgia Public Broadcasting show, *On Second Thought*, and knew that his wife would enjoy reading my book due to our shared heritage in Middle Georgia, family gardens, and cooking philosophies. And he was dead on.

Teri hails from Hazlehurst, Georgia, a small town just a little over an hour's drive down US Highway 341 from Perry. The countryside in our "neck of the woods" is filled with pine forests, slow-moving creeks, fields of cotton and soybeans, and old homesteads planted with fig trees, plum bushes, and scuppernong vines that run along fence posts and strung wire.

Our shared childhood is so familiar that Teri could have been featured as one of my kin in *Rise & Shine!* I relate in the memoir how my father would rouse me from bed on summer mornings to pick vegetables and fruit for the family table, and how at the time I truly despised that task. In a note she sent me the other day, Teri laments the same ritual from her days back home in Jeff Davis County. She includes, too, a similar lesson that I carry from those days of working stooped over a row of beans in the July heat.

My grandfather had a garden. I hated that garden! Mama would take a week of vacation and we would spend a week in that garden. A twelve-year-old finds no joy in getting up early to pick peas. It was pure torture. Papa thought it was a sin to let anything in the garden go to waste, so we harvested, shelled, blanched, and bagged everything. We had pear relish from Papa's pear trees, pickles, peas, butterbeans, creamed corn, corn on the cob, boiled peanuts, jars of tomatoes, and my favorite, fig preserves, year round. Papa wasn't a farmer though; he owned a funeral home. Gardening was just his passion. Papa's garden, even though I hated it as a young girl, taught me what real food is supposed to taste like.

And while Teri is now known throughout Southeast Georgia for her culinary talents, she did not start off as a commercial cook or chef. Her first career lasted eighteen years as a legal secretary, and after retirement, she ruminated on what she wanted to do. Her "ever wise" husband, as she describes him, offered the advice to "do something you love." She tells it this way:

I was always taking casseroles, sweets, and food to church, to sick people, and to anyone I could find who needed food. So I decided to open a small casserole store. My original business plan was to bake a few cakes, make a few casseroles, eat cookies with my friends, and do a few crafts! Well, this is the point of my life that I just say God had a different business plan. Somehow, I ended up owning a restaurant, writing for the newspaper, catering, and managing a cafeteria for the employees of the Hatachi-Mitsubishi plant!

When asked about her cooking philosophy, her thoughts reflect very much what I feel, and indeed learned from my relatives who worked their magic in the kitchen.

I'm not sure I have a developed philosophy. I just love to feed people good, familiar food. As you know in the South, the first reaction to births, deaths, illness—even moving to a new home—is "What can I cook?" I don't know what my customers are facing that day, but I do know that good, familiar food will make everything better!

Miss Sophie, the restaurant's namesake

Teri and her staff at "Miss Sophie's Marketplace" at the Mighty Eight Airforce Museum celebrated their tenth anniversary on June 30, 2016, a testament to Teri's cooking abilities, her warmth, and her hospitality. On her menu you'll find such Southern comfort-food favorites as fried pork chops, pot roast with vegetables, macaroni and cheese, sweet potato crunch, black-eyed peas, banana pudding, and a twelve-layer chocolate cake.

Her customers' favorite? Shepherd's pie. She says, "It isn't too exciting, but who doesn't love meat, potatoes, gravy, and cheese?" Indeed!

And to answer the question "why" on the name of her restaurant and her moniker? Well, take a look at this beautiful little girl pictured here.

She was only a year old when we started the business. We were looking for a name that sounded like a Southern grandmother or great-aunt. My husband added the "Miss" to her name one morning and we both knew that was it! She agreed to let me use her name at work, but she's the only Sophie at home.

The following is the wonderful story mentioned at the beginning of the chapter, and Teri kindly agreed to have it reprinted here. It was contributed to the April 20, 2016, edition of *The Savannah Morning News*. In it she writes about the special love she had for her grandmother, and the delicious, comfort-of-home chicken and rice dish that still remains dear to her after all these years. Enjoy.

Grandma Taylor

It's funny the things we remember about people in our lives. I've been thinking about my Grandma Taylor's yellow Chicken and Dumplings and her yellow Chicken and Rice. Both seemed better than anyone else's. I now know that the yellow came from the drops of yellow food coloring she put in the dishes, but that yellow dye made the dish ten times better for me as a child.

Grandma Taylor was my biological father's mother. My parents divorced when I was two and my mother got Grandma Taylor in the divorce! Grandma didn't take kindly to her son running off for years at a time and not helping support me. She often made that clear to him and to Mama!

Grandma married Mr. Taylor after her first husband died. I loved going to visit with them. Their house had a big fenced-in yard and screened porches on the front and back. The yard was full of big green plants and concrete benches. I loved to play outside while Grandma sat in the rocker on the porch. They had a little Chihuahua that patrolled those fences like a security guard. Grandma bathed the dog every Saturday in the back yard in a big washtub filled with soapsuds. I always thought he was so lucky to get to play in the water like that every Saturday. Sometimes after his bath, Grandma would rinse out the tub, fill it full of water again, and let me play in it too!

That washtub had many purposes. Grandma had a ringer washing machine under the carport. After the machine washed the clothes, she would feed them through the ringers to squeeze out the water and then toss them into the washtub for transporting to the clothesline. I thought those ringers were so cool!

Mr. Taylor died while I was still very young, and Grandma married Joe Leopold when I was in second grade. She brought him by our house for Mama to meet him before she married him. I can still see him sitting in the chair by the front door as she told Mama about him. He told us he was in the war and suffered from "shell shock," and I always thought that meant he was riding in the back of a truck when a bomb exploded, and he was shocked and scared.

Joe and Grandma liked to go dancing at the Moose Lodge. Grandma would dress me up and take me with them sometimes. I liked the pretty dresses she bought for me to wear. One time she even took me to the beauty shop and had my hair put up in barrel curls. I loved all those barrels on top of my head; I felt very pretty and grown up.

Grandma convinced me to eat my first tomato. We had gone to the farmers' market early one Saturday morning, and she purchased some bright red tomatoes. I turned my nose up at them when she sliced them for lunch, but she somehow convinced me to try one. For some odd reason, I have a vivid memory of sitting at the dining table on the screened porch next to the kitchen and tasting that thinly sliced tomato with black pepper specks and salt on top. It was acidic, salty, and so delicious that I ate the whole tomato. Perhaps my memory has comingled the love for my grandmother with the taste of that tomato, but tomatoes today can't hold a candle to the one Grandma sliced that day.

Sadly, Grandma went to heaven when I was in my early twenties, but she left me with so many precious memories. She was a great cook. By today's standards, she would be considered a simple cook. Her food wasn't fancy or gourmet; it was just good. I hope that someday my grandchildren's memories will comingle my food and my love and they will remember me as fondly as I do my Grandma Taylor.

—Teri Bell

Old-Fashioned Chicken & Rice

The secret in this dish is the broth. The rice absorbs the flavor of the liquid it's cooked in. In my opinion, a good broth requires bones and fat that can only be found in whole chickens or hens.

INGREDIENTS

1 (3-4 pounds) whole chicken, skin on

2 celery stalks, tops attached, roughly diced

1 medium onion, chopped, or 3 tablespoons dried onion

2 large carrots, roughly diced

6 cups water

1 teaspoon salt

¼ teaspoon black pepper

2 cups white long grain rice, such as Mahatma *(don't use instant rice)*

A couple of drops of yellow food coloring *(if the grandchildren are coming over)*

INSTRUCTIONS

1. Place chicken, celery, onion, carrots, water, salt and pepper in a 5-quart stock pot with a tight-fitting lid. Bring to a boil, then reduce heat to a simmer and cover.

2. Cook for 1 hour or longer, until the chicken is done.

3. Remove chicken from pot and set aside to cool.

4. Taste broth for salt and pepper and adjust if needed.

5. Return broth to a rolling boil and add rice and, if desired, food coloring.

6. Reduce to a simmer and cook for twenty minutes, stirring occasionally so that it does not stick to the bottom of the pan.

7. While rice is cooking, debone the chicken and chop or shred meat; discard the bones and fat. Add the chopped chicken to the cooked rice with a good sprinkling of pepper. Stir to combine. Serve while hot.

Serves 6

CHAPTER 13

MAMA LOVED ALTON BROWN

by JSB

Teri said that at her "Miss Sophie's Marketplace," the shepherd's pie is the best-selling dish. Now when someone mentions this Old World classic, I don't think about jolly old England and pub food, but of my Mama, Joyce Lou, who loved that dish and who also loved Alton Brown.

Mama was pretty old school in terms of her food until she was well into her fifties, preparing such standards as fried pork chops, stewed squash, fresh butterbeans, and peach pie. But as cooking shows became popular, and began competing with the soap operas, my little Southern Mama— from the metropolis of Clinchfield, Georgia—started spreading her culinary wings.

First there was Justin Wilson, who she thought was a hoot. She would laugh along and gamely drink a couple of glasses of wine while watching his show. She had several of Mr. Wilson's cookbooks and would fix up a number of his Cajun creations, just with a little less cayenne. Another favorite was Mr. Food, who came on 13WMAZ out of Macon, with his tag line, "Ooh! It's so good!" She also watched Nathalie Dupree and liked her food immensely, particularly her cheese straws. Moving north, Joyce Lou tuned in to the Barefoot Contessa regularly as well, and remarked that Miss Garten was "incredibly classy but not showy at all," a big compliment coming from Mama. She did not like pretensions one little bit.

Mama cooking in the kitchen

There were some shows, though, that she would not watch, those that she found "vulgar" or where they "talked dirty." Not naming names here, but many of you can guess which those were. Mama said you had to be happy in the kitchen, or your food would show it—a pearl of wisdom if there ever was about good cooking.

But of all the shows and chefs she did enjoy watching, she was enthralled with Alton Brown and his show *Good Eats*. Something about Alton just connected with my mom. She was fascinated and thoroughly enjoyed his explanations of why something worked, or wouldn't work, in a dish. She would remark time after time while watching his episodes, "Well, that makes sense," or "I'd never have thought of that." Too, I think she saw a little of his somewhat "geeky" side in me, and there was the fact that Alton grew up in Georgia. She found his recipes straightforward and easy to prepare, and his style comfortable in terms of engaging with his audience.

At some point she came across Alton's recipe for shepherd's pie, and it became one of her standards. It was a go-to dish for potlucks, a new neighbor moving in, or a Sunday night supper with a side salad and hot garlic rolls. She found that the pies would freeze well, too, so she could make them in advance and pluck one out of the chest freezer when she needed a dish at the last minute.

The recipe here is adapted from Alton's own, but a bit simpler. While Mama said she appreciated all the work he put into it, sometimes she didn't have everything it called for. Plus, she didn't care for the taste of lamb, so she substituted ground beef. But the gist is the same, and it really is the best shepherd's pie I've had this side of the Atlantic.

One regret is that Mama left us before I could take her to see Mr. Brown on tour. She would have loved it. And I think, if he'd met Mama, he'd have loved her, too.

Mama's Alton Brown's Shepherd's Pie

Besides trying new dishes as she entered her golden years, Mama also discovered that she could use a number of pre-packaged foods instead of starting from scratch, such as piecrusts or, in this case, mashed potatoes. If you don't feel like peeling and cooking your own, buy one of the 24-ounce packages of mashed potatoes you find in the grocer's refrigerator section. It is a perfect size.

FOR THE POTATOES

INGREDIENTS

1½ pounds white potatoes, peeled and cut into 1-inch cubes
    (or 1, 24-ounce packaged prepared mashed potatoes found in the
    refrigerated section of your local grocer)

¼ cup half-and-half (more as needed)

2 tablespoons butter

¾ teaspoon kosher salt

¼ teaspoon ground black pepper

Yolk of one large egg

INSTRUCTIONS

1. Cover the potatoes with water in a medium-sized pot and cover. Place on high heat, and bring to a boil.

2. When the water begins to boil, remove the lid and decrease heat to medium. Cook, stirring occasionally, until done, about 15 minutes. Drain the potatoes in a colander.

3. Put the potatoes back in the pot, and mash them until soft. Add the half-and-half, butter, salt, and pepper, and stir well to incorporate. Stir in the yolk and set the pot in the refrigerator, allowing the potatoes to cool.

FOR THE MEAT FILLING

INGREDIENTS

1½ pounds lean ground beef, or ground lamb, or mixture of the two

1 teaspoon kosher salt

2 tablespoons olive oil

1 cup chopped carrots, about 4 large

1 cup chopped onion, about 1 large

1 tablespoon minced fresh garlic, about 2 cloves

2 tablespoons flour

2 tablespoons tomato paste

1 cup low-sodium beef broth or stock

1 teaspoon Worcestershire sauce

2 teaspoons freshly minced rosemary

1 teaspoon freshly minced thyme

½ teaspoon freshly ground black pepper

1 cup English peas, either fresh or frozen

1½ cups grated sharp cheddar cheese

INSTRUCTIONS

1. In a bowl, mix together the ground meat and the salt.

2. Meanwhile, heat the olive oil in a large pot or Dutch oven. When hot, add the meat. Allow the meat to brown some, and then stir. Chop the meat into small pieces with a wooden spoon when stirring. Allow the meat to cook until completely done, about 10 minutes. Remove the meat from the pan, place in a bowl, and set aside. Pour off and discard all but about 3 tablespoons of fat from the pan.

3. Place the pan and reserved fat back onto the stove over medium-high heat. Add the carrots, and sauté for 2-3 minutes.

4. Add the onions, stir, and sauté with the carrots another minute or two.

5. Add in the garlic, stir, and cook another minute.

6. Add the meat back into the pan, and stir to mix together with the vegetables.

7. Sprinkle the flour into the pan, and stir to coat and thoroughly mix.

8. Add in the tomato paste, beef stock, Worcestershire sauce, rosemary, thyme, and black pepper. Stir to mix, and bring the filling to a simmer. Allow to continue simmering, stirring occasionally and being careful not to let the filling stick to the bottom of the pan, for another 3 to 4 minutes. Remove from heat and set aside to cool.

9. Preheat your oven to 400 degrees while the meat filling cools.

10. Add the peas to the filling, and stir to mix. Spread the mixture evenly into a lightly greased 11"x 7" baking dish with deep sides (or you can place the filling in 4 individual Corningware dishes or ceramic dishes).

11. Top with the cooked, mashed potatoes, starting on the sides to make a seal—this way the filling won't bubble up around the edges. Carefully spread the potatoes evenly over the meat with a spatula or large spoon.

12. Sprinkle the top with the cheese, and place the pan, or crocks, on a baking or cookie sheet.

13. Bake for 20-25 minutes until the filling is hot and the cheese has melted into the potatoes.

14. Remove from the oven, and allow to cool for about 15 minutes before serving.

Serves 4

CHAPTER 14

LOST IN TRANSLATION

by Sandra Gutierrez

With the help of good fortune and a publicist with connections, I landed a spot on a four-person panel at the Southern Independent Booksellers Association annual convention in fall 2015. It was there that I first met the talented and charming Sandra Gutierrez. Her reputation having already impressed me, hearing her speak in person gave me a further appreciation of her passion for food and her culinary skills.

Although born in the USA, Sandra was raised in Latin America and has for the last two decades enjoyed a very successful career as a food writer and culinary instructor. Her articles and recipes are found in newspapers and magazines around the world, including publications such as *USA Today*, *Huffington Post*, and *The Miami Herald*. She also has penned four critically acclaimed cookbooks. Her *New Southern-Latino Table* is a fascinating work that blends ingredients and traditions, marrying the foods of Latin America with those found in Dixie. A few of the mouth-watering offerings from this award-winning book are Jalapeño Deviled Eggs, Macaroni con Queso, and Latin Fried Chicken with Smoky Ketchup. Can you say *yum*?

Here Sandra tells of her first experience of being exposed to a Southern potluck dinner. It happened in Durham, North Carolina, many years ago. The story shows that good humor, friendship, and food all blend together, regardless of what language you speak.

I arrived in the South a young bride, barely twenty years old and fresh out of college. American by birth and Latina by heritage, I had everything to learn about my new home. And I mean everything. Oh, I spoke the language. After all, I grew up fluently bilingual in Latin America and attended college in the United States. However, as hard as it was to get used to the Bostonian accent (where the "r's" are not pronounced) while in college in New England, nothing could fully prepare me for the beautiful cadence and romance of the Southern drawl. It was love at first "y'all."

Sandra and her husband

The South I first encountered was filled with culinary history and a clear regional cuisine. Some of the food was strangely familiar—the pulled pork was somewhat similar to the "cochinito" I had grown up eating (drizzled with lime juice and chiles in place of vinegar sauce), the grits were made with the same hominy—or nixtamalized corn—that I used to make tamales and tortillas. Potato salads, coleslaw, layered cakes, and puddings were nothing new to me. Fried chicken ran through my blood, as did casseroles, pecans, and pickled shrimp. Yet I knew nothing of pimento cheese, hushpuppies, field peas, and chess pies. I had yet to meet my first ambrosia, taste my first okra, and savor my first mint julep.

Back in the day, there were few Latinos in Durham. In fact, it took eight years before we met anyone else from Latin America in the South, outside of the international student circle at the Fuqua School of Business at Duke University, where my husband studied.

It is no exaggeration to say that I stuck out like a sore thumb. My blonde and blue-eyed husband wasn't seemingly that different—until he opened his mouth to speak with a heavier Latin accent than mine and was met with confused looks. To say that we threw everyone off when they first met us is to put it mildly; people just didn't quite know what to do with us.

Which is why we were very excited when, after a few months of living in the South, we were finally invited to our first party—a potluck, to be precise. Our new friend wanted us to meet people so we wouldn't feel so lonely. The only thing, she said, was that I was to bring food to share with twenty other people.

Now, you must understand that the idea of a party was not foreign to us. However, we had never been invited to a potluck. In fact, we had never even heard of the term "potluck." Period.

I told my husband how sweet and welcoming this new friend was, but that she must not be doing so well financially because she needed me to bring dinner for twenty people. We agreed that she was very nice to offer to introduce us to new friends and left it at that.

The night of the party, we walked into her home with dinner for twenty people! From appetizer to dessert, I took enough food to feed an army: fifty Guatemalan tacos (rolled up like cigars and fried to golden perfection), a giant salad, chicken with sweet chile sauce, a huge rice casserole, and my pièce de résistance—two "impossible" cakes.

At first, our friend looked stunned as I presented her with dinner for twenty, as she had requested. Then she exploded in laughter. I was mortified at first, but it proved impossible not to join her when she pointed to the dining room table brimming with food—and I understood. Some things, it seems, do get lost in translation.

Suffice it to say that we made quick friends with everyone that night. At the end of the evening, we all walked out with plates of leftovers and with a story that no doubt everyone remembers to this day.

This recipe is really called "Impossible Cake," and it's a classic in many Latin homes (it's also known as "Magic Cake" or "Chocoflán"). The cake is half custard and half cake. First, caramel is poured into a Bundt pan. Cake batter follows, and then it's topped with liquid custard before it's baked in the oven, in a water bath. The heat causes the denser cake batter to produce gas, which makes it lighter than the custard; this change in density causes both layers to invert order. Once unmolded, the resulting cake is perfectly layered with the caramel sauce on the top, followed by the custard layer, and then the chocolate cake in the bottom.

As difficult as this cake sounds, it is one of the easiest recipes to make. The next time you're invited to a potluck, take this cake. It will make you many friends—about twenty—guaranteed.
—Sandra Gutierrez

Impossible Cake

INGREDIENTS

CAKE LAYER

1 box deviled chocolate cake mix

3 large eggs

1 cup water

½ cup vegetable oil

1 teaspoon ground cinnamon

FLAN LAYER

One (14 ounce) can of sweetened condensed milk

1 cup whole milk

5 eggs

1 teaspoon vanilla extract

¾ cup cajeta or dulce de leche, warmed until it's of pourable consistency

INSTRUCTIONS

1. Preheat the oven to 350 degrees.

2. Grease the sides and bottom of a large loaf pan (9"x 5"x 2") or a large Bundt cake pan.

3. Fill a large pot with water and bring it to a boil; keep it at a simmer while you work.

4. In a large bowl, combine the cake mix, 3 eggs, water, vegetable oil, and cinnamon; stir with a spatula until the batter is smooth. Set aside.

5. In a blender, combine the condensed milk, whole milk, 5 eggs, and vanilla; blend until smooth. Set aside.

6. Pour the cajeta or dulce de leche into the prepared pan, making sure to spread it all over the bottom.

7. Pour the cake batter from the bowl on top of the cajeta layer; top with the flan layer from the blender.

8. Cover the pan tightly with aluminum foil. Use a clean kitchen towel to line a large pan with high sides. Place the loaf pan in the middle of the large pan; place the pans in the middle of the preheated oven and pour 1½ inches of boiling water in the bottom pan (to create a water bath).

9. Bake the cake until a toothpick inserted in the middle comes out clean, about 1½ hours.

10. Remove the cake from the oven and let it cool completely at room temperature. Loosen the sides of the cake with a knife and invert the cake onto a large plate. Refrigerate until chilled.

Serves 12

CHAPTER 15

NEWLYWED CHICKEN AND DUMPLINGS

by Gayle Morris

M y friend Gayle Morris of Athens, Georgia, is a wonderful buddy and a Bulldog fan of the highest order. A woman of splendid tastes and varied interests, Gayle has traveled the world, exploring new cultures, faraway lands, and a myriad of cuisines. But, like me, the red-clay blood in Gayle draws her back home to Georgia, where she continues to make some of the best Southern dishes you can imagine. She once invited me to her mountain cottage for supper and served the most incredible chicken pot pie that had a homemade biscuit topping. It was so good I ate three helpings at one sitting . . . and literally gained two pounds overnight. That was ten years ago and I'm still talking about that pie; it was just that fabulous.

Besides being a seasoned cook and world traveler, Gayle is also known as one who is never without anything to say. Her anecdotes are as engaging, funny, and full of life as she is herself. Here she relays, in true Gayle fashion, the humorous story of one of her first cooking experiences, which involved a slightly demanding husband, a strong-willed mother-in-law, and a crock full of homemade chicken and dumplings. Several of us reading this know, as you'll hear from Gayle, that some kitchen disasters can produce laughable moments—with the passage of time.

Let's start with a little background information about myself and cooking. Having made the decision to marry my high school sweetheart sooner rather than later, as some of us did back in the day of 1958, I was ill prepared to tackle the cooking responsibilities that followed me into this choice. But, being the blessed child that I was, meaning I did not know I was not capable of anything I set my mind to (my Nannie's words exactly), I found myself in the kitchen with three "gifts" to bring me up to snuff on the cooking process. First and foremost was my husband, who wanted me to "cook like his mama." Second was that formidable mama, who in turn wanted me to feed her son well as she had always done. And third, but most important, was the miracle of having rented our first little house just two doors down the street from my wonderful, "I will teach you how to cook" mother-in-law. Yes, I was blessed!?

First, I needed to learn to make biscuits, which is not an easy task to start with. It's not like you can open up a box, pour in some milk, and they magically appear. My learning started with a wooden bread tray and the hard part of finding out that there was no measuring any of the ingredients. You had to "play it by ear:" sift flour into the middle of the tray... make a circle hole in the flour . . . scoop up lard with your fingers curved to form a cup . . . add to the flour . . . then pour buttermilk over the lard and start squeezing with your fingers to mix the lard and buttermilk while reaching over with your fingers and grabbing small amounts of flour to blend in as you go until it becomes "right." Now that last word, "right," is the secret to making good biscuits, and I do not have words to tell you what it means. You must feel it for yourself and do it wrong many, many times to finally learn what "right" is. So now on with the dumplings story.

It was a cold winter day, perfect for chicken and dumplings, and armed with instructions and the recipe from my sweet mother-in-law I began to prepare for the family gathering that night. I boiled my chicken in a large pot with a few diced carrots and onions until done, removed it from the broth and pulled the meat from the bones, and then added the chicken back to the broth. Then I made the biscuits, but instead of squeezing them into round shapes I rolled the dough out real thin, cut it into strips, and held it over the pot and pinched it off in inch-long pieces, which I then dropped into the broth, stirring with a wooden spoon occasionally to keep

Gayle with her daughter Gaye, 1960, about the time of the chicken and dumping incident.

them moving. My, my, what a sweet smell, and they tasted delicious. One of my wedding gifts was a heavy pottery bowl, and I decided to pour my beautiful, yummy chicken and dumplings into this lovely crock to carry the meal two doors down for dinner. I was about the happiest young cook in Athens that night.

I gently gathered the bowl, careful to wrap a towel around it to keep from burning my hands, and started for the door. I was dressed up cute in a new outfit and strutting with my bowl of dumplings, ready for my debut as a new young wife into the family circle of good cooks. Then, as I was walking across the living room toward the front door, the towel slipped. I grabbed for the bowl but down to the floor it went! Hardwood floors took my dinner away from me and left me with the greasiest, stickiest mess imaginable—a million pieces of forest-green pottery shards, mixed with my dumplings and chicken, were scattered from one end of the room to another. I screamed, I cried, I stomped my feet, and then I called down the street and declared that we had no dumplings for dinner.

I remember well looking at the mess on the floor, and the flour and dirty pots all over the kitchen, and declaring that I would never ever make chicken and dumplings again. Never!

But, after the hurt feelings became a dim memory, I gave it another try, and I have been making this dish now for forty-plus years. However, if I have to transport my chicken and dumplings, they are safely enclosed in a Tupperware container. Forget the crockery presentation.

—Gayle Morris

Chicken & Dumplings

Here is Gayle's magnificent recipe. Hint: If you don't feel like making dumplings, you can substitute 10-12 frozen biscuits, such as Mrs. B's or those from Pillsbury. Allow them to come to room temperature, dust a flat surface with flour, roll them out on the surface one by one, and slice them into strips as instructed below. But since chicken and dumplings is such a rare treat, homemade dumplings make the dish even more special.

CHICKEN

INGREDIENTS

1, 3-4 pound frying hen

2 quarts chicken stock

½ cup chopped onion

¼ cup chopped carrot

¼ cup chopped celery

1½ tablespoons chopped fresh thyme (or 2 teaspoons dried thyme)

1 tablespoon chopped fresh tarragon (or 1 teaspoon dried tarragon)

2 teaspoons chopped fresh rosemary (or ½ teaspoon dried rosemary)

½ teaspoon crushed black peppercorns

INSTRUCTIONS

1. Place the hen breast-side down in a large Dutch oven or stockpot.

2. Add the remaining ingredients to the pot; bring to a boil.

3. Reduce heat to a steady simmer, cover, and cook for 1¼-1½ hours, depending on the size of the chicken. Turn the chicken over the last half hour of cooking so that the breast is now facing upwards.

4. Remove the chicken from the stockpot and set aside.

5. Strain the stock into a bowl. Discard the herbs and vegetables. Return the now strained stock to the pot.

6. When the chicken has cooled, remove the meat, cut into bite-size pieces, and set aside. Discard the skin and bones.

DUMPLINGS

INGREDIENTS

2 cups all-purpose flour
½ teaspoon baking powder
¼ teaspoon baking soda
¼ teaspoon salt
¼ cup shortening
¾ cup whole milk buttermilk

INSTRUCTIONS

1. In a large mixing bowl, add the flour, baking powder, baking soda, and salt. Stir with a fork to mix.

2. Add the shortening to the bowl, and use your fingers to rub the shortening and flour mixture together until it is thoroughly incorporated.

3. Pour the buttermilk over the flour and shortening, and mix together with a fork until the dough forms.

4. Scrape the dough from the bowl with a spatula onto a floured surface. Knead the dough three or four times, and form a large ball. Place the ball back in the bowl, cover with plastic wrap, and place in the refrigerator. Allow the dough to chill for an hour.

5. Just before you are ready to cut out your dumplings in the following step, place the strained chicken stock onto the stove and bring to a low simmer.

6. Separate the chilled dough into three smaller balls. One at a time, place the balls on a floured surface, and with a floured rolling pin, roll each ball into rounds of about ¼ inch thick.

7. With a pizza cutter or knife, cut the dough into 1-inch wide by 3-inch long strips. Place on a cookie sheet.

8. When all the dumplings are made, drop them one by one into your hot stock. Gently stir as you go, dropping the dumplings into the stock but not atop one another. You don't want them to stick together.

9. When all dumplings are added, cover and allow to cook for 5-7 minutes, until just done.

10. Remove from heat, stir in the reserved chicken meat, and serve immediately.

Serves 6-8

CHAPTER 16

MY POTLUCK SAVIOR

by Ty Morris

Ty Morris—son of Gayle with the chicken and dumpling mishap—is quite the wine connoisseur and a wonderful cook. That wasn't always the case, though, as you'll read in his charming story below. And while I make a mean jar of pickled okra, Ty's spiced Southern spears outshine mine, hands down (no easy feat, mind you). He has grown into someone who really knows his way around a kitchen.

And on a total aside from the recipe featured here, I have to share that Ty's wedding was one of the most fun and memorable of nuptials I've ever witnessed. His fiancé, the lovely Beth Feingold, chose Chateau Elan in Braselton, Georgia, for the setting, and the guests were treated to a stellar weekend of golfing, dancing, spa treatments, and a round-the-clock open bar. And nothing gets my attention and my eyes more aglow, than free golf and flowing libations. On the evening of the wedding, while I went back and forth trying to decide whether to wear a white or black yarmulke (I had on a double-breasted, cream-colored dinner jacket and wanted to make myself as handsome as possible), some of my buddies came to the door telling me to head on back to the hospitality suite. Apparently the wedding would be late, as the rabbi was stuck in that incredibly insane traffic coming north from Atlanta. Two hours and many, many cocktails later when the service finally started, our group of fellows had morphed back twenty years into frat-hood. Thankfully the ushers had stuck us in the back of the ballroom, away from most of the guests, so our snickering and teenage antics could be ignored. My buddy Scott, another sizable guy like myself, and I were sitting on the edge of a huge hotel planter, and we got tickled about something. Trying to control our laughter, we lost our balance and both ended up sliding backwards into the stone container, our rears landing with a nice solid "thump" in the dirt. Which brought on another set of snickers and guffaws. Not a night to forget . . .

Anyway, here is Ty's thank-you to his mom, Gayle, as he tells how she helped him get his start in the kitchen.

When I graduated college and stepped into adulthood, cooking was a totally new concept to me. On my own and making my way, I learned quickly that food didn't automatically come with all the wonderful flavors I was accustomed to growing up back home—you actually had to work at making something to make it taste good. And I had no idea how one did that.

Just starting at my new job, I was asked to bring something to work for a potluck. I didn't have a clue what to make—it was one thing to whip up something edible enough for me to eat at home, but creating a palatable dish to present in public was a whole 'nother story. So, while I didn't know anything to make or how to make it, I did know who to ask: my mom. I called her up and she rattled off a fool-proof, delicious recipe from memory, which I found fascinating because I could not fathom how people did that sort of thing. She then walked me through each step, including where in the grocery store to find the ingredients I needed. I brought that dish into work the next day and was amazed by the compliments I received. I have now made this sweet potato casserole probably over a hundred times since—at first because it was the only dish I knew how to make, and then because it was consistently requested when people knew I was coming to a meal. For a long time, I still had to call my mother to be reminded of the steps and the ingredients, but now I, too, make the recipe by heart.

I always smile when I make this dish, and think of my mom. I've also grown in the kitchen, so now others call me when they are in need of culinary assistance. I guess I got good cooking genes. Thanks, Mama Gayle, for saving me at that first potluck, and for giving me an interest in how good food really can be.

—Ty Morris

* * * * *

Sweet Potato Casserole with Crunchy Topping

The following recipe is perfect for a side dish during the fall of the year, as it has those wonderful flavors we associate with autumn. However, it also a great complement to barbequed pork or chicken—the savory and the sweet pair together well.

FOR THE CASSEROLE
INGREDIENTS

2, 16-ounce packages sweet potato patties, such as McKenzie's or Flander's
½ teaspoon cinnamon
¾ cup whole milk
½ teaspoon vanilla extract
2 large eggs, lightly beaten
4 tablespoons butter, melted
½ cup sugar or more to taste
Crunchy Topping (recipe follows)

INSTRUCTIONS

1. Preheat oven to 350 degrees.

2. Spray a 9"x13" baking dish with vegetable oil.

3. In a large bowl, mash the sweet potato patties until smooth.

4. Add the cinnamon, milk, extract, eggs, butter, and sugar. Mix thoroughly and spread into the prepared baking dish.

5. Bake for 30 minutes.

6. Remove the dish from the oven, and crumble the topping onto the casserole. Lightly press down into the potatoes with a spatula. Return to the oven and bake another 10-12 minutes until the topping starts to brown.

7. Allow to sit and cool for 10 minutes before serving.

Serves 6-8

Crunchy Topping

INGREDIENTS

½ cup brown sugar

¾ cup corn flakes, finely crumbled

½ cup finely chopped pecans

6 tablespoons unsalted butter, melted

INSTRUCTIONS

1. Place all the ingredients into a medium-sized bowl, and stir to mix thoroughly.

2. Refrigerate and chill for 30 minutes.

3. Spread on top of casserole and bake as directed above.

*   *   *   *   *

So at the beginning of this chapter I allowed that Ty's pickled okra was, well, better than mine . . . not an easy admission. And with such a revelation, I figured I should share the recipe with you readers. His dish is adapted from that of another Georgia fellow, Alton Brown, and is really the best I've tasted. These spears are perfect for a Southern picnic served alongside some fried chicken and deviled eggs, or try one in a Bloody Mary!

Pickled Okra

Hint: When using okra, choose the smaller, shorter pods. The large ones can often be tough.

INGREDIENTS

2¼ pounds fresh okra

¼ cup kosher salt

2¼ cups unseasoned rice wine vinegar

2¼ cups water

6 small dried chiles, split open

3 teaspoons mustard seeds

12 sprigs fresh dill

6 whole cloves of garlic, peeled

3 teaspoons whole black peppercorns

6 pint-sized, wide-mouth canning jars, sterilized

INSTRUCTIONS

1. Rinse the okra in a colander and drain. Set aside.

2. In a saucepan, add the salt, vinegar, and water. Bring to a boil, and reduce to a steady simmer.

3. While the vinegar mixture is simmering, place 1 chile, ½ teaspoon mustard seeds, 2 sprigs of dill, 1 clove of garlic, and ½ teaspoon peppercorns in the bottom of each sterilized jar.

4. Alternating stems up and down, pack the okra into the jars.

5. Pour the hot liquid over the okra into the jars, until just reaching the top of the okra.

6. Seal the jars, and store in a cool place for at least two weeks before serving.

Makes 6 pints

* * * * *

Before moving on from this chapter, I wanted to add another wonderful way to fix okra as an appetizer. My friend Mary Ann Smith in Savannah brings this delicious dish to potluck parties because she knows how much I enjoy it. And these easy-to-make little babies fly off a plate during cocktail hour. Serve them at your next gathering and you'll taste why they are so popular.

Pickled Okra & Ham Roll Ups

INGREDIENTS

1 pint (16-ounce) jar of pickled okra

1, 8-ounce container cream cheese, at room temperature

2 dashes Texas Pete or other hot sauce

Couple of pinches (about ⅛ teaspoon) of black pepper

½ pound thinly sliced smoked ham

Fresh parsley for garnish

INSTRUCTIONS

1. Drain the okra and gently wipe dry with paper towels. Trim off the ends of each okra spear so that they are the same width. Set the trimmed spears aside, and discard the ends.

2. In a bowl, combine the cream cheese, Texas Pete, and black pepper. Whip until you reach a consistency that is easy to spread.

3. Place an individual slice of ham on a tray or flat surface, and dab it dry with a paper towel if damp.

4. Spread the dried side of the ham with a thin layer of the cream cheese mixture.

5. Place one or two spears, or one spear and a sliced portion of another, across one short side of the ham slice, leaving a small amount of ham on the end, about ¼ inch.

6. Roll up the slice, starting with the okra side, like a jelly roll. Set aside on a platter.

7. Continue the steps to use all the slices of ham.

8. Cover and refrigerate 4 hours or overnight.

9. Just before serving, slice the roll-ups into ½-inch thick rounds, and serve on a decorative platter. Garnish with fresh parsley springs.

Serves 12 for hors d'oeuvres

CHAPTER 17

BIG MAMAS: THE SOUTH'S TITLED NOBILITY

by JSB, Wes Goodroe, Sherry Witherington,
and Martha Giddens Nesbit

While Southerners love their mamas, we *adore* our grand-mothers. Forget Daddy: if Mama won't let you do it, ask Grandmama. The bond is such that we often bestow special names on them, too—"Grandmother" just doesn't say enough to express our love and affection. A friend of mine was graced with "Grand-Martha," and she was indeed grand. Another I know is called "Honey" by all her progeny, and another is known as "Gee-Gee." Many go by Nonnie, and on my mother's side, our family's adoration was given to "Ninnie." And then we have the prominent set of matriarchs who have their own special distinction: those grandmothers of such bearing, stature, and renown that they are honored as "Big Mama."

People from north of the Mason-Dixon Line might mistake the descriptive to mean that the woman is large, or rotund. Sometimes this is true—in one story you'll read in a moment, Miss Junnie Akins is indeed statuesque. But in most cases, the title is not due to the lady's size. Some of our Big Mamas are little bitty things who don't weigh 100 pounds soaking wet. (On the same token in terms of monikers not making sense, I also know of two men—both over six feet tall and weighing many stones—who are nicknamed "Tiny.")

No, the "Big" in Big Mama comes in most instances from either the intense love accorded to her by the family or, in some cases, her incredibly strong personality, bearing, and presence.

Every town in the South has at least one Big Mama in residence. There might even be more than one in a family, and they then are distinguished in some way—maybe with their Christian names in the honorary, such as Big Mama Louise and her sister-in-law, Big Mama Nanette. Or sometimes in a clan they are designated by who was first in line and who earned the title at a later date. Then they are known as "Big Mama" and "Little Big Mama," respectively. Again, "little" here does not equate to size but in this case means she was not the first of the Big Mamas in the family.

Wes's Mom with her parents, Grandpa and Big Mama Junnie Akins

In my discussions and porch chat with folks while writing this book, Big Mamas came into the conversation time and again. Three contributors submitted accounts of the admiration and love they carry for those special ladies in their family. You'll find those charming and heart-warming stories, and some outstanding recipes, in the following few pages.

And all hail and laud Big Mama, our region's esteemed class of nobility.

The Best Friend a Boy Could Ask For

by Wes Goodroe

My buddy Wes Goodroe and I fished in the same slow-moving creeks and wandered through the same ancient oaky woods while growing up together in Middle Georgia. Wes was known for his prowess on the football field, and he always knew how to have a great time. And while Wes hasn't been under the stadium lights in many years, he still knows how to enjoy himself to the fullest. He is a classic good ol' Southern boy at fifty-four, and we're still in touch lo these many years after Westfield High.

In the recollections below, this big-hearted and big-statured fellow gives us a wonderful glimpse into the life and kitchen of his maternal grandmother, who was lovingly known to him as "Big Mama Junnie." The bond was such between these two that Wes would even give up time on campus while in college to race back home and visit with Miss Junnie. There aren't too many teens I know of who would do that today. But I suppose if your grandmother is your best friend as is the case here, you'd welcome the chance for such time together just like Wes did. Here is his story.

My maternal grandmother, Junnie Akins, was from a tiny stop-in-the-road called Tippetteville, Georgia, population thirty-five or so, located right on the county line separating Dooly and Houston County, Georgia. We all called her "Big Mama," as she was over six feet tall, an unusual height for a woman even by today's standards. She was orphaned at a young age, and pretty much left to fend for herself until she met my Granddaddy.

The two of them started off life together with limited means. Granddaddy had served in the Civilian Conservation Corps during the Depression, working as a foreman building levees in the bayous down in Louisiana; he returned home to Georgia and started sharecropping, growing cotton. Through hard work and his sense of business, he eventually became very successful at the trade, and later in life he was the state's largest cotton producer. By the time the mid-seventies rolled around, he also owned numerous heads of cattle, and had an inventory of over a million dollars worth of John Deere tractors and equipment.

But despite their success, money never changed Big Mama. She was, her entire life, very shy around other people, particularly non-family members. I guess it is because she never learned to read or write, but she was still one of the smartest and most wonderful women I've ever known.

Like Granddaddy, Big Mama was an entrepreneur; she didn't let a lack of education keep her from making a dollar. She started her own egg business, and brought me in at age five as her "partner." She was making enough money to stuff $20 bills (and Juicy Fruit gum) in my pockets whenever I visited, telling me it was my share of the hens' efforts. I spent a great deal of time with her growing up, and those memories are some of my most prized possessions. We wouldn't do anything you might call special—maybe walk through the cow pastures together and count the cattle, and she'd point out the different plants bordering the barbed-wire fences, telling me which ones were edible or which you could use for medicinal purposes. Other times we'd go to different fishing holes around that side of Dooly County, and catch a mess of bream or catfish for dinner. She also taught me how to drive on those fishing excursions, and I was behind the wheel mastering a clutch before the age of nine under her guidance.

We also cooked together; she was a master in the kitchen. She had an enormous garden with sweet corn, purple hull peas, okra, tomatoes, squash—all the Southern favorites. Our favorite foods, besides those homegrown vegetables, were fried chicken, fried tripe, and of course her banana pudding! I enjoyed her company and cooking so much I'd drive home from college on any given afternoon just to sit and visit with her in her kitchen, and have one of her glorious suppers. And if she knew I was coming, there'd be one of her big, creamy banana puddings waiting on me in the refrigerator. She was the best friend a boy could ever ask for, and a stellar grandmother. Still to this day I tear up thinking of her; I loved her dearly.

—Wes Goodroe

*　*　*　*　*

What a testament to a grandson's love, stretching now almost six decades. Here is Big Mama Junnie's incredible banana pudding recipe shared by Wes. It is made, of course, from scratch, with a rich custard topped with sweet meringue. This dish can be served hot right out of the oven or chilled overnight in the fridge. One of the secrets of this dish is to make sure you pour the custard over the wafers and fruit right when you bring it off the stove. The hot liquid will cook the soft bananas a bit, which allows their flavor to marry with the custard.

Big Mama Junnie's Banana Pudding

INGREDIENTS

⅓ cup all-purpose flour

1½ cups sugar, divided

¼ teaspoon salt

3 large eggs, separated

1½ cups whole milk

1 cup heavy whipping cream

2 teaspoons vanilla extract

36-40 vanilla wafers

4 large or 5 medium-sized ripe bananas, peeled and sliced
    into ¼-inch circles

INSTRUCTIONS

1. Preheat oven to 425 degrees.

2. Sift the flour into a medium-sized heavy saucepan. Add 1¼ cups of the sugar and the salt, and stir with a fork to mix.

3. In a mixing bowl, lightly beat the egg yolks with a fork. Add the milk and cream and whisk all together until thoroughly incorporated.

4. Pour the egg mixture into the saucepan, whisking as you pour.

5. Place the saucepan over medium heat and cook, whisking frequently, for about 12-15 minutes, until a smooth and thick custard forms. It should easily coat the back of a spoon. Be careful during the cooking process so that the custard does not stick to the bottom of the pan. You may need to adjust the heat down to medium low.

6. Remove the pan from the stove; set aside and whisk in the vanilla extract.

7. Spread a small amount of the custard—a very thin layer—on the bottom of a 2-quart baking dish. Cover the custard with a layer of wafers and then half of the bananas.

8. Pour about ⅓ of the remaining custard over the bananas, and continue layering the wafers, bananas, and custard, ending with the custard on top.

9. To make the meringue, beat the egg whites over high speed until stiff in a bowl; gradually add the remaining ¼ cup of sugar and continue beating until stiff peaks form.

10. Spoon the meringue over the top of the pudding, spreading to cover the entire surface and onto the edges of the dish. Make sure to seal the edges with the meringue so that it does not shrink onto the pudding, leaving a gap of custard.

11. Bake in the preheated oven for about 5 minutes, or until the meringue is slightly browned.

12. Cool slightly before serving, or chill.

Serves 6-8

Big Mama's Two-Day Brunswick Stew

by Sherry Witherington

Sherry Witherington was raised in Stewart County, which forms the "hip" of Southwest Georgia on the Alabama border. Only 6,000 folks inhabit these 450 acres, which is a full third of the size of Rhode Island (population 1 million+). The county sits alongside the famed Chattahoochee River and is a landscape covered in forests and farmlands stretching from one horizon to the other. The closest city is Columbus, which is a lonesome forty-mile drive to the north.

Growing up in such a sparsely populated rural setting can teach you many things, such as how to maximize what you have on hand and the importance of working with your neighbor to make things happen. Sherry has taken those lessons to heart. She has been involved with social work for

Sherry on her wedding day with her Mother, Big Mama,
and her fellow dish-washer sisters, Angela and Trina

most of her years since being crowned homecoming queen and serving as valedictorian at Greenfield Academy. She is, in her own words, a "convener, strategizer, linker, arranger, problem solver, coach, and conflict-resolver," serving as a Director of Community Support for Georgia Family Connection Partnership.

Sherry also learned a love of home and cooking while growing up in a family that had close ties to farm-to-table food, hunting, and fishing. That love has stayed with her, and she claims that her favorite place to be is in her kitchen with an apron on—just like the one her Big Mama used to wear—surrounded by family and friends. She and her husband, Olin, live in the country on a dirt road outside of Griffin, Georgia (complete with three horses and a cow), in a wonderful home that is made for entertaining. Sherry says it isn't unusual for them to have a couple dozen or more people over for a cookout. And the following recipe she shares for stew is a perfect dish to serve such a crowd.

I know you'll enjoy Sherry's story about life with her parents, her fellow dishwashing sisters, and the centerpiece of the family, Big Mama. While you'll laugh at her descriptions and smile at her warmth, I also bet you'll get a lump in your throat when she talks about missing Big Mama. What wonderful memories she has from those days in the Georgia countryside.

The rituals surrounding food as I experienced them growing up during the sixties and seventies in rural Southwest Georgia are forever etched not only in my memory but also in my DNA. There were no large, chain grocery stores; no fancy or fast food restaurants; no "official" farmers' markets; no famous chefs. What we had in that impoverished part of the state were hard-working folks who grew and/or killed much of what they ate and shopped for the rest at one of several small, family-owned grocery stores. Then they went home to a modest kitchen without all the amenities and put together a hearty meal that stuck to your ribs and provided comfort to your soul. Most of us had no dishwashers except for those people "lucky" enough to have daughters to do the honors. That was my introduction to the world of food.

Our rituals for gathering food were simple—drive the three miles to town and visit the local Suwannee Store, almost every day, where Mr. John would cut our chicken, pork chops, and cubed steak, and grind the hamburger meat, just like we wanted it. We would walk the four or five short aisles to choose between Sunbeam and Colonial bread, decide between the two sizes of ketchup, and buy the iceberg lettuce. There were also those highly anticipated times when generous neighbors who had large gardens would call and invite us over to pick peas and butterbeans. Of course, the best time to do that on those sultry summer days was first thing in the morning. That way, we avoided the worst heat of the day and got the peas shelled in time to make it to the city pool—the only place we had for gathering with our friends.

Daddy was an avid fisherman and hunter, so that yielded many meals for us of fish, venison, doves, and rabbit. I ate so much of those things growing up that I thought I'd never want to see them again . . . and yet, all these years later, I miss Daddy and the plentiful nature of the wild game. Although I have to say I don't miss Daddy storing catawba worms in the refrigerator so he could preserve them for the next fishing trip! Mama and all three of us girls were terrified of those ugly worms when they were in the yard on the tree, so you can imagine how we felt when Daddy walked in the house with them dangling off his wide-brimmed fishing hat. He'd pull them off the hat, drop them in a paper sack, and in the refrigerator they'd go. I still have flashbacks of the few times those worms crawled out of the bag and ended up loose in our refrigerator. I'll leave it to your imagination how that played out between Daddy and Mama.

Preparing breakfast, dinner, and supper was a family affair in our house—especially at night when we were all home together. Mama was the baker in the house and also the one who made casseroles and salads. But on some days, Daddy saw it as his job to cook the peas and beans—slowly boiling the fatback or streak-o-lean to season those fresh vegetables. Then there was the meat to fry—what would it be tonight...chicken, chops, cubed steak, fish, doves? So many good choices. And it goes without saying that no meal was complete without bread, some meals "calling for" biscuits and some for cornbread. In the early years, my sisters and I learned how to do the important things, like peeling the potatoes for those yummy home-made mashed potatoes, grating cheese for Mama's mac and cheese, chopping nuts for dessert...all of which we loved doing. Throughout all those years at home, our parents taught us how to cook the same down-home, soul food that they did, and I still carry that preference with me today.

What follows a meal is the inevitable, dreaded cleanup. Earlier I said that most folks didn't have a dishwasher—I'm not even sure they existed then—but in our family we had three, and they had names: Angela, Sherry, and Trina. We divided the work into three categories—washing, drying, and cleaning the counters and table, and then we rotated duties. It definitely made for quicker work and taught us a lot about teamwork that we carry with us to this day. On one particular day following an extended family gathering hosted at our home, while at my post washing dishes, I looked out the window to see Mama and two of her sisters turned over backwards in the swing with their feet straight up in the air. They were laughing so hard, and I started laughing too, as it seemed like poetic justice that they were flat on their backs on the ground since they left me and my sisters to do the dishes while they "retired" to the swing.

The only grandparent I ever knew was Big Mama, my maternal grandmother, Mrs. Lois Mitchell Hobbs. She was so special to me and always called me her Sherry-Baby. She was a woman who loved to cook and loved to eat. She always had food to offer when you went to her house, and she expected you to eat, even though once you obliged, she would tell you that she thought you'd put on some weight. She was so committed to cooking and eating that we couldn't make the drive from Richland to Stockbridge to see my aunt, which was no more than two and a half hours, without Big Mama getting up at the crack of dawn to fry chicken, bake a cake, and make potato salad to take with us. We'd always stop at a roadside picnic table across from a church just outside Thomaston to eat that meal. I'd give anything to do that one more time with her.

Big Mama and I shared a love of stew, and sometimes when Daddy would kill a rabbit, she would make a big pot of rabbit stew. I can still remember the flavor and comfort I found in that stew. I think it's safe to say that it conveyed an act of love to me. I don't have ready access to rabbits today, so I've modified her recipe to include the meat that is readily available. This would probably be called a "Brunswick stew"—one filled with pork and chicken and vegetables. Big Mama wasn't much on writing recipes down, and if you've ever made a homemade stew, you know that it's not an exact science, but I've worked to get this as close to her version as I can. I hope as you make this, you'll remember your own rituals around food and how they brought your family together in ways that reach deep into your soul.

—Sherry Witherington

Big Mama's Two-Day Brunswick Stew

This stew makes a wonderful main dish and pairs well with something like broccoli slaw and the "must-have" cornbread. Count on at least twenty-four main-dish servings and of course more if you're serving the stew as a side to another main dish. It's like many dishes that improve over the course of several days, so it's a great recipe to make in stages during the week for a party you're hosting on the weekend. It also reheats well but must be done slowly in a heavy-bottomed pot. You could microwave a single-serving portion, but I wouldn't try to microwave a family-size bowl. You will normally need to add additional broth (chicken or beef) when reheating as the stew tends to thicken as it sits in the refrigerator. It also freezes well. The recipe can be halved to make a smaller quantity, but I always make it in the larger portion for sharing and/or freezing for a quick meal later! —SW

INGREDIENTS

8 pounds Boston butt

2 cups water

4 pounds mixed chicken pieces—bone in but skin removed

3 cups frozen seasoning blend (onions, peppers, celery),
    use fresh if preferred

16 ounces frozen silver queen or white corn niblets

1, 20-ounce tube of frozen white creamed corn, thawed

3, 14.5-ounce cans petite diced tomatoes

1 can original Rotel tomatoes (use hot if more heat is desired)

3 cups ketchup

2 cups Heinz 57 sauce

¼ cup Worcestershire sauce

1 tablespoon vinegar

6-8 cups chicken stock

2 cups pork stock (or the amount produced by cooking the pork)

2 tablespoons salt, or to taste

1 tablespoon ground black pepper, or to taste

INSTRUCTIONS

Note: This stew is easiest to make if done in 2 parts.

DAY 1

1. Season the Boston butt with salt and black pepper. Place it with two cups of water into a crockpot sprayed with cooking spray. Cook on high until it is fall-off-the-bone tender, 6-10 hours or overnight. You can also place the butt in a large roasting pan, covered with foil, and bake in a 250-degree oven until done, about 4-6 hours.

2. When done, allow the meat to cool so that you can easily handle it. Drain the stock into a bowl, cover, and set aside.

3. Pull the meat from bone, discarding fatty parts. Shred or chip the lean meat into small pieces; however, do not pulverize or use a food processor.

4. Season the chicken with salt and black pepper, and place the pieces into a large boiler, covering generously with water, and bring to a boil. Stir, reduce heat to a steady simmer, and cook until falling from bone—probably around an hour if using large breasts.

5. Remove the chicken from stock and set aside. Strain the stock into your pork stock, cover, and refrigerate (to use on day 2).

6. Debone chicken and chip up into small pieces; again, as with the pork, do not use a food processor.

7. Place the chipped pork and chicken into a large bowl, cover, and refrigerate overnight.

DAY 2

1. Remove pork and chicken stock from refrigerator. Skim and discard the fat that has solidified on top. Heat the stock enough to liquefy, as it will be somewhat congealed. Set aside.

2. To begin to build your stew, use a very large stockpot (ideally about 12 quarts) with a heavy bottom (the stew scorches easily, so you want to have a good heavy bottom on the pot). Spray the bottom with cooking spray.

3. Add the refrigerated, chopped chicken and Boston butt to the pot.

4. Add the seasoning blend, creamed and niblet corn, diced tomatoes, Rotel tomatoes, ketchup, Heinz 57, Worcestershire, and vinegar. Stir to mix.

5. Add about two thirds of the stock to the pot. Do not add too much stock at this stage, as you don't want this to be too "soupy"; it's meant to be thick and meaty. Depending on the consistency you want, you can add more broth (it is fine to use chicken or even beef broth from a carton if you run out of your own pork and chicken stock).

6. Add salt and pepper to your taste or to accommodate any dietary restrictions. Stir well to mix all ingredients thoroughly.

7. Bring the stew to a gentle simmer on medium heat. Stir occasionally while the stew is heating. When at a simmer, turn the heat to low

and cover with a lid. Simmer for 3-4 hours to blend all the flavors. Remember to stir frequently during the cooking, as the stew will easily stick to the bottom of the pan. Add more stock or broth as needed.

8. When finished, serve immediately. Can be refrigerated for two days, or frozen.

Serves 24 as a main course

A Catfish Mulldown

by Martha Giddens Nesbit

When I first moved to Savannah back in the 1980s, I kept hearing the name "Martha Nesbit" in almost any food conversation that would come up at a cocktail party or around someone's dinner table. Come to find out, there was a whole lot of substance behind that buzz. At the time, Martha was the food editor for *The Savannah Morning News*, and arguably the area's leading expert on entertaining and dining. I was soon introduced to the lovely lady through a mutual friend, and with a bit of great luck and good fortune, Martha featured me and my New Year's Eve menu in her ongoing column, "Good Cooks." During our lunch interview, we learned that we had a great deal in common: our families are from small Georgia towns, we love to make people happy with food, and we both take to heart Julia Child's sage advice that "You don't have to cook fancy or complicated masterpieces—just good food from fresh ingredients."

Since that article twenty-five-plus years ago, Martha has published a number of popular cookbooks. My copy of her first, *Savannah Collection*, is worn and a bit tattered from years of use. (Her recipe for Greek Salad found in *Collection* is the best I've ever come across.) And her recipes for coastal favorites, such as a Low Country Boil, Crab Cakes, and Oyster Perlou, have been repeated and shared both far and wide—a Savannah party wouldn't be perfect without one of Martha's dishes being offered on the buffet.

Through her talent as a hostess and author, Martha has received some well-deserved recognition from her peers. Bobby Flay perched himself in Martha's kitchen to film a segment of his popular TV show, and Paula Deen turned to her fellow South Georgia native to help orchestrate several of her own cookbooks. And in a scene worthy of its own short story, my friend found herself waltzing across the dance floor with none other than the renowned Mr. Craig Claiborne.

One of the secrets of Martha's success, I believe, is her ability to draw on her Southern roots for inspiration, utilizing fresh, farm-to-table ingredients to create her simple but magnificent dishes. Also, she cooks with love.

Here is one of her delicious and entertaining culinary memories that contains such love, along with some fresh, just-out-of-the-water Georgia catfish and an indomitable grandmother.

Martha's Big Mama, Mary Lane

My Big Mama and Big Daddy—Mary and Emory Lane—lived in Bulloch County, Georgia, on a working farm, meaning that they worked from dawn to dark to feed the cows, pigs, and chickens, plant the crops, then harvest them and "put them away." They also raised their three children— Jones, Alice Jo, and Betty.

To unwind, my Big Mama loved to fish, and if you're thinking I'm going to tell you a sweet little story about how she would invite me to be her fishing buddy, dishing out gems of wisdom and culinary tips, you are sadly mistaken. My Big Mama loved to fish alone. She'd send me and my cousin Mary Ann and any other available grandchildren out into the yard to dig around the root of the trees for worms. When she felt we had found enough of the wiggly, slimy creatures, off she'd go in her peddle pushers for some peace and solitude to one of the ponds on their property, or to the Ogeechee River down the road. She was probably not supposed to be on the Ogeechee by herself in a boat, but no one had the nerve to tell her this. My Big Mama was a woman you did not mess with.

I remarked recently to my Aunt Betty, my mother's younger sister and Big Mama's youngest daughter, that Big Mama had never once taken me fishing. "You should probably be grateful for that," Aunt Betty said. "When you went fishing with Big Mama, you had to sit still and not talk and stay out until after dark." My Big Mama did not come home from fishing until she was good and ready.

Big Mama and Big Daddy were like everyone else living during the Depression—scratching out a living, making do, reusing and recycling, and eating whatever fish, fowl, or critter was available. Sometimes, all Big Mama could catch was catfish, and that meant that supper would most assuredly be fried fish and catfish mulldown. Now, a mulldown is any of those Southern dishes that actually "season up" and "get right" while they are sitting on the back of the stove. So, if you were making a mulldown, you'd start it early enough in the day so that it could "mulldown" for a couple of hours before serving. I suppose, then, that mulldown is both a noun and a verb, right? Hope you enjoy!

—Martha Giddens Nesbitt

Catfish Mulldown

This dish is great on a cold winter's night served with hot biscuits and a bowl of creamy grits.

INGREDIENTS

Vegetable spray or cooking oil

2-3 pounds boneless catfish fillets, halved

2 cups of water

1 large onion, chopped

4 medium baking potatoes, peeled and cut into 1 to 1½-inch cubes

1 teaspoon salt

½ teaspoon finely ground black pepper

2, 15-ounce cans of chopped tomatoes

6 slices of bacon

4 tablespoons unsalted butter

1 bay leaf

A few shakes of Texas Pete or other favorite hot sauce

INSTRUCTIONS

1. Spray a large, heavy-bottomed pot with vegetable spray. Place the catfish and 2 cups water in the pot and bring to a boil, then reduce heat and simmer for about 20 minutes, until catfish is cooked through.

2. Remove the fish and set aside.

3. Strain the broth and return it to the pot.

4. Add the onion, potatoes, salt, and black pepper. Bring to a gentle simmer and allow to cook over low heat until the potatoes are tender, about 20 minutes.

5. Add the tomatoes and juice and allow this to cook 10 minutes more.

6. Meanwhile, fry the bacon until very crisp and break it into pieces; reserve about 2 tablespoons of the bacon drippings.

7. Add the fish, bacon, butter, bay leaf, and drippings to the stew. Add a couple shakes of hot sauce. Turn off the heat, cover, and let the stew "mulldown" for 2 hours. If too thick, add a bit of water.

8. Reheat on low when ready to serve.

Serves 6

* * * * *

I mentioned that Martha's recipe for Greek salad was the best I've ever tasted, so I figured I should share it with you here. Martha attributes the original recipe to Mrs. Pauline Georges, one of many fabulous cooks of Greek descent who are from Savannah.

Greek Salad

INGREDIENTS

1 head of Romaine lettuce (or other crisp lettuce), washed and coarsely
chopped

2 green onions, finely chopped

2 stalks celery, finely chopped

1 cucumber, peeled, seeded, and chopped

1 ripe tomato, chopped

1 green bell pepper, cut into thin julienne strips

1 cup crumbled Feta cheese

½ cup large black Greek olives, sliced

Greek Salad Dressing (recipe follows)

INSTRUCTIONS

Place all salad ingredients except for the Feta and olives in a large
mixing bowl. Pour the dressing over the salad, and toss to coat. Serve
the salads in individual bowls and top with the Feta and olives.

Serves 6

Greek Salad Dressing

INGREDIENTS

½ cup olive oil

¼ cup vegetable oil

⅓ cup freshly squeezed lemon juice (This is the key to the recipe!)

1 teaspoon kosher salt

¼ teaspoon freshly ground black pepper

1 clove of garlic, minced

¾ teaspoon dried oregano (or 1½ teaspoons fresh oregano)

¼ teaspoon sugar

INSTRUCTIONS

Place all ingredients in a jar. Shake well. Keep refrigerated until ready
to serve.

Makes 1 cup

CHAPTER 18

THROUGH ELLIS ISLAND TO SAVANNAH

by John Nichols

D ue to our famed St. Patrick's Day celebration and the fact that Georgia was the last Crown Colony in the U.S., most folks think Savannah is a city filled with people mostly of Irish and British descent. However, being a major seaport, the Hostess City of the South is a melting pot of many different nationalities. One group of denizens that has contributed heavily to the culinary reputation of the city is the Greeks. The annual Savannah Greek Festival, which will soon enter its seventieth year, is one of the most popular events in the Southeast for foodies. Thousands flock here for the celebration of Hellenic culture and history, and the dishes that are offered up—all handmade by locals—will make your taste buds sing. Pastitso, dolmades, souvlaki, roasted lamb, baklava, ravani, and kourabiedes are all featured throughout the weekend.

I mentioned one such splendid cook in the previous chapter, Mrs. Pauline Georges, and featured her delicious Greek salad recipe. Another such descendant is John Nichols, a local restaurateur and caterer. John is the proprietor of the historic Crystal Beer Parlor, a Savannah institution of the highest order. The first owners reportedly ran illegal hooch and operated a speakeasy there during Prohibition, and the parlor has been a local landmark ever since. The lines for lunch and supper stretch out the door of the old brick building, but it is well worth the wait once you get inside, pour yourself into one of the commodious leather booths, and sample the food. John has kept the classics on the menu that have been offered for generations, including the enormous chili-cheese burgers, luscious crab stew, and fried Vidalia onion rings. But he did put a bit of a Greek twist on the offerings when he purchased the establishment years ago, adding such items as an Aegean Sampler—with homemade hummus and stuffed grape leaves—along with "My Mama's Greek Salad" and a lamb burger that will make any meat lover swoon.

John started cooking as a teenager, and learned authentic old-country secrets and techniques in his family's kitchen. These lessons taught to him by his beautiful and vivacious Yiayia (Greek for "grandmother") have rooted John in classical cooking, and so he has the incredible culinary advantage of being not only Greek but also Southern. John relates to us here his family's story of coming to America, and how the love learned in cooking has provided him with a wonderful and full life in the cooking arts. He has also given us one of Yiayia's best recipes, one that John says is a family favorite: Fasolakia Yiahni (in Southern terms, that's green beans cooked in a tomato sauce).

Gia mas, y'all!

My grandfather, Paul Rousakis, seeking a better life in America for himself, came through Ellis Island as a teenager from a small village in Greece in the early 1920s. He worked in a little grocery store in down-town Savannah owned by another Greek who had emigrated some years earlier. He saved his money by sleeping in the stock room of the store and eventually had enough to open his own. As time went by, his business became successful, and he sailed back to Greece to find a bride. Upon his arrival, the reason for his return spread quickly throughout the village, and meetings were arranged with families of eligible daughters. Of course, discussions took place over food and wine in the local taverna. As was the custom, the young man and his prospects didn't speak—the families discussed arrangements. My grandmother, Antigone, was the last of many young girls presented, and my grandfather was immediately taken with her. After a wedding and reception in the village, my grandfather and his eighteen-year-old bride sailed to America. Arriving in New York, he bought furniture for the house in Savannah and promised her she would

Paul and Antigone (Yiayia) Rousakis

never wear the same dress twice. Until the Great Depression, he kept that promise.

Over the years, she gave him four children—a son, John; my mother, Maria; and her two sisters, Julia and Alice. I never had the chance to meet my grandfather; he died a year before my parents married. Their children would produce twelve grandchildren, so Sunday dinner at Yiayia's house was always an event! Coming through the front door of her house, I can still remember the heavenly aromas emanating from the kitchen. When we came in, Yiayia would always be at the stove cooking, dressed to the nines, but she'd stop long enough for hugs and kisses. Besides the rich pasticcio, the roasted lamb, or her luscious fried chicken, one of my favorites was a dish called fasolakia yiahni, which is made of fresh green beans simmered in tomato sauce with carrots, onions, potatoes, mint, and parsley—a perfect accompaniment to her fabulous fried chicken!

Yiayia Antigone died in 1975, my senior year of high school. I'm so thankful for all the Greek women in my family who made every meal a special and memorable occasion. I swear I don't know how they got it all done. I learned her recipe for fasolakia yiahni from my mother and make it often. It's definitely a crowd pleaser! And as time has progressed, those lessons of love and cooking become more and more special—they are my personal treasures.

—John Nichols

Fasolakia Yiahni
(Green Beans in Tomato Sauce)

This dish is delicious served alongside roasted lamb or chicken.

INGREDIENTS

2 large yellow onions, chopped

¾ cup olive oil

1, 15-ounce can tomato sauce

2 teaspoons salt

1 teaspoon ground black pepper

2 pounds fresh green beans (my grandmother liked to leave them whole, and so do I)

1½ cups chopped fresh parsley

½ cup chopped fresh mint

2 large potatoes, peeled and cut into thick wedges

2 large carrots, peeled and sliced

1 cup cold water

INSTRUCTIONS

1. In a large pot, sauté the onions in the olive oil over medium heat until tender.

2. Add the tomato sauce, salt, and pepper and simmer for about 15 minutes.

3. Add the green beans and remaining ingredients. Cover and simmer for about an hour or until the beans are tender, stirring occasionally.

Serves 6-8

CHAPTER 19

PRESIDENTIAL CARAMEL CAKE

by Luke Usry

M r. Luke Usry is a dapper young Middle Georgia native with an artistic soul. And I love having friends like Luke, folks who are much more complex—and interesting—than what appears just on the surface.

You might not guess that a young man living on a farm in rural Peach County—an Episcopalian with a business degree from UGA who looks very much at home in seersucker and Ralph Lauren—would be a fan of the Grateful Dead or the late outsider photographer Diane Arbus. (Though he does dig into his Georgia roots by admitting his admiration of our Flannery O'Connor.) His sense of style extends, too, when naming his animals, with one cat called Althea, after the famous song by his favorite band mentioned above, and the other Calliope, chief of all the muses known for the sound of her voice. That must be one melodious kitty.

I like to think of myself as an older version of Luke. I've got the Georgia roots, worked in business for the last thirty years, and served on the vestry of my church, St. Paul's Episcopal in Savannah. But then I love to write, as does Luke, and my musical tastes are varied from the CPA norm, ranging from Johnny Cash and Loretta Lynn to the B-52's and REM. I have one dog named after a character in *Sunset Boulevard*, Max, and another named after an Irish bar, Murphy, as well as cat named after a president, Roosevelt.

And speaking of presidents, I guess I need to move on to Luke's story here.

JIMMY CARTER

24 October 2008

To Mrs. Usry's Third Grade Class
Byron Elementary School
Byron, Georgia

I really enjoyed my visit with you yesterday,
and thank you for letting me read my book to you. I
hope all of you will read as many books as you can.

I read all of your letters to me, and enjoyed
the messages and the pictures.

Maybe sometime you can all take a bus over to
Plains and see our school house, which is just like
it was when I was in the Third Grade.

Love, and best wishes,

Jimmy Carter

p.s. Marle, thank you for inviting me – and for the
cake!

*Letter from President Carter to Mrs. Usry's third grade class;
he thanks Marle for the cake in the postscript.*

Luke is the son of two of my dear friends from our 4-H days harkening
back to the late 1970s. His dad is my buddy Jody, a strappingly handsome
Georgia native who grew up in the piedmont town of Gibson. And his
lovely mom is Marle (nee' Carter) from down in the southwest part of the
state near Plains. Here Luke gives us a funny and engaging anecdote about
Marle, the Secret Service, a former U.S. president, and a mouth-watering
caramel cake.

In addition to being a gifted educator, my mother Marle is a pro-foundly talented culinary artist. If I referred to her as such in her presence, she would, of course, disavow that title from the bottom of her servant's heart. But no amount of humility on her part can erode the fact that she makes the best caramel cake in Georgia. A confection crafted meticulously from a recipe honed through years of trial and error, Marle's cake enjoys a diverse fan club that includes every family member, friend, or stranger who has the privilege of enjoying a slice. But the most noteworthy member of that fortunate few who laud her Southern-born masterpiece is Nobel Laureate and former U.S. President Jimmy Carter.

For those of you familiar with the Carter family, my mother is Billy's daughter, which makes her Jimmy's niece. Her tradition of baking him one of her prized caramel cakes every year at Christmas has stood as long as I can remember. But out of all the cakes she has baked for Georgia's beloved statesman, there's one in particular that we will always remember.

Back the early 2000s, Mamma was teaching third grade at Byron Ele-mentary when she learned that Uncle Jimmy was scheduled to travel from Plains to Macon and speak at Mercer University. Byron Elementary being right on the way, she sent Uncle Jimmy an e-mail on a whim, promising one of her cakes if he would schedule a stop at the school to read to her students. Now, to say that President Carter is a busy man is about the biggest understatement I can think of, so Mamma didn't exactly get her hopes up.

Over the next few weeks, she forgot about the e-mail altogether. That was, until the day before Uncle Jimmy's Mercer appearance. When the school secretary called down to her classroom over the intercom system, I'm sure Mamma was expecting news of a student's forgotten lunchbox, an early dismissal, or one of the many innocuous messages relayed throughout the school every day. Any-thing except a request to come to the front

Marle and her Uncle Jimmy

office and greet the two United States Secret Service agents there asking to speak with her.

To back up, my mother is not the kind of person who goes around introducing herself as "Jimmy Carter's niece." That has nothing to do with a lack of love for her uncle but everything to do with her overflowing reservoir of couth. She also is the last person you would suspect of running a counterfeiting operation or calling in bomb threats to the White House, so the office staff were understandably curious and a little on edge. Actually, that's the second biggest understatement I can think of. Everyone from the principal to the school nurse was in a frenzy, shocked and terrified by the presence of these foreboding, stern-faced agents standing in the middle of the front office at quiet little Byron Elementary.

They were there, of course, on behalf of Uncle Jimmy. It is standard procedure for Secret Service protection details to send agents ahead of time to any location the president plans to visit in order to establish a security plan, and that's exactly why they were there. And so, after supper that night, Mamma stayed in the kitchen until the hour neared my bedtime. And, the next day, Uncle Jimmy appeared as promised to read his children's book, "The Little Baby Snoogle-Fleeger."

On his way out, after all the photos were snapped and the hands shaken, he hugged my mother's neck and kissed her cheek with a smile before looking into her eyes and saying, very seriously, "Now where's my cake?"

—Luke Usry

* * * * *

The layers of this cake are made rich with cream cheese, and one bite of the icing will make you sigh with contentment. Besides being President Carter's favorite, caramel cake was also my mom's favorite, and two of them were served at her eightieth (her final) birthday party. The episode was funny and pure "Mama," a lady who had strong opinions on her food and what she wanted served. We had the luncheon at the esteemed Savannah Yacht Club, which provided us with an extensive menu of wonderful desserts. Mama passed them all by and told me that she wanted "one of Joyce

Giles's caramel cakes." Joyce is my cousin, and a magnificent baker—with caramel cakes being one of her specialties. So the pastry chef at the Yacht Club was spared any efforts on that day, as Joyce boxed up two of her prizes and drove them from Unadilla all the way to Savannah for the celebration. I think Marle would have been proud of them too.

Presidential Caramel Cake

INGREDIENTS

3 sticks salted butter, softened to room temperature

8 ounces cream cheese, softened to room temperature

3 cups sugar

6 large eggs, at room temperature

3 cups all-purpose flour, sifted

2 teaspoons vanilla extract

Caramel Icing (recipe follows)

INSTRUCTIONS

1. Preheat oven to 325 degrees.

2. Grease and flour three 8-inch or two 9-inch cake pans.

3. In a large mixing bowl, cream butter and cream cheese until fluffy.

4. Add sugar to the bowl and mix well.

5. Add the eggs one at a time, mixing well after each.

6. Slowly add flour and mix until just incorporated.

7. Mix in the vanilla, and pour into the prepared cake pans.

8. Bake layers 20-25 minutes until toothpick inserted in center comes out clean.

9. Remove the layers from the oven and place on wire racks. When completely cooled, spread Caramel Icing (recipe below) between the layers and on tops and sides of the cake.

Serves 12-16

Caramel Icing

INGREDIENTS

1 cup (2 sticks) salted butter

4 cups sugar, divided

1 cup evaporated milk

INSTRUCTIONS

1. In a large, heavy saucepan (I use a Dutch oven), melt the butter over medium heat.

2. Add 3½ cups sugar and the evaporated milk. Increase heat and bring to a rapid bowl, stirring constantly with a whisk to prevent sticking.

3. Remove the saucepan from the stove and set aside.

4. Caramelize ½ cup sugar until it resembles a golden honey color. To do this, add the reserved ½ cup sugar to a cold non-stick pan and slowly heat the sugar on low heat for approximately 4 to 4½ minutes, stirring constantly to prevent scorching.

5. Place the sugar and milk mixture back on the stove on low heat. Slowly pour the caramelized sugar into the sugar and milk mixture, stirring the mixture as you pour. (A wire whisk works best for this.) The caramelized sugar may harden a little when poured into the sugar and milk mixture. If this happens don't panic; the sugar will melt as you stir and the mixture comes to a boil.

6. Continue to cook over medium heat until icing comes to a slow boil. After icing begins to boil, cook for approximately 7 more minutes until a hard ball is formed when a small amount is dropped in cold water. (Stir constantly the entire time icing is cooking to prevent sticking and scorching.)

7. Remove from heat and beat 12-15 minutes until creamy enough to spread on cake. (I use a stand mixer. This step may take a little longer if you are using a hand mixer.) If icing gets too thick to spread, you can add a little milk and beat again until creamy. Spread icing on completely cooled layers. ENJOY!

CHAPTER 20

A WHIFF
OF CHILDHOOD

by Virginia Willis

Virginia Willis. The name sounds as easy and lovely as a warm summer breeze blowing through the needles of a long-leaf Georgia pine. I first heard of Virginia several years ago, and as the days progressed, there was more and more talk of this Southern chef achieving recognition far and wide.

While our Georgia native is a graduate of both L'Academie de Cuisine and L'Ecole de Cuisine La Varenne, has cooked for countless celebrities, made *lapin Normandie* with Julia Child, and is in development for a series on PBS about the global influence of Southern cuisine, she continues to be approachable, kind, and gracious. This distinguished James Beard award winner remembers her roots in all that she does in terms of cooking, and those wonderful family lessons she learned in the kitchen with her mother and grandmother remain with her as she garners one milestone after another.

Virginia and I first met in person in November 2015; we were both presenting at the popular Mistletoe Market in my hometown of Perry, Georgia. Thousands of people come from across the country to attend this holiday celebration, and I was there with my first book, *Rise & Shine!* Upon learning that Virginia was a part of the lineup as well, I made sure to receive an introduction. She was everything I expected: warm, engaging, and gracious.

When starting this book, I very much wanted a recipe and story from her because Virginia's philosophy on cooking mirrors my own feelings about food: "… simple is best. I try to use the finest ingredients and…do as little to them as possible to let the flavor of the actual food shine through—a style I like to call 'refined Southern cuisine.'" And when I wrote her to ask if she'd share a special story and recipe with us, she, in her generous spirit and genuine sense of hospitality, readily agreed. Here is her contribution, and as you read it you'll be able to feel the love and smell the incredible aromas that come from her family's kitchen to yours. Enjoy.

Virginia and her Grandmother Louise Wingate Baston (photo by Terry Allen)

I grew up eating beef stew Mama prepared in her slow cooker: rich hunks of meat bathed in dark brown gravy, thickened with flour, and flavored with a generous slug of my grandfather's homemade wine. She'd make a big batch and we would enjoy it for several nights, each night yielding a richer, fuller stew as the flavors increasingly mingled and married. One of my favorite lunch spots serves "yesterday's soup." That could be an argument for making this stew ahead and refrigerating it overnight before serving.

Sometimes, instead of beef, Mama prepared stew with meat from a deer my father shot or that was given to us by an uncle or a neighbor. (I grew up calling it deer meat and never called it venison until I went to culinary school.) Venison is meaty, full-flavored, and lower in fat than beef, so it responds well to long, slow cooking. Mama would often serve it with rice, potatoes, or buttery egg noodles. It was simple, satisfying country cooking.

Food memories are precious things. The sense of smell, more than any other sense, is intimately linked to the parts of the brain that process emotion. One whiff of this stew and I am immediately transported to my childhood. And some of my best memories happened in the kitchen, learning at Mama's and my grandmother Meme's side. I inherited their love of fresh, home-cooked meals, as well as their sense of hospitality, which were guiding values in my family. As the years have passed, I have held on to what they've taught me, and those lessons have served me well.

And beef stew remains one of my favorite dishes in the entire world, and is one of my favorite dishes to prepare. The hearty aroma of a bubbling soup or sumptuous stew is destined to whet appetites and bring folks into the kitchen. Soups and stews make memories. Steamy kitchen windows and tantalizing aromas in the air often mean a slowly cooked winter stew is simmering and gently burbling away in the kitchen. When it's cold and wet outside, few meals satisfy and satiate our souls and stomachs like a steaming bowl of hearty goodness. There's also something rewarding about making a pot of stew. Perhaps it's because stew is greater than the sum of its parts.

Following proper techniques and using good ingredients pretty much ensures a satisfying bowl of stew. Julia Child supposedly once said, "If you understand the technique, you don't need a recipe." The first thing a budding chef learns in cooking school is how to make soup and stews. Soup and stews are so much more than tossing a bunch of stuff in a pot, topping it with water or stock, and boiling away. Having said that, a perfect stew, when put on the right course, practically cooks itself. The subtle layering of flavor is what transforms good food into great food.

The most important ingredient in beef stew is, undoubtedly, beef. Never choose stew meat already in precut cubes. It's more expensive and you have no idea if you're getting, for example, leftover bits from the shoulder or rib-eye, two wildly different cuts that won't cook at the same rate. All stew meat is not the same. Instead, purchase a large piece of meat and ask your butcher to cut it, or cut it yourself. The best cuts for stew are rump roast, chuck pot roast, sirloin tip, top round, and bottom round. Also, you may have seen the USDA stamp on your meat, a purplish-blue insignia made of food-safe ink stamped directly on the beef. Young beef is categorized as prime, choice, select, or standard. The terms commercial, utility, cutter, and canner refer to more mature meat. I don't advocate eating anything less than select.

The second consideration is to create the fond. This is done by first browning the meat in the pot and then cooking the vegetables in those brown bits of goodness to take on the flavor of the meat. The third point to consider is the vegetable foundation. From France's mirepoix of onion, carrot, and celery to Latin American sofrito made with tomatoes, onions, peppers, and garlic to the famous Holy Trinity of Cajun cooking made with onion, celery, and green bell pepper, nearly every cuisine in the world starts with a simple vegetable base. For my take on Beef Bourguignon, the vegetables must be "sweated"—cooked over low heat—to reduce the liquid and concentrate the flavors. Aromatics in the form of bouquet garni, a bundle of herbs and spices, are then added to enhance the flavors. The stock is the vehicle for all the flavors. It's what drives the stew, so using the best-quality stock is essential.

Bon appétit, y'all!

—Virginia Willis

Old-Fashioned Beef Stew

This recipe is a marriage of my mama's slow cooker stews and a traditional country stew I learned in France. Don't be tempted to skip browning the meat. If you do, the resulting stew will be thin and tasteless. Browning the meat makes all the difference. Also, I find that after cooking for hours, the carrots, onion, and celery are quite soft. Instead of serving mushy vegetables, I puree them into the sauce, making it extra creamy without added cream. This is also why I suggest cooking the meat in cheesecloth—so you don't have to "bob" for the cubes of meat in the cooking liquid. Serve it the day of cooking or, as Mama did, over the course of a few days. —VW

INGREDIENTS

3 pounds lean rump roast, chuck pot roast, sirloin tip, top round, or bottom round, cut into 2-inch cubes

1 (750-ml) bottle red wine, preferably Pinot Noir

1 carrot, cut into 1-inch pieces

1 stalk celery, cut into 1-inch pieces

1 onion, coarsely chopped

4 slices thick-cut bacon, cut into lardons

2 tablespoons canola oil, plus more if needed

Coarse salt and freshly ground black pepper

1 tablespoon all-purpose flour

2½ cups beef stock or low-fat, reduced-sodium beef broth

Bouquet garni (5 sprigs of thyme, 4 sprigs of flat-leaf parsley, 2 fresh bay leaves, and 10 black peppercorns, tied together in cheesecloth)

1 tablespoon tomato paste

2 cloves garlic, finely chopped

8 ounces white button mushrooms, halved, or quartered if large

Cooked noodles, potatoes, or rice, for accompaniment

INSTRUCTIONS

1. To marinate the beef, place the cubes in a large glass or stainless steel bowl. Add the wine, carrot, celery, and onion. Cover and refrigerate for at least 2 hours or overnight.

2. Line both a baking sheet and a large plate with paper towels. Remove the beef from the marinade and transfer to the prepared baking sheet. Pat the meat dry with paper towels.

3. Strain the marinade, reserving separately both the vegetables and the liquid.

4. To cook the beef, heat a large skillet over medium-high heat. Add the bacon and cook until the fat is rendered and the bacon is crisp, about 5 minutes. Remove the bacon with a slotted spoon to the prepared plate to drain. Reserve until ready to serve. Pour off all but 1 tablespoon of bacon fat from the pan.

5. Decrease the heat to medium, add 2 tablespoons of the canola oil, and heat until simmering.

6. Season the beef with salt and pepper. Sear the beef in two or three batches without crowding the pan until nicely browned on all sides, about 5 minutes. Transfer to the prepared baking sheet when done. (For ease of removal later, if you would like, wrap the beef cubes in a cheesecloth sack and tie with cotton butcher's twine.) Set aside.

7. Add the reserved vegetables from the marinade and cook until they start to color, 5-7 minutes. Sprinkle on the flour and toss again to lightly coat. Cook, stirring constantly, until the flour turns brown, 2-3 minutes.

8. Transfer the vegetables and cheesecloth-bound package of beef to the insert of a slow cooker. Add the reserved marinade liquid and enough stock to barely cover the meat. Add the bouquet garni, tomato paste, and garlic. Seal with the lid. Cook on high heat for 3 to 4 hours or low for 6 to 8 hours.

9. Remove the bouquet garni and discard. Transfer the cheesecloth-bound packet of beef or remove the individual pieces with a slotted spoon to a bowl. Discard the cheesecloth.

10. Using an immersion blender, puree the sauce and vegetables remaining in the insert until smooth. (Or, once the beef is removed, ladle the sauce and vegetables into a blender and puree until smooth, a little at a time.)

11. Return the reserved beef to the sauce. Add the mushrooms and continue to cook until tender, about 30 minutes.

12. Add reserved bacon. Taste and adjust for seasoning with salt and pepper. Serve piping hot with noodles, potatoes, or rice.

Serves 6-8

CHAPTER 21

MAMA THARPE, GANNY, & MAMA

by Kathryn Barfield Rigsby

G rowing up in Perry and Middle Georgia, I knew most everyone in three counties, or at least who their families were. So when I first spotted this cute-as-a-button blonde girl sitting a few pews over from me at St. Paul's Episcopal one morning, I wasn't surprised that she struck a bell with me. Come to find out, she was one of the Barfields from back home! Kathryn had just moved to Savannah after graduating from Georgia Southern (a Perry favorite institute of higher learning, and my alma mater) and was looking for a house of worship. She fell in love with our little English-style country church, and soon became fast friends with all the members. She is a sweet soul, as pretty inside as she is out. We enjoyed many years together in our adopted town of Savannah, sharing warm memories and stories about life in Houston County; we both so love home, family, and good food.

To our dismay, Kathryn moved to Atlanta several years ago, and we still miss her at St. Paul's. However, she and I have continued our friendship, and she was one of my biggest promoters when *Rise & Shine!* was first published. An avid reader and promoter of Southern literature, Kathryn serves as the President of the Friends of the Library in Gwinnett County. She helped arrange for me to give a talk to benefit the library, and what an incredible event it was. There were well over 100 people in the audience, and the chef prepared the luncheon menu with recipes from my cookbook:

Kathryn with her Ganny, Margaret Stalnaker, and her Mom, Kitty Barfield

Southern shrimp rolls, tomato pie, and a salad of roasted beets, pears, and chevre, finished off with my Aunt Polly's coconut cake. I was so grateful for Kathryn's support, but, as we both agreed, it all goes back to being from the same small town, where people cheered one another on for happiness and a good life.

Here Kathryn tells us about three lovely women who helped mold her into who she is today, and the cooking and life lessons they imparted. You can tell from her writing that—while she may be living in the big ATL—her heart is still back home in Middle Georgia.

I grew up in a family of good cooks, starting with my great-grand-mother. While she passed away about a year before I was born, I've always felt as if I had known her through the stories told to me by my family. Mama Tharpe, as she was called, was born Lucia Reddy in Houston County, Georgia, and married Earnest Feagin Tharpe. She was as straight-laced as they come, and my great-grandfather, Papa Tharpe, though a true Southern gentleman, dearly loved to tease her.

One night their new minister—who was sight impaired—came to Sunday supper. Well, Mama Tharpe had a still for making the church's Communion wine, and it was located in the butler's pantry next to the dining room. During the meal, it started "working off" and making all sorts of noises. The minister was alarmed, not knowing what all the commotion was about. Papa Tharpe, calm as ever, told him, "Don't worry, Preacher . . . it's just Lucia's still working off." Mama Tharpe was mortified because Papa Tharpe never told the minister the wine was for church!

And speaking of wine and spirits, Mama Tharpe's whiskey sauce recipe has been in the family for years. It is great poured over pound cake or any other kind of plain cake. Often she would color the sauce to match the holiday occasion.

The kitchen that this sauce was made in for decades was recently moved seven miles from its original location and placed next to my parents' house in Centerville, Georgia. The kitchen, along with the house, was built in 1853 and is one of the oldest structures in the county. While the house is no longer standing, my Mama and Daddy are lovingly restoring the kitchen.

Next in the line of family cooks was Ganny. I know that all grandmothers are special, but not all grandmothers are a grandchild's best friend, as was my Ganny. As I child, I loved visiting with her and learning about family members from stories she would tell me. I asked her to write many of them down for my birthday one year, and I will always treasure the recollections she shared with me.

Ganny made every meal special, whether it was decorated pancakes or a birthday cake whose layers were an explosion of rainbow colors. One of my favorite things she made was her lemon chess pie. She helped me make it one year for the county fair when I was in the seventh grade for a Home Economics project. I won first prize! To this day it is one of my go-to and most requested recipes. I almost always make it when I am serving seafood, as it is a great dessert to compliment fish and shellfish. My sweet Ganny passed away two years ago at age eighty-nine. I was lucky to have her in my life for forty-two years. I miss her every day, but when I cook with her recipes, I feel just a little closer to her.

Then there is my beautiful Mama. When I decided to major in Home Economics in college, ready to learn to cook, my mother gave me the much-used and well-loved aluminum tube pan that had belonged to Ganny, along with a handwritten copy of Mama's cream cheese pound cake recipe. Mama has the most beautiful handwriting of anyone I have ever seen. It almost looks like calligraphy. I was excited to make my first "from scratch" cake. I followed the recipe just as Mama had written. But I noticed that when I took the cake out of the oven after the time written on the recipe, the cake was nowhere near done. Back in the oven it went, and thirty minutes later it still wasn't ready.

After I consulted with my mother and assured her that I had followed her instructions to the letter, she asked me to read the recipe to her word for word. Well, in Mama's elegant script, what read "1 8 ounce cream cheese" came across to me as "18 ounce of cream cheese," and that is the amount I used! We had a big laugh over that baking tragedy and have had a running joke over the "18-ounce pound cake" now for more than twenty-five years. Of course, I've kept that handwritten recipe along with the pan, and with those stories written down by Ganny, I am making some very special memories at home, and especially in my kitchen.

—Kathryn Barfield Rigsby

Whiskey Sauce

INGREDIENTS

1 cup sugar

1 egg

1 stick unsalted butter, melted

Whiskey of your choice to taste (I suggest starting off with ¼ cup)

INSTRUCTIONS

1. In a mixing bowl, cream the sugar and egg together until well mixed.

2. Pour the sugar and egg into a saucepan, and slowly drizzle in the melted butter while cooking over low heat. Stir constantly until a creamy texture, about 2-3 minutes.

3. Drizzle in the whiskey, stirring constantly, until thoroughly incorporated and heated through. Do not at any time along the process allow the mixture to come to a boil.

4. Pour the topping on your cake of choice as a glaze.

Makes about 1¼ cups

Lemon Chess Pie

INGREDIENTS

2 sticks unsalted butter, at room temperature

2 cups sugar

5 eggs, beaten

⅓ cup lemon juice

2 tablespoons cornmeal

2 tablespoons flour

1 teaspoon vanilla

Pinch of salt

1 unbaked pie shell

INSTRUCTIONS

1. Preheat oven to 350 degrees.

2. In a large mixing bowl, cream the butter and sugar.

3. Add the eggs, lemon juice, cornmeal, flour, vanilla, and salt. Mix well and pour into the pie shell.

4. Bake for 1 hour or until the center of the pie becomes firm.

Serves 6

CHAPTER 22

HOT SHOT

and

AUNT OPAL'S KITCHEN TABLE

by Debra Brook

ebra Brook is another Middle Georgia kindred spirit who has settled in Savannah. While we did not know one another as children—she grew up in Macon and I in Perry—we've become friends down on the coast. We met years ago when she served on the board of directors for the Flannery O'Connor Home Foundation. I had hosted a fundraiser event for the museum at my house, and we began a lively chat that has carried forward.

A CPA and attorney, Debra started cooking in the early 1960s with *Betty Crocker's Cookbook for Boys and Girls*. Today she and her husband Mike Kemp—a banker—like to prepare farm-to-table, locally sourced food in their home in the historic neighborhood of Isle of Hope. Shaded under centuries-old live oaks and featuring a wide, front porch veranda, it is the perfect spot to sip a libation and nibble on a tomato sandwich.

Debra gives us two humorous stories for *Cook & Tell*, along with two family recipes that are worthy of your own table. The first features an industrious mama who knew how to handle a passel of hot peppers, while the second tells about a great-aunt, her kitchen table, and a unique salad.

Prepare to be entertained!

My family serves beans and peas with Hot Shot. No, not the ant and roach solution. It's a recipe that's been in the family for decades and is best when vine-ripe tomatoes and Vidalia onions are plentiful. About thirty years ago, my mother ordered a chicken dish with salsa at Buck's restaurant in Decatur, and when it arrived she said, "Oh, I get salsa now. It's kind of like Hot Shot." And it is…but it isn't. I don't know where the recipe originated, but I recall my great-grandmother, Mama Freeman, making it, so it's been around for at least fifty years. If you find yourself with peas or beans, vine-ripe tomatoes, and Vidalia onions, make some Hot Shot. It's

Debra's great-grandparents,
Gordon Lee and Pearl Smith Freeman

good stuff. Or, as my Daddy would say, "It's good enough to make a puppy dog kiss his Mama." Note: Hot Shot, like revenge, is best served cold.

As an aside, when we were first married and before he was properly trained, my husband Mike went to the Dekalb Farmer's Market for the ingredients for Hot Shot and returned with a plastic bag full of Kung Pao peppers—one pound of them! I needed one pepper. I made the Hot Shot and took the one pound of Kung Pao peppers (minus one) to my mother. Never one to waste anything, she donned swim goggles, a surgical mask, and rubber gloves and made hot pepper jelly. Lots of hot pepper jelly: it takes about ¼ cup of hot peppers to make six 8-ounce jars of hot pepper jelly. That was almost thirty-five years ago, and I think Mom still has some of that jelly in her pantry.

The moral is: when life gives you hot peppers, make pepper jelly.

Here is the family recipe for the great condiment, Hot Shot. Just remember: you only need one hot pepper to make a batch!

—Debra Brook

Hot Shot

INGREDIENTS

1 teaspoon salt

1 teaspoon sugar

1 teaspoon ground black pepper 1 small Vidalia or other sweet onion, finely chopped

1 cup or so cider vinegar

2 large vine-ripe tomatoes, finely chopped with juice reserved

1 hot (jalapeno, serrano, Kung Pao) pepper, seeded and finely chopped

INSTRUCTIONS

1. Place the salt, sugar, black pepper, and onion in a non-reactive (oh, alright, Pyrex) bowl.

2. Add the cider vinegar to cover, and stir.

3. Add the tomatoes, reserved juice, and hot pepper and stir.

4. Add just enough additional cider vinegar to barely cover, and stir.

5. Cover and store in the refrigerator.

6. Serve with black eyes, pink eyes, crowders, butterbeans, or lady peas.

Makes about 2 cups

* * * * *

Speaking of piping hot peas, I have to put in an aside here along with a recipe. We had a freezer full of peas each year from the summer harvests in Middle Georgia. As I've written before, and it lent the title *Rise & Shine!* to my previous book, it would be an early-morning family outing to pick all sorts of Southern produce, including an extensive variety of peas: crowder, black eyes, purple hulls, lady finger, white acre, and pigeon. When they were brought home it was time to shell, and we all pitched in for that job, too. My father offered on many occasions to buy my mom an electric pea sheller to save time and aching fingers. She always refused, though; she said that those shellers tore up the peas and left bits and pieces scattered about. After all the work of picking and shelling, Mama and Carrie—my nanny—would blanch the peas, spread them out atop towels laid across the kitchen table, and let them cool and dry before bagging them and placing them in the deep freeze.

Mama always added a slice or two of pork side-meat or streak-o-lean to her pot of peas, along with a good dash of salt, a little black pepper, and maybe a cayenne to give the dish some heat. Sometimes, too, just before the peas were done, she'd throw in a handful of small pods of young okra. I cooked a pot of pink eyes the other day—it was ages since I'd had any—and when I lifted the lid off the pot and smelled that wonderful aroma of fresh farm-picked peas wafting up, all I could think about was my mama and home.

It reminded me, too, of a funny exchange between my mom and one of her friends, Lula Batchelor, who is related to my brother-in-law. We were at a family dinner, and Miss Lula had brought a big bowl of butterbeans for the buffet. They smelled heavenly and looked wonderful. Mama ladled some onto her plate and said "Lula, these butterbeans are delicious. What did you season them with?" And Miss Lula answered in kind of a whisper, "Side-meat." Mama looked at her and said "Really? I didn't see any in the bowl."

"Well, Joyce," Lula continued, still whispering across the table, "I took the meat out and threw it away before I put the beans in the bowl. Julie and the rest of the kids just raise Cain about 'fat this and fat that,' and I didn't want to hear them yapping about it. You know you can't cook a decent pot of beans without a little meat. So just don't say anything to get them started!"

Miss Lula is right. Chicken stock helps, but to get a true pot of real Southern peas, you need to throw in a little bit of pork to make it right. Here is how Mama, Miss Lula, and so many women for decades made their peas (and I do, too).

Southern-style Peas with Okra

INGREDIENTS

4 cups good-quality, low-sodium chicken stock

2 or 3 slices pork side-meat, or about ½ cup of smoked ham, cut into 1-inch cubes

1 green cayenne pepper

½ teaspoon of salt, or to taste

Scant ¼ teaspoon finely ground black pepper

4 cups fresh black eyes, crowders, purple hulls, or other Southern peas (butterbeans can be cooked with this recipe as well)

12 small pods of fresh or frozen okra (do not use large or thick pods, as they tend to get "woody")

3 tablespoons butter (optional)

INSTRUCTIONS

1. In a large pot, place the stock, meat, cayenne pepper, salt, ground black pepper, and peas. Stir to mix and bring to a boil.

2. Reduce heat to a steady simmer, and cook uncovered, 25-30 minutes until tender, depending on the type of pea. If cooking butterbeans, the timing will be less, around 20-25 minutes. Stir the pot occasionally. Skim off any foam that may arise and discard. Be careful not to let the liquid totally evaporate. Add more stock, or water, if needed.

3. Place the okra pods in the pot about 5 minutes before the vegetables are done. Stir.

4. Remove from heat and add the butter, stir until melted, and serve. These reheat easily and can be cooked ahead of time before serving. They also freeze nicely if there are any leftovers.

Serves 6-8

★ ★ ★ ★ ★

Now back to Debra and her next story.

Aunt Opal's Kitchen Table

Aunt Opal and Uncle Henry lived and farmed in Chiefland, an old-fashioned part of Florida forty miles southwest of Gainesville. For several years in the seventies, we visited them at Thanksgiving. The women and girls stayed in the (uninsulated) cement block farmhouse. The men and boys went to the huntin' camp, a collection of ramshackle (uninsulated) RVs without benefit of plumbing, where they were joined by Uncle Henry's male friends and relations.

The men were well armed, and during the day hunted wild boar and turkey. At night they told tall tales around the fire and tried hard not to freeze to death. During the day the women toured nearby Manatee Springs State Park and local sinkholes and at night tried hard not to freeze to death. Aunt Opal and I shared a sofa bed that was located by a classic Florida picture window, and I remember thinking that I might not survive the night despite the fact that I was wearing every item of clothing I'd brought. A ceramic gas heater made the kitchen the only warm room in the house.

There was also an old wooden table in the kitchen. The first time we visited, I was in my teens and Aunt Opal was an ancient seventy or so. I was dumbfounded when, in response to a question from my mother, Aunt Opal immediately dropped to all fours and crawled under the kitchen table. Was there something about this great-aunt that I didn't know? Did mental illness run on this side of the family? No! This was before smart phones and computers, and Aunt Opal had long since figured out that a piece of paper could be lost, but she always knew where the kitchen table was, so she recorded all important information (birthdates, anniversaries, Social Security numbers, how old the bull was, etc.) on the underside of that table.

Aunt Opal and Uncle Henry raised cattle and contained them with an electric fence that was, of course, too big a temptation to be ignored. My brothers, sister, and I each had to touch the electric fence just so we knew what it was like to be a cow. Trust me on this, you don't want to be a cow.

Thanksgiving dinner at the huntin' camp was an adventure. The women folk who corresponded to the hunters showed up with a huge turkey (it was a Butterball—wild turkey are scrawny, wild-tasting things) and all the fixins' including those classics, swamp cabbage and squirrel and dumplings. I have to say that the squirrel and dumplings were a little greasy for my taste. I was raised eating squirrel, but we fried it.

On Saturday night, my dad treated Aunt Opal, Uncle Henry, my grandparents, and the rest of us to dinner at the Island Hotel at Cedar Key where the adults indulged in Hearts of Palm Salad with Ice Cream Dressing and fried mullet. We children were a little circumspect about any salad dressing that boasted of containing ice cream, peanut butter, and mayonnaise—and was green.

But even so, we enjoyed this unique salad, and whenever I think of Aunt Opal, I recall days in Chiefland, Cedar Key, and this old Florida concoction.

—Debra Brook

Hearts of Palm Salad
with Ice Cream Dressing

INGREDIENTS

4 cups thinly sliced iceberg or green leaf lettuce

1 cup diced pineapple (preferably fresh)

½ cup pitted dates

1 tablespoon minced candied ginger

2 cups thinly sliced hearts of palm, preferably fresh

Ice Cream Dressing (recipe follows)

INSTRUCTIONS

1. In a large bowl, toss the lettuce with the pineapple, dates, candied ginger, and half of the hearts of palms.

2. Arrange this mixture on 4 salad plates, in shallow bowls, or on a platter.

3. Spoon the Ice Cream Dressing over the salad and garnish with the remaining hearts of palm.

Serves 4

Ice Cream Dressing

INGREDIENTS

⅓ cup vanilla ice cream, softened slightly

⅓ cup mayonnaise

3 tablespoons peanut butter

1-2 drops green food coloring

INSTRUCTIONS

To prepare the dressing, combine all of the ingredients in a blender and blend to a paste.

CHAPTER 23

'MATER LIPS

by JSB

Until the late seventies, there weren't any restaurants in Perry where teenagers could hang out except for the Tastee Freeze and the Dairy Queen, and space inside those spots was limited. Then one fine day Shoney's decided our little town was a prime market for Big Boy Burgers and the incredible fifty-item breakfast bar. As kids, our favorites on the menu included the hot fudge cake and the restaurant's signature dessert, that pièce de résistance, fresh strawberry pie. One of the funniest food memories from my years in high school actually happened under the eyes of Mr. Big Boy, with his checkered red and white overalls and pompadour haircut.

One afternoon several of us had piled into a booth, and Miss Ruby, the sixty-ish waitress who was our favorite—she of the blackest hair, the reddest lips, and most sardonic disposition—came to take our order.

The lone girl in our group, "Bonny," promptly ordered a slice of strawberry pie. Miss Ruby looked at her, raised one of her moon-shaped, penciled-on eyebrows, and said, "Honey, you ain't got any business eatin' strawberry pie, what with that bad case of 'mater lips you're sportin'. If you gonna get something sweet, get the hot fudge cake."

Bonny turned a dark shade similar to the color of pie she was ordering, and sucked in her badly chapped lips until there was only her chin and nose showing. While Miss Ruby was giving her lecture of foods to avoid when suffering from a cracked smile, another waitress stopped by our table to offer her two cents. Perry was a small town where everyone knew everyone else and opinions were freely shared.

"Lord a mercy, Bonny!" she said, shaking her head. "You follow Ruby's advice, sugar, and stay away from that pie." With that, she sashayed off, still shaking her head.

Bonny slunk a little lower in the oversized, eight-seater booth.

"'K, sweetie," Ruby continued, pencil on pad, "it's a fudge cake, right?" Not waiting for Bonny's response, she said, almost to herself, "Better leave off that red cherry as well."

When the orders were taken and Ruby had left the table, there was an incredibly awkward silence. After a few moments and then I couldn't help it anymore; I had to ask, "What in the world did she mean by 'mater lips?" Bonny gave me a dark look. My best friend Chris, the smartest of the bunch as well as a master of rural vernacular sayings as his family was from the hinterlands of West Georgia, explained. "It's a countrified description for chapped lips caused from eating an abundance of acidic foods, like toma-toes. And Miss Ruby was relating that strawberries, being so tart, would only make"—he stopped, and cut his eyes over to Bonny—"the 'mater lips worse off."

Having had her peeling and red-rimmed smile critiqued enough, Bonny gave us a mighty "go-to-hell" look, threw down her napkin, and scooted out the booth, high-tailing it to the door, all of us craning our necks as she stomped along the tile floor.

Clueless, as boys can be, we were all rumbling at once: "What got into her?" "Boy, she sure is touchy today." "Geez, why is she so mad?"

When the cherry-less hot fudge cake was delivered, we all took forkfuls and shared it around the table, still wondering, through bites of chocolate and ice cream, why in the world our friend was so darn moody sometimes.

Whenever I drive by a Shoney's now, which is rare as most have closed, or see a recipe for a strawberry pie, I think about those days of high school, Miss Ruby, and Bonny, who surprisingly still speaks to me and claims me as a close friend. Thank goodness for her forgiving nature and strong belief in the Golden Rule.

I wanted to recreate this nostalgic Shoney's dish with more berries and less sugar. I poured through countless recipes and finally came up with the following adaption. The glaze is infused with the taste of the fruit, and the crust gives a wonderful citrus and nut surprise that complements the sweet berries. Hopefully a bite of this will put you right back in one of Big Boy's burnt-orange Naugahyde booths, where you spent time as a kid laughing and joking with your family and friends. Just don't eat too much, or you might have to pull out your Chapstick!

JB's Better-than-Shoney's Strawberry Pie

INGREDIENTS

2 quarts ripe strawberries, tops removed

¾ cup sugar

2 tablespoons cornstarch

1½ teaspoons reduced sugar Sure Jell

1, 9-inch graham cracker crust (recipe follows)

Fresh whipped cream for garnish

INSTRUCTIONS

1. Set one quart of the whole strawberries aside.

2. In a food processor, puree the remaining quart of berries. Spoon into a mixing bowl.

3. Mix the sugar, cornstarch, and Sure Jell in a small bowl with a fork; add to the pureed berries.

4. Pour the berry mixture in a pot and place over medium heat; stir with a spatula until the mixture comes to a gentle boil.

5. Cook for another 2-3 minutes, stirring constantly, until the foam that formed is no longer visible and the mixture has cleared and become thick. Set aside to cool.

6. When the filling has completely cooled to room temperature, fold in the remaining quart of whole strawberries (if some are very large, cut in half).

7. Gently fold the filling into the prepared graham cracker crust and spread out evenly. Refrigerate for two hours or until thoroughly chilled. Garnish with a dollop of whipped cream.

Serves 6

Graham Cracker Crust

INGREDIENTS

1½ cups graham cracker crumbs

½ cup very finely ground pecans

¼ cup sugar

2 tablespoons orange zest

½ teaspoon cinnamon

5 tablespoons sweet unsalted butter, melted

INSTRUCTIONS

1. Preheat oven to 350 degrees.

2. In a bowl, mix together the cracker crumbs, pecans, sugar, zest, and cinnamon.

3. Add the melted butter, stirring to mix well.

4. Place the crumb mixture into a pie pan. Press down evenly with your hands or the back of a spoon, smoothing it into the bottom and up most of the sides of the pan.

5. Set the pie shell in the oven and cook for 5-6 minutes for the crust to set. Remove and allow to cool to room temperature before adding filling.

*   *   *   *   *

Since I mentioned hot fudge cake, I figured I should include it here as a recipe. There's nothing like this decadent dessert to finish off a meal, or just to have as a special treat on a Saturday afternoon.

This dish is pretty simple to make. While I always tout "made from scratch" and fresh ingredients, there are some good commercial varieties, especially in the dessert category, that you can use to save time. And the results can be very close to what you would spend hours trying to create on your own.

For this recipe, I use a base of Ghirardelli dark chocolate brownies. These babies are just plain luscious, and as close to homemade as you can get. I continue on using another store-bought gourmet commodity,

Häagen-Dazs Vanilla Ice Cream. The folks at Häagen-Dazs make their ice cream with the best of ingredients, and it isn't inflated with air to make it appear more voluminous. For the topping, you can choose a variety of pre-made chocolate sauces; Ghirardelli has their own, as does Stonewall. Just be sure to purchase one made with good, dark chocolate.

Hot Fudge Cake

INGREDIENTS

1 box Ghirardelli dark chocolate brownies, any variety*

1 jar chocolate sauce, such as Ghirardelli Premium Chocolate Sauce or Stonewall Bittersweet Chocolate Sauce

1 pint Häagen-Dazs Vanilla Ice Cream

½ pint heavy cream, whipped

4 Maraschino cherries

*Note: I like to substitute strong coffee or espresso in place of the water called for in the recipe. This gives a wonderful taste to the brownies.

INSTRUCTIONS

1. Prepare the brownies per the directions on the box. Set aside and allow to cool slightly.

2. Heat the chocolate sauce in a small saucepan until warm but not simmering.

3. Cut the brownies into approximately 4x4-inch squares. With a spatula, set each brownie on a dessert plate.

4. Place a scoop of ice cream on each brownie.

5. Drizzle the warm chocolate sauce over the ice cream and onto the plate.

6. Top with a dollop of whipped cream, and adorn with a cherry.

7. Serve immediately.

Serves 4

CHAPTER 24

SWEET IRENE

by Linda Rogers Weiss

L inda Weiss of Charleston, South Carolina, and I have struck up a warm friendship based on our mutual love of Southern food and culture. Linda is one of those considerate, kind, and generous people to whom folks naturally gravitate. I'm lucky to have her as a friend, as well as a culinary inspiration.

While Linda has called the Holy City home since 1966, her roots are in Southwest Alabama's Marengo County.* There, she discovered the art of cooking and garnered a lifelong appreciation of Southern food at the home of her grandmother, Irene. Linda has taken those lessons learned in rural Alabama and melded them into a career in the culinary arts after a long and successful profession in real estate (and, on an interesting note, Ms. Weiss loves anything to do with aviation and has her pilot's license). With stints studying at LaVerenne at the Greenbrier and at Le Cordon Bleu, Linda is now a food writer and instructor, and previously served as the food editor for *South Carolina Homes & Gardens* magazine. She has two cookbooks to her name, *Memories from Home* and *Seasoned in the Kitchen*. She maintains three blogs on cooking and entertaining, and her work has been featured in several newspapers and magazines throughout the USA.

In her recollection below, Linda takes us back to rural Alabama and introduces us to her talented grandmother and her uncle, Ben, who was an editor at one of the state's leading newspapers. Their correspondence on food has stayed with Linda now for more than six decades, and she shares some of those classic recipes here with us in *Cook & Tell*.

*A total aside from the story here, but I found this trivia fascinating: Marengo County was settled by the first European Americans in 1817, followers of Napoleon Bonaparte who were exiled from France after his downfall. The county is named in honor of the Marengo Battlefield near Turin, Italy, where Napoleon defeated the Austrians in 1800.

My grandfather met my grandmother, Irene, when he was a student at Alabama Polytechnic Institute (now Auburn University). He was sent to her father's farm to check the pecan orchard. There, he fell in love at first sight with this young home economics teacher.

Marriage didn't happen right away. My grandfather went out west to the University of Montana and worked in the "Badlands." But they missed each other, and my grandfather, James Marvin Rogers, went back to Auburn to marry his sweet Irene. I know this because after Mama Irene died, I found the letters that the two of them had written to each other in an old trunk in the back bedroom of their house. The letters were in bundles, wrapped with pink ribbons. Just as you would expect.

Their home life began in my grandfather's hometown in Marengo County in Southwest Alabama, 200 miles away from her family. They had three children, and my grandmother, conscious of her religious duty to God and family, became a pillar of the church and the community. She played the piano for the only church in town for over forty years. She also played light operas for our grammar school plays and occasionally taught music.

My grandmother was a wonderful cook who canned and preserved whatever grew in her garden. What she wasn't growing, someone else was, so the women gardeners in our small community exchanged food quite often. She also loved to make jelly from the elderberries that grew on the fence by her house, and fig preserves from the trees in the backyard. As children, my sister and I had friends who lived close by, and when visiting with them, we always ended up in the "cave" of a honeysuckle bush talking about how hungry we were. One of us would run to my grandmother's, go into the pantry, get a jar of fig preserves, grab a sleeve of crackers and a knife, and race like the wind back to the "cave," where we had the best

Sweet Irene and her
devoted husband, James

snack you could ever put in your mouth. I'll bet there are a half-dozen silver engraved knives under that bush to this day. I still love fig preserves on crackers.

My dad's youngest sister married a newspaperman, Ben Reeves Davis, who was from Birmingham. Uncle Ben loved my grandparents and would come up and hunt at the old Rogers place, staying with them. He became the executive managing editor for the Montgomery Advertiser Journal. The journal published recipe supplements in the newspaper. Uncle Ben, knowing that my grandmother loved recipes and that few were available back then, would mail the supplements to her. These were the latest recipes as well as old family recipes for what women were cooking in Alabama at the time. After Mama Irene died, I found the stack of papers pushed back in her kitchen pantry. I put them in a paper bag, stuffed them down in her old churn, and brought them home to South Carolina.

Not too long ago, I pulled out these old and yellowed news clippings to see what she had saved. I found that many of the crackled pages contained dishes that my grandmother had prepared over the years. As I sorted through the recipes, many memories of home came flooding back, particularly the recollections of the wonderful food that came out of Mama Irene's kitchen. What a treasure trove I had on hand—a culinary legacy left to me by Uncle Ben and my dear, sweet grandmother.

One of the best recipes I came across, one of my favorites, was for Okra Spoon Patties. I pulled out some frozen okra and got to work recreating this dish. My gracious, they were good! I wanted to share this recipe with you, which was published by the Birmingham News in 1955. I've adapted it for a modern kitchen, and I do hope you enjoy it. By the way, these would be perfect served alongside a roasted chicken and mashed sweet potatoes, or they make a unique appetizer as the start for a Southern dinner party.

—Linda Rogers Weiss

Okra Spoon Patties

INGREDIENTS

2½ cups water

½ teaspoon salt

1¾ cup fresh okra, sliced crosswise ¼ to ½ inch thick

1 large egg, whisked

8 Club or Ritz crackers, finely crushed

¼ teaspoon salt

⅛ teaspoon black pepper

Vegetable oil

Mayonnaise-Dijon Sauce (recipe follows)

INSTRUCTIONS

1. Bring the water and salt to a boil, and add the okra. Cook for about 10 minutes until tender. Remove from heat and place in a colander to drain. Allow to cool for 5 minutes or so.

2. In a mixing bowl, add the whisked egg and crackers, salt, and pepper.

3. With a spatula, press down on the okra to remove most of the moisture. Measure out 1 cup of the okra, and add it to the egg and crackers. Mix well.

4. In a large skillet (I prefer a black cast iron), add enough oil to cover ¼ inch and heat over medium high.

5. By the tablespoon, drop the okra mixture into the hot oil. Don't overcrowd the pan—otherwise, the patties will not come out crisp. You should be able to fit about 6-8 in a batch.

6. Allow to brown on one side, about 1-2 minutes or so. Turn, and allow to cook another 1-2 minutes or until both sides have browned. Place on a platter covered with a paper towel.

7. Complete the second batch.

8. Serve immediately with the following sauce.

Serves 6-8

Mayonnaise-Dijon Sauce

INGREDIENTS

3 tablespoons Duke's mayonnaise

2 teaspoon Country Dijon mustard

INSTRUCTIONS

Mix well, and serve with okra patties.

* * * * *

As I mentioned at the beginning of this chapter, Linda is a generous person who is constantly sharing encouragement, good wishes, and recipes. When asked to be a part of *Cook & Tell,* she didn't send me just one recipe but instead took the time and effort to scan and provide several wonderful dishes from her grandmother's collection. I found a number fascinating, with many of them taking me "back home," and figured that you all would like to try a few as well.

The following recipe Linda sent from her grandmother's collected clippings is for tea cakes. These simple but delicious cookies were a constant in our home growing up, and if you are from the South, I'm sure you ate your share of tea cakes as well. This recipe is attributed in the newspaper to a Mrs. Henry Fowlkes of Birmingham. A similar recipe can be found in *Southern Cooking*, and in her notes, the renowned author Mrs. S. R. Dull says, "This is without any exception the best tea cake or cookie recipe I have ever used."

Be aware that this recipe makes a lot of cookies. You could easily half it and still have a few dozen treats to share.

Grandmother's Tea Cakes

INGREDIENTS

2 cups sugar

1 cup butter, at room temperature

5 cups all-purpose flour

1 teaspoon baking powder

Pinch of salt

3 egg yolks and 3 egg whites, beaten separately

1 teaspoon vanilla

INSTRUCTIONS

1. Preheat oven to 375 degrees.

2. In a mixing bowl, cream the sugar and butter.

3. In a separate bowl, sift together the flour, baking powder, and salt. Set aside.

4. Add the beaten yolks and vanilla to the sugar and butter mixture. Stir to mix.

5. Add the sifted dry ingredients, and finally the beaten egg whites.

6. Work the dough until thoroughly mixed, and then turn onto a floured board or surface. Knead the dough until smooth, and roll out into a thin disc, about ¼ inch thick.

7. Cut out into rounds or any desired shape, and place on a lightly greased cookie sheet. Be careful to space them apart so that they do not touch.

8. Cook until the edges just begin to brown, about 7-8 minutes. Be careful as these delicate cookies can burn easily. Remove from the pan and cool on a wire rack.

Makes 5-6 dozen cookies

* * * * *

The next recipe is for a wonderful bread that placed first in a cooking contest held by the *Birmingham News*, featured in the Sunday, September

4, 1955, edition; the title of the article was "From the 'Sunset Years' Comes Top Recipe of Alabama." The winner was Miss Elizabeth Mason of Talladega. Miss Mason was a retired nurse who loved to cook, and lived in an assisted-living home called The Sunset Inn. (By the way, the inn is still in business sixty-plus years later.) The paper's food editor, Sue Scattergood—don't you love that name?—said this about Miss Mason: "She is a dear little lady who has spent a most useful life in the nursing profession who now chooses to spend her retirement years in a home where she will not be living alone."

Thanks to Miss Mason and Miss Scattergood for this delicious bread. It is basically a light biscuit dough flavored with cheese and onions. And yes, it is much better than those boxed brands you can buy. It slices nicely and also makes wonderful small muffins. I served this recently with barbequed pork tenderloin and a big green salad, and it was an excellent menu.

Sunset Bread

INGREDIENTS

½ cup chopped onion

1 tablespoon bacon drippings (or vegetable oil)

1½ cups all-purpose flour

2 teaspoons baking powder

½ teaspoon salt

¼ cup shortening, such as Crisco

1 egg, beaten

½ cup whole milk

1 cup sharp cheddar cheese, grated and divided

2 tablespoons butter, melted

INSTRUCTIONS

1. Preheat oven to 400 degrees.

2. Cook the onion in the bacon drippings over medium-high heat until tender and light brown, about 5-6 minutes. Remove from heat and set aside.

3. In a large bowl, sift together the flour, baking powder, and salt.

4. Add the shortening to the flour, and work in with your fingers or a fork until the mixture looks like coarse meal.

5. Add the beaten egg and milk. Stir until just moistened; do not over mix.

6. With a spatula, gently fold in half the cheese and all the sautéed onions.

7. Add the dough to a greased and floured round 8-inch or 9-inch baking pan. With a spatula or the back of a spoon, spread the dough evenly across the dish.

8. Sprinkle the top of the dough with the remaining cheese, and drizzle with the melted butter.

9. Bake for 20 or 25 minutes until done and the top becomes a golden, light brown color.

10. Remove from heat and serve immediately. It can also be served at room temperature.

Serves 4-6

*   *   *   *   *

While this cake contains no eggnog, it has the taste of the holidays and makes a beautiful presentation on your sideboard or buffet table. It is also delicious served at teatime with a cup of Earl Grey or a small glass of sherry. This wonderful recipe was from a Miss Patty West of Sylacauga, Alabama, and was printed in the *Birmingham News* in September 1955. Miss West states in the recipe, "Truly, this is a novelty cake—somewhat similar to a fruit cake but delightfully different."

Lemon Eggnog Cake

INGREDIENTS

1 pound unsalted butter

2 cups sugar

2 ounces lemon extract (2 small bottles)*

4 cups all-purpose flour, with ¼ cup reserved and set aside

1½ teaspoons baking powder

6 eggs

1 pound white (golden) raisins

2 cups chopped pecans

½ cup confectioner's sugar for decoration

INSTRUCTIONS

1. Preheat oven to 350 degrees.

2. In a large bowl, cream together the butter and sugar.

3. Add the lemon extract (yes, 2 ounces is correct!).

4. Sift together the flour and baking powder into a separate bowl.

5. Alternately add the sifted ingredients along with the eggs, one at a time, to the creamed sugar and butter. Beat well.

6. Lightly toss the ¼ cup reserved flour with the raisins and pecans, and add to the batter. Stir to mix.

7. Pour batter into a greased and floured loaf pan and bake for 1 hour and 20 minutes.

8. Allow to cool, and then invert on a cake plate. Sprinkle the top with the confectioner's sugar.

Serves 10-12

*Note from JSB: I am not a fan of lemon extract, so I would very finely zest 3 large lemons and use that instead of the flavoring. However, the recipe is still delicious as originally presented.

* * * * *

This final offering is one of Linda's own adaptations that incorporates the wonderful Southern vegetable used in the okra patty recipe with another Dixie staple, grits. These hoecakes would make your foodie friends sit up and take notice at your next dinner party. According to Linda, "I was over on John's Island and picked up a bag of stone ground meal. I love cornbread with my summer vegetables, but I like hoecakes too. Our cook used to make them for us. Hoecakes have a little crispness that you don't get with cornbread. When the hoecakes were done, I served them with a little red pepper jelly. Delicious alongside fresh butterbeans or peas, and they are darn good."

Okra & Jalapeno Hoecakes with Red Pepper Jelly

INGREDIENTS

1 cup stone ground cornmeal (I used Geechie Boy brand Stone Ground White Cornmeal)

¾ teaspoon baking powder

½ teaspoon salt

¼ cup finely chopped onion

½ cup thinly sliced or chopped fresh okra (use smaller, more tender pods)

1 teaspoon finely diced fresh jalapeno, or to taste

1 egg, beaten

3-4 tablespoons whole milk

Vegetable or peanut oil

1 small jar Red Pepper Jelly

INSTRUCTIONS

1. Add the cornmeal to a bowl, along with the baking powder, salt, onion, okra, and jalapeno. Mix together.

2. Add the beaten egg and 3 tablespoons milk, and stir to mix. It should be a thick consistency, enough to ball on a spoon. If too thick, add more milk—a tablespoon or less.

3. Heat about ½ inch of oil in a heavy skillet over medium-high heat until the oil begins to move in the pan.

4. Use a small scoop to put drops of batter into the pan. Flatten the hoecake mounds slightly with the back of the scoop. Brown on one side, then turn over and brown hoecakes on the other side. Do not overcrowd the pan or allow the hoecakes to touch one another. Depending on the size of your pan, you may have to make two batches.

5. Remove from the heat to paper towels to drain. Place on a serving platter alongside a bowl of pepper jelly.

Serves 6-8

CHAPTER 25

MEMORIES
FROM MELINDA

by Melinda Lowder Palmer

Bill and Melinda Palmer reside under the historic oaks of Belfair Plantation in Bluffton, South Carolina, and are two the most genuine and gracious hosts that I know. A guest is always greeted with warm hugs, big smiles, a little music playing in the background, and a favorite libation when walking through their door. These two charming people are the epitome of what I call relaxed sophistication; they have and enjoy the best life has to offer, and they express their hospitality with an ease and grace that looks as if they were born to entertain.

Hailing from small towns in North Carolina, Bill and Melinda never forgot the life and lessons learned during their childhood in the country. While they just spent a week in New York at the Waldorf for their fortieth anniversary, this couple still appreciates the taste of a good tomato sandwich or a spoonful of homemade pimento cheese. And Melinda, who has carried on those cooking traditions from back home, can set a magnificent table with some of the finest food found in the Southeast.

My friend tells us in this chapter about her Sundays growing up, and the special dishes that were lovingly prepared for family gatherings by her mom, aunts, and grandmothers. From the story, you can easily tell where Melinda learned the art of cooking—and understand why she is such a renowned hostess today.

Melinda with her Mom and Grandmother Almond on the Blue Ridge Parkway, 1953

Having been blessed to be born "Southern," I was taught from a young age the importance of church, family, and food—and precisely in that order. Sundays were spent in church for Sunday school and the worship service. Even when we slept over at a friend's house, we had to be in church come Sunday morning. Typically after the midday service we gathered at home and had "dinner"—when I was growing up in the fifties and sixties, the noon meal was called dinner as in most Southern households. Supper was your evening meal.

Anyway, after dinner we then were off visiting relatives. I loved driving out to see my great-grandparents, Hal and Sophia Almond, who had a real working farm near Millingport, North Carolina. There were horses, mules, cows, pigs, chickens, ducks, and a fish pond. Even though they had indoor plumbing, my sisters and I would beg to use the outhouse— such a novelty! And the well under the big oak tree supplied the coolest, best-tasting water that we sipped right out of the ladle. In the summer, Grandpa Hal always had a watermelon chilling, just waiting for us. But the best part of the visit was Grandma Sophia's custard and fruit pies, always sitting on her pantry shelf. And she cut her pies into fourths—no skinny slices here! No matter how young or old, how big or little, everyone got exactly a quarter of a pie.

My maternal grandparents, Reynolds and Ruth Almond, always hosted family holiday meals, which were truly food events. Grandmother would prepare not only a roasted turkey and ham but also some sort of beef, along with an assortment of veggies that were canned or frozen the previous summer from her garden. The sideboard in the dining room would be filled with desserts, including cakes, pies, and her special persimmon pudding. Sweet iced tea was the beverage of choice to wash it all down.

Grandmother Ruth had six sisters and one brother. The Fink sisters (their maiden name) gathered each Monday for the noon meal. The host planned the menu and delegated the dishes. While these get-togethers were social, they also included a little unspoken cooking competition and a bit of gossip. Many people throughout the community would have "paid good money," as they say, for an invitation, but these meals were closed sessions. Once, however, they did permit the local newspaper to do an article on the festivities. Many recipes were shared during these times.

Other fond food memories included church events, such as covered dish suppers, or when my parents' Sunday school class hosted a barbeque. Talk about a buffet! On those occasions, my mom always brought her famed potato salad, a town favorite. There was never any left in the bowl!

I'm truly blessed to have grown up surrounded by such wonderful Southern cooks who instilled in me a love of food, cooking, and then the joy of sharing it with others.

—Melinda Lowder Palmer

* * * * *

Persimmons are hard to find these days; as with hard Kieffer pears, their trees are now mostly on old farm homesteads or along country roads. Your best bet is to search the local farmers' markets in early fall. If you can't find persimmons, you can substitute large, purple plums, which are usually available year-round in most grocery stores.

Persimmon Pudding

INGREDIENTS

2 cups persimmon pulp (or plum pulp if substituting)

3 eggs, slightly beaten

1¼ cups sugar

1½ cups all-purpose flour

1 teaspoon baking soda

1 teaspoon baking powder

½ teaspoon salt

½ cup butter, melted

2 cups whole milk

1 teaspoon vanilla extract

1 cup raisins

Whipped cream for topping

INSTRUCTIONS

1. Preheat oven to 325 degrees.

2. In a large bowl, add all ingredients (except for the whipped cream) and stir until mixed well.

3. Pour into a lightly greased baking dish, and cook for 1 hour or until firm in the middle.

4. Allow to cool slightly before serving. Serve with a dollop of freshly whipped cream.

Serves 6-8

* * * * *

Here is another of Melinda's culinary treasures. Her copy is written in her mother's handwriting. When you fix this dish and sample it for yourself, you'll taste why Mrs. Lowder's Potato Salad has been so popular for decades.

Mrs. Lowder's Potato Salad

INGREDIENTS

3 pounds white potatoes, peeled and cut into 1-inch cubes

½ cup sweet bell pepper, chopped finely

½ cup celery, chopped finely

½ cup fresh tomatoes, seeded, and chopped into ¼-inch pieces

½ cup sweet pickle, chopped finely

½ cup Vidalia or other sweet onion, chopped finely

4 hard-boiled eggs, chopped finely

¾ cup real mayonnaise, or more to taste

1 teaspoon yellow mustard

Salt and black pepper to taste

INSTRUCTIONS

1. Place the potatoes in a large pot and cover with 2 inches of cold water. Bring to a boil, stir, and reduce to a gentle boil. Cook until soft, but not mushy, 10-12 minutes.

2. Drain the potatoes in a colander.

3. Place all ingredients in a large mixing bowl and fold together gently with a spatula or large spoon. Be careful not to break the potatoes into too many pieces.

4. Cover and refrigerate 4 hours or overnight before serving.

Serves 6-8

CHAPTER 26

GOD BLESS OPHELIA

by Chuck Beard

O n the tour for my first book, *Rise & Shine!,* I received the privilege of being asked to present at the renowned Southern Festival of Books in Nashville. The second privilege presented with this invitation was to have freelance writer, editor, and author Chuck Beard moderate my talk. What an impressive young man, both professionally and personally. Some moderators just glean through a book and hit the high spots, but not Chuck. He read *Rise & Shine!* as if he were researching an important paper for a college final. His questions were well thought out and insightful, and in the end he had me thinking about some of my stories in a different context than I had before.

And through his series of questions, and then our brief conversations, I found—as does all of Nashville it seems—that Mr. Beard is a classic Southern gentleman: well read with an impressive mind, wonderful manners, easygoing personality, and warm, sincere smile. I was happy to have made such a new friend. I could sense his popularity firsthand as we strolled the grounds of the state capital and alongside the book vendors at the festival. Young and old stopped to say hello, shake his hand, or give him a hug. That popularity was then reconfirmed when I placed a photo of the two of us together on Facebook; I received about a hundred "likes" on the post, while he outpaced me, garnering what seemed like a gazillion.

Through our time with one another, I mentioned to Chuck that my next book project would compile stories and related recipes from Southern cooks, and asked if he had anything he would like to share. He immediately answered, "Absolutely! Fifi Rolls!" He then went on to tell me, as he writes in the following story, about the indomitable Ophelia Butts, her bond with his family, and the most delicate and delicious rolls found anywhere in the South. I know it is a story, and recipe, that you'll thoroughly enjoy. And, if you are in Nashville, look Chuck up at his store, Eastside Books. Stop by, say hello, and plan to be charmed by this engaging and wonderful fellow.

On the grounds of the state capital in Nashville with Chuck Beard

My ninety-year-old mother, Mary Anne Reynolds Beard, recently recalled Ophelia "Fifi" Butts walking down Glen Lily Road in Bowling Green, Kentucky, to work every Monday through Friday. Standing at around five feet tall, if she was wearing her thick-soled shoes, Fifi was a young teenager in those days who cooked and cleaned for a living around town.

Originally hired by my great-grandparents, Fifi made quite the impression, career, and lasting legacy in my family. She worked for my great-grandparents until they passed away. Then she worked for my grandparents and great-aunt and uncle as well before cementing her place in our family lore by continuing to help my parents until just before her death in the late 1980s.

In my immediate family of eleven children, Fifi was much more than help to my mother; she was a sous chef, disciplinarian, mentor, and friend all wrapped into one soul. Simply put, she was family. When you think about it, Fifi spent more time with my family than some people live in a lifetime. She was in her late seventies when she retired to the Upper Room in the sky.

Mother claimed that Fifi's original nickname, the one that didn't stick over the long haul, was B.S. due to the white bobby socks she wore as part

Ophelia, back center, with Chuck's Great-grandmother Patricia Nusz, his Grandmother Patty Reynolds, and his Aunt Trisha, at Trisha's first communion, 1977

of her personal uniform every day of her life. She also wore any and all shoes that were given to her, no matter what size. To complete her daily uniform, she was always seen with a pristinely clean and lightly starched white outfit.

Fifi married Sam Hayes, a retired employee of the historic L&N Railroad who was twenty years her senior. Together they had one child, a son, who died at birth. After that, Sam didn't live much longer. So it came to be that Fifi said she had many loves in her life, and, besides Sam, those loves were her prized chickens. Every night, when all the daily work was completed, she would collect and carry every last bit of leftover scraps of food she could find to take home to feed those darn chickens. On a fairly personal note, I distinctly remember one incident with those chickens in particular that I cannot erase from memory.

I was seven years old, playing with siblings and cousins in my grandparents' side yard when, from out of nowhere, Fifi came storming out of the house and into the yard in full stride. She said she was aimin' to wring a chicken's neck and there was simply no stopping her. She was on a mission. All of us kids stood still with mouths wide open in amazement as Fifi finally caught and indeed wrung that chicken's neck right in front of us. Before that moment, none of us knew it was even possible for a chicken to literally run around the yard without a head. The children were running and the follow-up screams were deafening, but fried chicken was on the dinner table a few hours later. They just don't make 'em like that anymore. God bless Fifi.

And while this wonderful lady spent her lifetime cooking, cleaning, and changing cloth diapers while helping raise umpteen numbers of children, she is also forever known for her incredible potato yeast rolls. These delicacies have become a family classic, bringing back wonderful memories of our friend whenever we gather for a birthday, holiday, or special gathering. Even those of our family who have come along after Fifi passed—never having the pleasure of her company—make special recognition of this culinary legacy. I hope that when you make our "Fifi Rolls," they will bring sweet smiles to the faces of you and your loved ones, just like they do for me. From our house to yours, enjoy. And again, God bless Fifi.

—Chuck Beard

* * * * *

Chuck's mother graciously shares Ophelia's recipe; these rolls are perfect served next to a big pot roast or platter of fried chicken for a classic Sunday dinner. If any are left over, which is a rare occurrence, rewarm them in a hot oven, slice, and insert a piece of ham for breakfast. Or create your own Southern slider with a scoop of chicken salad instead for a quick lunch treat. There are a dozen ways to enjoy these delicacies.

Fifi Rolls

INGREDIENTS

1½ cups warm water

1 package yeast (2¼ teaspoons or ¼ ounce; I use Fleischmann's Rapid Rise Yeast)

⅔ cup sugar

1½ teaspoon salt

1 cup melted shortening, divided

2 eggs (slightly beaten)

1 cup peeled and cooked white potatoes, mashed, at room temperature

7-7½ cup all-purpose flour (plus additional for flouring your board)

INSTRUCTIONS

1. In large bowl, dissolve the yeast in warm water. Allow it to sit for about 5 minutes.

2. Stir in sugar, salt, ⅔ cup of melted shortening, eggs, and potatoes. Mix until just incorporated.

3. Sift half of the flour into the potato mixture and stir until easy to handle. Sift in the remaining flour and continue mixing to make a soft dough.

4. Turn the dough onto a lightly floured board. Knead until smooth and elastic, about 5-7 minutes.

5. Brush the top of the dough with some of the additional melted shortening.

6. Lightly grease another large bowl and place the dough into it, greased-side up. Cover with a damp cloth.

7. Set the greased dough in a warm spot in the kitchen and allow to rise and double in size, about 1 hour.

8. About 2 hours before baking, roll out the dough to a thickness of ½ inch and cut into rounds.

9. Dip each roll into melted shortening and fold over into your baking pans. Allow to rise, about 1 hour.

10. Bake in a preheated 400-degree oven for 10-12 minutes, or until a light brown.

Makes about 4 dozen rolls

CHAPTER 27

MEMORIES OF A TENNESSEE JAM CAKE

by Nicki Pendleton Wood

n the previous chapter I mentioned being part of the Southern Festival of Books in Nashville, and there is another story coming here about that wonderful trip. But before I introduce our next Southern cook and storyteller, who hails from the Music City, let me share two "It's a Small World" experiences that happened there.

First, I was standing in line at a coffee shop just outside Tennessee's state capital and started chatting with the fellow in front of me. After introducing ourselves, we looked at each other as if we were thinking, "That name sounds familiar...." Come to find out, I was talking with Harrison Scott Key, who not only lives in my hometown of Savannah but also resides just a few blocks over from me in the same historic neighborhood of Ardsley Park. We had both heard of one another back home, but had never met in person until that morning—500 miles away from our respective doorsteps! Harrison was at the festival speaking about his highly successful memoir, *The World's Largest Man*. If you have not read it, buy a copy and prepare yourself to be thoroughly entertained.

The second less-than-six-degrees-of-separation happened at the "Authors in the Round" fundraiser party, which is held at the historic War Memorial Plaza in downtown Nashville. *Nashville Scene* described it as an event "...where each round table pairs guests with one of 40 visiting authors (and each guest gets a copy of their book). Individual tickets for

Nicki's grandmother, Myrtle Harrington Qualls, 1968

the SFB fundraiser are $200. There'll be drinks at the outset and drinks at the end, with time in between for occasional drinking." Those of you who know me realize that I was looking forward to this party. And I was very fortunate to have been chosen as one of the forty author guests.

During the "drinks at the outset," I sidled up next to one of the many bars in the outdoor plaza and started a conversation with a fellow named Walker while waiting for a whiskey. When he found out where I was from, he mentioned that he graduated from Sewanee with a fellow from Savannah by the name of Will Belford. Well, I live right across the street from Will's mama and daddy, and have known him since he was a kid. Come to find out, too, my new friend had attended Will's wedding—as had I—and was at the pre-wedding party Tom, my partner, and I hosted for the newlyweds earlier that week. Then—okay, y'all, this is too many coincidences—who just happens to be the guest author at Walker's table later that evening? Yep, yours truly, JSB. God has fun moving the pieces around on the chessboard sometimes, don't you think?

Anyway, now that I've gone around my arse to get to my elbow with asides about never knowing who you'll run into, let me get to the next story and featured recipe. This one is contributed by one of Nashville's own, the charming Nicki Pendleton Wood.

Nicki and I met that night of the Authors in the Round at the beginning of the banquet. All forty of the authors were gathered at the foot of the auditorium stage, and one by one were introduced to the audience with a picture of ourselves and a photo of our book presented on a huge movie screen. Standing next to me was Nicki, whose *Southern Cooking for Company* had just been released. Her book features more than 100 Southerners who share their "show-off" recipes that they pull out when guests are coming over. Nicki is quite the talent in the kitchen, and besides being an honored author, she is also known as a restaurant reviewer and cookbook editor.

We enjoyed one another's brief company as the festivities started to unfold and have kept in touch since the festival, sharing recipes, tidbits about upcoming events, and comical stories about the rigors of a book tour.

Here Nicki gives us a story about her granny and an old-time favorite, Tennessee Jam Cake—a rich confection that was one of my favorites growing up as a child. The popularity of this cake has waned; you don't see too many of these anymore at a family reunion or at Christmas. Maybe some of you reading this book will help change that by showing off this classic on your next holiday sideboard. Thanks for sharing, Nicki, and it was great meeting you in "the small world" of Nashville!

Summer blackberry picking was a tradition on my grandparents' Tennessee farm. Around July 4, aunts, uncles, and cousins dressed in our berry-picking outfits: long sleeves, jeans tucked into socks, bug spray all over. And underdrawers because everyone knows chiggers crawl until they're blocked, and then they bite. For buckets, we cut off the tops of plastic gallon milk jugs, threaded a belt through the handles, and strapped them to our waists. We aimed to pick a gallon each. That's about eight gallons of berries.

Fresh berries with cream was our post-picking treat. Then we cranked blackberry ice cream. The rest of our haul was frozen or made into preserves or jam in a weekend-long session of simmering, ladling, and sealing. At Thanksgiving and Christmas, the preserves reached their highest purpose in Tennessee Jam Cake, a lightly spiced cake frosted with a rich buttermilk penuche frosting. It was a favorite of both my granny and my mom.

Jam cake is fairly common in the upper South—recipes for it date back to the late nineteenth century and originate from northern Kentucky through central Tennessee to north Alabama.

My grandmother's recipe was a straightforward spiced buttermilk cake with blackberry jam, pear preserves if she had them, and hickory nuts or pecans. My in-laws' family (Giles County, Tennessee) had a more elaborate version that included both molasses and sugar, pear preserves, dates, and raisins.

My granny and I were very close, and I loved cooking with her. We poked fun at each other's styles and tastes. I cringed at her unseasoned spaghetti sauce. She cringed at how much pepper I put into the chicken. We once made the worst peach pie I ever tasted, because we each insisted on a little change here and there.

Memory is a powerful thing. I probably only saw Granny make this cake once, and the frosting twice. It stuck with me, though, and when I dug out the recipe, I made it as easily as if I'd been making it my whole life.

—Nicki Pendleton Wood

Tennessee Jam Cake

INGREDIENTS

1 cup (½ pound) butter, softened slightly

2 cups sugar

5 large eggs

1 cup blackberry jam

1 cup pear or strawberry preserves

1 teaspoon baking soda

½ cup whole milk buttermilk

3½ cups all-purpose flour

1½ teaspoons ground allspice

1 teaspoon cinnamon

½ teaspoon nutmeg

½ cup cocoa

1 cup coarsely chopped pecans, toasted (optional)

2 cups raisins (optional)

Buttermilk Frosting (recipe follows)

INSTRUCTIONS

1. Preheat the oven to 325 degrees. Grease two 8-inch cake pans. Dust lightly with flour or cocoa. (Note: If you don't want to mess with layers, bake the cake in a tube pan for about 1-1½ hours.)

2. Beat the butter and sugar until very well combined.

3. Add the eggs and beat for 2 minutes.

4. Beat in the jam and preserves.

5. Dissolve the baking soda in the buttermilk and add to the batter.

6. Combine the flour, allspice, cinnamon, nutmeg, and cocoa in a small bowl. Add to the batter and beat just until combined.

7. Stir in the pecans and raisins, if using.

8. Spoon the mixture into the prepared pan, spreading the thick batter into the corners.

9. Bake about 30 minutes or until the cake springs back when pressed, a knife inserted in the center comes out clean, or the cake pulls away from the sides of the pan. Cool in the pans for 15 minutes before turning out.

10. Spread the frosting between the layers, on the sides, and on top of the cake.

Serves 12-16

Buttermilk Frosting

INGREDIENTS

½ cup whole milk buttermilk

1 cup granulated sugar

5 tablespoons butter

½ teaspoon baking soda

INSTRUCTIONS

1. Combine the buttermilk, sugar, and butter in a large (3-quart) saucepan. Bring to a boil over medium heat, stirring often.

2. Stir in the baking soda and keep stirring—the mixture will foam up. Cook, stirring, until the mixture reaches soft ball stage (235-240 degrees). Let cool slightly before frosting the cake. (At this stage, the frosting has a glaze consistency—if you want a spreadable texture, beat it with an electric mixer for a few minutes to thicken it.

CHAPTER 28

WELSH RAREBIT RIVALRY

by Barbara Salter Hubbard

Carter and Barbara Hubbard met at the University of South Carolina forty-plus years ago, and it was love at first sight. Carter relates that he was advised by friends to take chorus as an elective his freshman year, because (1) if you attended each class you were assured of an "A," and (2), more important, you could meet lots of pretty girls. He goes on to tell that on his first day, in walks this petite, dark-haired beauty with enormous blue eyes and an angelic voice. Carter turned to his buddy and fellow classmate and said, "I'm going to marry that girl." And they've been in love and together ever since.

As Barbara tells in the following story, her husband is from Virginia aristocracy. His father was a petroleum executive, and his mother undertook the restoration of the Monroe House, where the future President James Monroe practiced law, in historic Fredericksburg. Carter inherited a magnificent original oil portrait of Elizabeth Monroe, James's wife; it hangs with distinction in the Hubbards' Savannah home.

My husband, Carter, is from an old Virginia family. The youngest of five children, he was raised in a formal upbringing, rich in tradition. One of their favorite customs was having Welsh Rarebit at large gatherings such as Christmas, Easter, and reunions. As the years passed, each sibling developed his or her own version of the original recipe. One brother added

To Carter and Barbara —
This book has some delicious recipes — especially page 118 — I am delighted with Allan Jones' line drawing of our house —
With much love and best wishes for a happy Christmas!
"Mom"
Christmas 1975

A note inscribed to Barbara and Carter by Carter's mother
in the **Virginia Hospitality Cookbook**.

hot pepper to his, and one sister even took a shortcut with Velveeta (which proved, as you can imagine, unsuccessful to the palate).

During a family reunion several years ago on Tybee, all eighteen family members gathered in one of the island's large, rambling beach cottages for a week's stay. Each sibling and spouse was assigned an evening meal. In the spirit of familial rivalry, those occasions became a contest to see who could outdo the other. Themes were created along with hats, decorations, *and even fireworks and sparklers after dinner. And of course, a Hubbard family gathering just wouldn't be the same without Welsh Rarebit. On the final day, different versions of the recipe were to be prepared—the ultimate test of sibling rivalry. At the end of the meal, most pots were barely touched, while one was empty. Not much was said about it after that since I, the in-law, was the one with the empty pot. I don't think Carter's sisters were particularly amused that this interloper had scooped up the cooking prize. Fortunately, they still love me! The tradition now, to save everyone's culinary feelings, is that whoever is hosting the dinner or the event is the one who prepares the Hubbard Welsh Rarebit.*

—Barbara Salter Hubbard

* * * * *

I've been fortunate to sample this rich and satisfying Welsh Rarebit at the Hubbard home several times over our decades-long friendship. The original recipe is from Carter's mother, which she submitted and subsequently had published in the 1975 edition of *Virginia Hospitality*, a cookbook presented by the Junior League of Hampton Roads. I've adapted their family classic to include ale or stout, giving it more of an English influence and taste. Served over toasted sourdough bread, with a side of bacon and fresh fruit, it is a delicious way to start a special day or end a magical evening.

Welsh Rarebit

INGREDIENTS

3 tablespoons unsalted butter

3 tablespoons all-purpose flour

1 teaspoon dry English mustard

½ teaspoon kosher salt

⅛ teaspoon onion powder

⅛ teaspoon sugar

¼ teaspoon ground white pepper

1 teaspoon Worcestershire sauce

½ cup porter beer, stout, or dark ale

1 cup cream

8 ounces sharp Cheddar cheese, shredded

Two dashes hot sauce

6-8 pieces of toasted sourdough bread

INSTRUCTIONS

1. In a medium-sized boiler, melt the butter over medium-low heat.

2. Whisk in the flour, and mix until smooth, cooking 2-3 minutes until hot and bubbly. Do not allow the mixture to brown.

3. Add the mustard, salt, onion powder, sugar, white pepper, and Worcestershire. Whisk until smooth.

4. Add the beer, stout, or ale, and whisk until fully mixed. Allow the mixture to heat through, but do not allow to simmer.

5. Pour in the cream, and whisk until thoroughly mixed.

6. When hot, but again not to the point of simmering, add the cheese a few tablespoons at a time, stirring along the way. When fully heated, add the hot sauce, stir, and serve over toasted sourdough bread.

Serves 6-8

Monroe House

The Monroe House, Carter's childhood home, as depicted in **Virginia Hospitality**. The Hubbard Welsh Rarebit recipe was featured on the following page.

CHAPTER 29

LESSONS OF A COUNTRY KITCHEN

by Rebecca Aultman Cheatham

I knew of Becky Cheatham before actually meeting her; it seems that everyone in Savannah had some connection with this lovely lady who was so involved with health care and education. I think we first met doing committee or board work back in the late 1980s—Becky served on a slew of boards, including time on the vestry of the Christ Church Episcopal, the Mother Church of Georgia. Or maybe we met at church? Anyway, it doesn't matter; we've been friends now going on thirty years. We've also become closer in the last decade, as her lovely daughter, Margaret, married Carter Clark Hubbard, Junior, son of our dear friends Barbara and Carter whom you read about in the previous chapter. Tom and I are so fond of both clans that we gave Carter and Margaret a wedding party, which included, in true Savannah style, a large buffet and open bar. Each invited guest brought a gift-wrapped ornament to decorate the soon-to-be married couple's first Christmas tree. What a fun evening and party!

Becky grew up in Sylvester, an agrarian community in South Georgia with ties to cotton, peanuts, timber, and soybeans. The folks down there are also known for their gardening, and Becky's family, like my own up the road just a few miles away in Perry, spent their summers picking, shelling, and "puttin' up" any number of crops.

Becky's story here harkens back to her days in the country, and is an example of how we Southerners—who grew up on fresh, farm-to-table food—won't let any fresh vegetable or fruit go unused.

"Waste not, want not!" Those were words to live by in the rural community where I grew up. If they're not in the Bible—and I'm not entirely certain they aren't—well, they ought to be. And they were echoing in my head the morning after my daughter Margaret's beautiful wedding. Yes, the lessons of a country kitchen resonate down decades, even when you move to Savannah and do your gardening out of clay pots.

The town of Sylvester, tucked away in Southwest Georgia, calls itself "The Peanut Capital of the World" these days. While my family's main crop was timber, we always had a large garden. My family has been coaxing food or cash—in the form of naval stores or lumber—out of the Worth County dirt for 200 years or so now. Summer mornings were spent canning and freezing fruits and vegetables because "idle hands are the Devil's workshop" was also considered a guideline for rearing satisfactory children. Even when the garden wasn't producing, the kitchen stayed busy with the fruits of Daddy's hunting and fishing. No matter what time of year, life revolved around the kitchen activity, and it was always happy and good.

When I became an adult, guided by a close friend, I got back into freezing fresh vegetables like peas, butterbeans, squash, and pears or whatever was plentiful. Making jams, jellies, barbecue sauce, and pickles became a regular part of my summer and a way of reconnecting with my earlier life. I discovered how good it felt to share what I'd preserved as gifts that friends literally could not buy themselves.

When I grew up, I hit the road for the "big city" of Savannah, about 200 miles from Sylvester and a world away. I'd earned my Master's degree in Speech Pathology from the University of Georgia, and went to work at the Savannah Speech and Hearing Center in June 1972. Early in my career, I received a subpoena to testify in a court case. I remember being very frightened about appearing in court as an expert witness, but I wound up marrying the judge several years later. He liked to tell people he gave me

Margaret and Carter, Jr. at their wedding reception. Little did they know that they would be eating the centerpieces at Christmas!

a "life sentence." We married on October 9, 1976, and enjoyed thirty-two years together. He died in 2008.

When Margaret got married in November 2007, we reflected the season in the table decorations at the reception. Apples, oranges, and cranberries filled the bottom of large glass hurricane lamps, with beautiful floral arrangements on top.

On Sunday morning after the wedding, I awoke to the images of the day before and the knowledge of all that fruit in a storage room at the Savannah Yacht Club. With all those centerpieces and decorations, there was just too much food there to go to waste! The mother of the bride was back on the scene that morning, armed with plastic bags. But what to do with the bounty?

The oranges were easy. They were turned into my family recipe for ambrosia and frozen for Thanksgiving. But what about the cranberries and apples? Then I remembered how treasures are often buried in the small-time productions of Southern club and church recipe collections, which all Southern cooks accumulate sort of as an obligation. I found a recipe for cranberry chutney in **Pleasures Unlimited**, the Tifton Garden Club cookbook.

That chutney, made of wedding décor leftovers, was such a success that it has become a family favorite at Thanksgiving. It also lasts a couple of weeks at least, again personifying the "waste not, want not" mantra that led me to discover it in the first place.

—Becky Aultman Cheatham

Becky's Wedding-Bell Cranberry Chutney

This chutney will pair excellently with cornbread dressing, roasted fowl, or ham. Too, you can serve it at cocktail hour atop a round of Brie for an hors' d'oeuvre.

INGREDIENTS

1 pound fresh cranberries

2 cups sugar

1 cup water

1 cup orange juice

1 cup seedless golden raisins

1 cup chopped apples

1 cup chopped walnuts

1 tablespoon freshly grated orange zest

1 teaspoon ground ginger

INSTRUCTIONS

1. Over low heat, cook the cranberries, sugar, and water for about 15 minutes, stirring often.

2. Remove from heat and add all other ingredients, stirring to mix.

3. Cool to room temperature, place in a bowl, cover tightly, and refrigerate.

Makes about 1 quart

CHAPTER 30

SUNSHINE, BLACKBERRIES, & DADA DASHER

by Walter Dasher

Alice and Walter Dasher are two of my favorite people in Savannah, and it is always a pleasure to see them. Often, like so many of the folks I know with busy lives, we find ourselves having to catch up with one another while in the check-out line at Publix, instead of over a cocktail or dinner. But wherever I run into this couple, it is always a joy.

While Alice is diminutive in stature, she fills up a room with her distinctive, wonderful laugh, and her twinkling, mischievous eyes make your soul smile. Walter is a bit more reserved, a charmingly soft-spoken and gracious gentleman of the first order. Both being incredible foodies, and with Walter a professional chef of renown, it was fitting that this couple met and fell in love at La Toque, a splendid restaurant that was located in the heart of Savannah's historic district. They have now been married for almost thirty years.

Walter has had a following of fans for decades, dazzling Savannah gourmands at the venerable Chatham and Oglethorpe Clubs, the Savannah Yacht Club, and the spectacular 45 South. His dishes and creations range from one showstopper to another, but it is a simple recipe, inspired from his days of boyhood spent with his grandparents, that he selflessly brings to us here. This story shows that, even at the heart of great chefs, the days of childhood dishes shared with family are some of our most memorable times of life, especially in the South.

It was another time, growing up in the South in the early 1960s. Granddaddy would take me blackberry picking. He was good friends with the ranger of what's now known as the Savannah Wildlife Refuge, 30,000 acres of freshwater marshes, tidal creeks, and coastal woodlands. The two of us would traipse up and down the refuge's dirt-covered back roads to pick (and eat, of course) from the endless bushes of blackberries. I never even noticed the Southern, summertime sun beating down on us while we cherished the sight of every colorful berry. I'd drop each, one by one, into my homemade pail with coat hanger as a handle, smiling as I heard the sweet-sounding thunk when it hit the metal inside. The mere thought of what Dada (my grandmother) would create with these finds made our efforts all the more gratifying.

Dada made jams and sauces and cakes and muffins and just about everything else you can think of, but my all-time favorite were her lattice-top pies. She was a superb cook, as many grandmothers are, self-taught and never referenced a cookbook—just cooking from her heart and experience. Many things inspired my decision to become a chef, but the very first influence, hands down, would be Dada's pies that accompanied her award-worthy Sunday lunch after church.

Dada and Grandaddy Dasher

If you can possibly imagine anything better than a blackberry pie, it was her pineapple upside-down cake. A few years ago, I pulled out her handwritten recipe and started to improvise. Could I change it into a blackberry upside-down cake? Should I try to make two perfect recipes into one?

Why would I do that? Why not?

I baked, modified, converted, tweaked, added, adjusted, and tasted until "Dasher Version 100.0" hit the mark! My cooking companion and wife, Alice, finally gave it the thumbs-up, and I knew it wasn't going to get any better.

This dessert reminds me of why I became a chef, it honors three special people in my life (Granddaddy, Dada, and Alice), and it is so darn tasty! I hope you think so, too. And if you stain your white linens with the black-berries, call Alice, not me!

—Walter Dasher

Blackberry Upside-down Cake

INGREDIENTS

FOR THE TOPPING

6 tablespoons unsalted butter

¾ cup packed light brown sugar

2 pints of fresh blackberries

FOR THE BATTER

1½ cups all-purpose flour

2-3 teaspoons ground cinnamon

2 teaspoons baking powder

¼ teaspoon salt

6 tablespoons unsalted butter, at room temperature

1 cup granulated sugar

2 large eggs

1 teaspoon vanilla extract

¼ cup Grand Marnier, divided

Zest of one medium lemon (finely done on a microplane)

2 tablespoons freshly squeezed lemon juice

INSTRUCTIONS

FOR THE TOPPING

1. Prepare a 9-inch cake pan with a parchment paper round, and butter and flour the entire pan including both sides of the parchment.

2. Preheat oven to 350 degrees.

3. Melt the butter in a medium-sized skillet. Add the brown sugar and simmer over moderate heat, stirring constantly until all the sugar is melted, about 2½-3 minutes. Remove from heat.

4. Pour the topping evenly in cake pan, spreading out gently with a spatula if needed.

5. Carefully place the blackberries in an even, tight layer on top of the sugar layer. Set aside.

FOR THE BATTER

1. In a mixing bowl, sift together flour, cinnamon, baking powder, and salt. Set aside.

2. Beat the butter in a large bowl with an electric mixer until light and fluffy, then gradually beat in granulated sugar. Add eggs one at a time, beating well after each addition. Scrape down sides with spatula to make sure all is incorporated.

3. Beat in the vanilla extract and 2 tablespoons Grand Marnier. Add half of the flour mixture and beat on low speed just until blended. Beat in the zest and lemon juice, then add the remaining flour just until blended.

4. Spoon the batter over blackberry topping and carefully spread evenly. Bake in middle rack of oven until golden, about 35 minutes, or until a tester comes out clean. Let cake rest in pan about 5 minutes, and then remove from the oven, immediately running a knife around the sides.

5. Invert a plate over cake pan and flip the two over, holding both firmly pressed together. Sprinkle the two remaining tablespoons Grand Marnier over the cake, and allow to cool before cutting.

Serves 6-8

CHAPTER 31

PARTY LINES & BUTTERBEAN WISDOM

by Cindy McDonald

've known my friend Cindy McDonald since we were five years old, and have a photograph showing the two of us onstage at our kindergarten graduation ceremony—she in a pretty little dress and me with a bowtie. Over the years we grew to be close friends. I often sought out her company, as she always had a sweet spirit and gentle heart, even in those incredibly awkward and trying days of our early teens. I've always felt a warm affinity for my friend, too, because of the deep affection she has for animals; even in grade school her stories were about dogs and horseback riding. Today you'll find in her yard felines, pups, chickens, and other varieties of God's creatures that she loves and cares for.

Cindy comes from a well-known family in our hometown, in part because of her spirited and lovely grandmother, Mrs. Alice Connell. Mrs. Connell was widowed at an early age, when Cindy's mom was just twelve years old, and left to raise three children on her own. Folks in Perry admired her tenacity and determination, as Mrs. Connell worked hard to make certain that each of her children finished high school and graduated from college—not an easy task for a single mother in the 1940s and '50s.

Cindy remembers her grandmother with great humor, respect, and love—and in our Southern tradition, many of those memories involve something from the family dining table, or garden.

I don't know if many of y'all remember, but years ago most homes shared a telephone line called a "party line." Grandma Alice of course, since she was our next-door neighbor, was on our party line. Well, this sounds fairly reasonable in theory, but Grandma Alice had a tendency to talk A LOT. I distinctly remember that most of the time if we picked up our phone to make a call, Grandma Alice would already be on there, talking with one of her good friends such as Miss Irva or Miss Opal, and they would go on for hours. The comical part is, if we were finally able to get a dial tone and call someone, Grandma Alice would inadvertently pick up her phone, hear the conversation, and just join in, asking who we were talking to and introducing herself, inquiring who their parents were and if they might need any vegetable, fruit, or jelly...you name it, and she had it. We did not appreciate this at the time, but looking back now it's pretty darn funny! Grandma Alice loved to talk on the phone so much that one day while I was unloading groceries at my mother's place, I saw a huge plume of black smoke coming from up the field by grandmother's house. The party line was long gone by this time, and we had our separate lines. I tried to call her and got the usual busy signal. The smoke got darker, and then I could see flames taller than the trees, so I started running up the field. Long story short, Grandma Alice got to talking on the phone with one of her sisters and forgot she was burning trash, and from that day forward there was one less barn on the property!

Speaking of the farm, Grandma Alice took her gardening and her vegetables seriously . . . very seriously! One morning I woke up to the sounds of sirens and horns and all kinds of chaos. I jumped up and looked out the window, where I saw that all the commotion was coming from the road right in from of Grandma Alice's driveway. I threw on some jeans and a shirt and ran up the field to see what was going on. When I got there, it was obvious Grandma had been in some type of minor car accident and a policeman was questioning her. I walked up closer to hear what was being said. The policeman asked, "Ma'am, why were you in such a hurry to get out of your driveway? Is there some emergency?" (Keep in mind that Grandma Alice was in her late seventies at the time.) She told him to step to the back of the car and he would see why she was in such a rush. I walked around there, too, expecting to see something awful like

Grandma Connell

a wounded animal or something that needed help. When she lifted the lid I could have died of embarrassment; her car trunk was heaped full of green beans, peas, and corn. She told the officer that it was indeed an emergency, for she needed to get to the cannery in Byron immediately, or all of the fresh vegetables would be wilted and no longer fresh in this heat!

He laughed a little bit, wrote her ticket, and went on his way.

When he left, I was looking at my grandmother, who was usually very well dressed and put together. But that day her hair was kind of messy and her shirt a little wrinkled, and then I noticed something white in front of her slacks. I told her she had something on her pants—the kind of pants with an elastic waist that all older women wore at that time (she called them pull-on pants). Anyway, she looked down and started laughing, looked at them a little more and started laughing harder, and then finally mustered out, "I was in such a rush to get to the cannery that I not only put my pants on backwards but inside out as well!" We both had a good laugh, and then she changed her clothes and straightened out her hair and we were off with the vegetables to Byron for a day of heat and humidity at the cannery.

Along with her humor, though, Grandma Alice was also a very wise and insightful woman. I learned many lessons both from her actions and her words. An example of her prudent judgment came about from what was a hurtful disappointment. Grandma Alice had recently sold a large tract of land located just outside of town, and most people in Perry mused that she had made a great deal of money. Sadly, this was not the case. My grandmother believed people at their word, and she had dealt with a realtor she thought was her friend. The key word here is "thought." Anyway, at that time I was in middle school and furious of how my grandmother had been treated. This was a time when young people weren't allowed in grownup conversations, so I couldn't say anything. I kept my tongue until I could no longer hold it in. It was the following spring, and we were planting the garden. I cautiously brought the subject up by saying, "Grandma, aren't you mad about what that lady did with your land?" She replied that she was disappointed, but that was all she chose to share.

This annoyed me greatly, and I expressed that to her. Then she asked me what I was doing, to which I replied, "Sitting in the 100-degree heat planting butterbeans, why?"

She kept planting and didn't look up but asked me what I'd be doing in a couple of months in this same spot, and I said, "More than likely sitting in the 100-degree heat picking butterbeans." She let out a little laugh and said, "Well, the kind of seeds those kinds of people plant won't produce anything good, and they will have to live with that, while we'll be eating our butterbeans."

—Cindy McDonald

* * * * *

After reading this story each of you are probably thinking, "I would love to have known Mrs. Connell." She was just a lovely person, one who had a special place in our hometown. A lady of determination, great wit, and conviction, and someone with the type of insightful wisdom that could convey a life lesson in a parable using a simple butterbean. There aren't many who come out of such a mold anymore, if any.

Here are a couple of favorite offerings that Grandmama Alice would have had on her table, ones she would have invited you over to try if she had picked up on your party line.

The first is succotash, which combines those wonderful butterbeans and another favorite, fresh corn. While those are the key ingredients, there are a number of variations on the dish that have been "revamped" by modern chefs. Some are quite good, but others I think try a little too hard to give the dish a "twist." One popular way to prepare succotash in some of the "new" Southern restaurants is to blanch the beans and serve it al dente. I'm sorry, y'all; I just cannot, and will not, eat a crunchy butterbean.

The dish here is simple yet delicious, and the soft, *cooked* butterbeans along with the bright taste of the newly picked corn is quite a combination. You can serve it hot or cold.

Succotash

INGREDIENTS

1 tablespoon vegetable oil

1 cup chopped Vidalia or other sweet onion

1 quart low-sodium chicken stock

1 quart fresh baby butterbeans (if using frozen, I prefer McKenzie's Petite Deluxe brand)

½ fresh jalapeno pepper, seeded

2 quarts water plus 1 tablespoon kosher salt

4 ears of fresh corn, shucked and silked (if using frozen, 4 cups of kernels)

¼ teaspoon black pepper

3 tablespoons butter

Salt to taste

2 tablespoons cream (optional)

2 tablespoons fresh chopped chives or green onions for garnish

INSTRUCTIONS

1. In a medium-sized pot, heat the oil over medium high until hot. Add the onion and cook, stirring occasionally, until soft, about 3-4 minutes.

2. Add to the pot the chicken stock, butterbeans, and jalapeno. Bring to a boil, stir, and reduce heat to a steady simmer. Cook for 20-25 minutes or until soft (the timing will depend on the size of your butterbeans).

3. While the butterbeans are cooking, prepare the corn. Bring the water and salt to a boil, and add the corn. Cook for 5 minutes and remove from heat. Then drain the corn and allow it to cool.

4. When the butterbeans are done, pour them into a colander and drain. Remove and discard the jalapeno.

5. Cut the corn kernels from the cobs, and set aside.

6. To finish the dish, melt the 3 tablespoons of butter in a medium-sized pot (the one you cooked your butterbeans in will do). Add to the pot the butterbeans and corn. Season with the black pepper and salt, and toss to coat with the butter. If you would like a creamy finish to the dish, mix in a few tablespoons of cream.

7. Serve immediately, or chill for a succotash salad. Garnish with the chopped chives or green onions.

Serves 6-8

* * * * *

Another favorite that came from Mrs. Connell's garden was yellow-neck squash, one of the "Three Sisters" along with corn and beans. As we could not find Miss Alice's recipe, my friend Linda Weiss of Charleston (see chapter 24, "Sweet Irene") has lent us her version of an outstanding casserole using this Southern vegetable. The presentation is lovely, and it should prove to be a favorite on your menu for a Sunday dinner or buffet supper. This dish is excellent teamed with roasted ham, green beans, sliced tomatoes, and hot, buttered biscuits.

Squash Soufflé

INGREDIENTS

2 pounds yellow-neck squash

1½ cup onions, chopped

1 cup water

20 Club or Ritz crackers, finely crushed

4 eggs, separated

2 cups sharp cheddar cheese, grated

1 cup whole milk

1½ teaspoon Kosher salt, or to taste

⅛ teaspoon black pepper

INSTRUCTIONS

1. Preheat oven to 400 degrees.

2. In a large pot, add the squash, onions, and water. Bring to a gentle simmer, cover, and cook until very tender, about 20 minutes or so. Stir occassionally.

3. In a colander, drain all the water from the cooked vegetables and add them to a large mixing bowl. Mash until pureed.

4. Add the crackers, egg yolks, cheese, milk, salt, and pepper. Stir to mix.

5. Beat the egg whites until stiff peaks form. Fold the beaten whites into the casserole mixture with a spatula.

6. Spread the casserole into a buttered baking dish and cook until done, about 30 minutes. The casserole is done when the top becomes slightly brown and the center is firm. Let sit 10 minutes before serving.

Serves 6-8

CHAPTER 32

TASTING HOME

by Amy Paige Condon

Amy Paige Condon is one of the nicest and most genuine people found on God's green earth. I dearly love her company, and just writing this introduction makes me smile.

Along with her engaging and affectionate personality, Amy is also a renowned writer and a fabulous cook. A native of Fort Worth, she discovered her love for both passions at an early age and says this about herself: "I came into this world with a big, adventurous appetite, born to a tequila-loving Texan and a whisk-wielding mama who could bake birthday cakes that made you scream with delight."

Amy wrote her first story in Mrs. Henry's first grade class at Lee Britain Elementary in Irving, Texas, and, according to her, "From that moment on, I was hooked." Fast-forward a few decades and Amy now occupies the desk of editor-in-chief at *Savannah Magazine*, *Savannah Homes*, and *Savannah Weddings*. She has also co-written two nationally acclaimed cookbooks, *The Back in the Day Bakery Cookbook* and *Wiley's Championship Barbeque Cookbook*. Additionally, she teaches Creative Writing at Georgia Southern University.

In terms of cooking, our little girl from the Lone Star State was baking before she even met Mrs. Henry. Amy shared with me that "At the age of four, when all the other kids in the neighborhood were headed off to school, I was despondent. I wanted to go so badly. So Mom told me she would make 'school' for me at home. She taught me how to count, figure up fractions, and measure, and I became the chief cornbread maker for the family. Around the same time, she gave me my first cookbook, Gold Medal Flour's 'My First Cookbook,' which I still have. And I started collecting cookbooks from them on. I have more than 150 now."

Amy had an extremely close relationship with her mother, one that was solidified in the kitchen, starting with those prized pages from Gold Medal. She brings to us a story here about that love, which continued on through the emotional and physical ravages of illness and could shine through in the form of a homemade chicken pie. As Amy says, "You cook as an act of love and healing for one another." How true a statement, particularly for those of us in the South.

I've tried, but I cannot pinpoint exactly when Mom's homemade chicken pot pie became part of our homecoming rituals. The summer of 1996 stands out in my memory. My third year living in Miami was emotionally and professionally draining to the point that I began to question every decision I had ever made, including moving halfway across the country. All I wanted was to come home to Fort Worth, Texas, and have my mom take care of me for a few days. When she asked what I wanted for dinner after I got off the plane—enchiladas or chicken fried steak—I simply sighed and replied, "Can we just stay in?"

And so, every time I returned to her table, a savory chicken pot pie filled with finely chopped carrots and celery and topped with a buttery crust marked our first meal together. She always served it with a crisp iceberg lettuce salad on the side and a pitcher of unsweetened iced tea that had enough lemon squeezed in it to make you wince. For Mom and me, food was our touchstone, our shared language when we disagreed (which was often). The table was our communion.

On the occasions when she would visit me wherever I was living— Miami, New Smyrna, Savannah—I, too, served a chicken pot pie. As I grew more adventurous and confident in the kitchen, I started putting my own spin on it. I added onions and garlic into the vegetable medley. Instead of using a can of condensed cream of chicken soup, I made my own béchamel sauce with chicken stock and bouillon to layer flavors. Sometimes I poached the chicken breasts in white wine and rosemary.

Amy's mom, Barbara Lee Polly, holding a prized chocolate cake she'd baked.

Other times I deboned a roasted chicken. Sometimes I made my own crust from scratch. Each time was a little different. Some of these flourishes she liked. Others not so much.

On the occasion of Mom's seventieth birthday, Aunt Teresa and my cousins Cheryl, Rachel, and Megan all came to celebrate. We shared a periwinkle cottage on Tybee Island, and we made a chocolate cake bathed in ganache and Mom's deep-dish chicken pot pie for the birthday dinner. Mom would have commandeered the kitchen, but she was so frail from chemotherapy she simply sat at the table and sipped an orange soda. Because of the toxic cocktail of carboplatin and Taxol, she had neuropathy and couldn't stand for long. Her steps were unsteady and her hands shook uncontrollably. Her skin was like translucent velum—so easy to tear, bruise, and bleed. But she glowed from the inside and she laughed, mustering just enough energy to mark another year lived.

She had barely eaten anything for the past several months. The chemo had made everything taste like metal. But, after she took her first bite of the chicken pot pie that night, she smiled and nodded her head. "This is good," she said, slowly savoring. "This is good." She ended up eating everything on her plate.

On a Sunday in December eight months later, after my husband and I had returned from her funeral in Fort Worth, I could think of no comfort food I needed more than her chicken pot pie.

Bone tired and bleary from grief, I took my time with every step, somehow finding the patience she always had in the kitchen and that I often lacked. I baked it in the blue-speckled quiche pan that she had given me when I first moved away from home.

When I pulled it out of the oven, a bit of the cream sauce had bubbled over one of the crimped edges, caramelizing the crust. I broke it off and popped it in my mouth. Hot, salty, and tender, it tasted like home.
—Amy Paige Condon

Chicken Pot Pie

INGREDIENTS

1, 9-inch pie crust (your favorite recipe), prepared, chilled, and set aside

4 boneless, skinless chicken breasts, poached in white wine with a bouquet of fresh rosemary and thyme, cubed and then set aside

2 tablespoons unsalted butter

2 tablespoons all-purpose flour or cornstarch

1 tablespoon chicken base, such as Better Than Bouillon Roasted Chicken Base

1½ cup whole milk, heated

1 cup chicken stock, heated

1 teaspoon sea salt

½ teaspoon freshly ground black pepper

2 tablespoons canola oil or other fresh vegetable oil

2 carrots, peeled and finely diced

2 celery stalks, finely diced

1 medium sweet onion, peeled and finely diced

2 garlic cloves, peeled, smashed, and finely diced

1 teaspoon poultry seasoning

Pinch sea salt

Couple of grinds of black pepper

INSTRUCTIONS

1. Preheat the oven to 425 degrees.

2. In a heavy-bottomed saucepan over medium heat, melt the butter and then stir in the flour or cornstarch, chicken base, salt, and pepper. Stir constantly until the flour cooks down and bubbles, but not browns, approximately 2 minutes.

3. Stir in the hot milk and chicken stock, continuing to stir until the sauce thickens, approximately 3-5 minutes.

4. Turn the heat to low, then add the chicken and stir.

5. Place the oil in a skillet on medium-high heat. Add the carrots, celery, and onion, and sauté until the celery and onions are translucent, approximately 5 minutes.

6. Add the garlic and sauté two minutes more. Sprinkle the poultry seasoning, salt, and pepper over the vegetables, and give them another stir.

7. Add the vegetables to the chicken and sauce, then stir until well incorporated.

8. Remove the pan from the heat and pour the pie filling into a pie plate.

9. Roll out the pastry dough over the top, crimp the edges, and cut little holes in the top of the pastry to let air escape.

10. Brush a little fresh cream or an egg wash over the pastry. Set the pie plate on a cookie sheet or a jelly roll pan and place it in the preheated oven. Bake for 25 to 30 minutes, until the crust is browned and the filling is bubbly.

11. Remove the pie from the oven and let cool 5 minutes before serving. Enjoy heartily with a chilled pinot gris.

Serves 6

Notes from Amy: Feel free to use a lightly seasoned rotisserie chicken to save time, if necessary. There's nothing wrong with using prepared cream of chicken soup instead of making your own sauce. Same goes for a refrigerated pastry round. You'll cut lots of time, which will give you more to spend with loved ones.

CHAPTER 33

SMALL HANDS FOR PIMENTO CHEESE

by Damon Lee Fowler

Whenever someone asks me for a how-to guide on Southern food, I direct them to Damon Lee Fowler and his nine critically acclaimed cookbooks, such as *Essentials of Southern Cooking* (Lyons Press, 2013). His works give an instructive and educational—as well as enjoyable and delicious—explanation of our region's cuisine. Damon is not only an excellent cook, mind you, but also quite the authoritarian on Southern food.

We're another set of kindred spirits, and our friendship has gone back several years now in Savannah. Damon grew up in a small town in the upcountry of South Carolina and practiced architecture for more than a decade (having graduated with honors from Clemson University). And while small-town fellows from the Deep South can always find a great deal of fertile common ground to share and discuss—particularly those who enjoy cooking and bourbon—I think our shared professions really helped us click. While Damon worked for years as an architect, I'm a CPA and practiced in the financial world before entering nonprofit management. Both careers require incredible attention to detail and are tightly structured: a number is a number is a number, and a right angle can only be that, a right angle. Those staid traits don't often coincide with a love of entertaining and creativity in the kitchen, but when they do, they result is someone of such ilk as Mr. Fowler (and I hope you think, at least to an extent, JSB!).

And besides being an excellent chef, Damon is also an engaging conversationalist; he can entertain you for hours with stories, anecdotes, and amusing asides that go right along with one of his magnificent dishes. Just read this excerpt from his website, and you can see why I very much wanted him to be a part of *Cook & Tell*!

Southerners love to tell stories, and our favorite stories (aside from the ones about our crazy—er, I mean eccentric—family) always seem to involve food. If there isn't actually food in our mouths, we're talking about it: what we just ate, what we're eating at the moment, and what we plan to eat next. If you understand that, then you are either a Southerner or an Italian, in which case, come on in and we'll swap stories and recipes. If you don't get it, then come on in and have a seat anyway: you need to be educated.

Besides, the only thing a Southerner loves better than eating is having a new audience for our stories.

I know you'll enjoy the lovely passage below that Damon brings us, which is a beautiful example of the intersection of our love of Southern food and storytelling that he just described above.

If my childhood summers could be condensed into a single taste, that taste would be pimento cheese. Not ice cream. Not fried chicken from a picnic basket. Not even a sun-warmed, ripe tomato from the garden. Just that simple and yet sublime duet of cheddar and pimento peppers, held together with just enough mayonnaise to make it spreadable. Making it with my maternal grandmother, whom I knew as "MaMa," is one of my earliest and best culinary memories, and is probably the reason that I associate it so keenly with summer.

At some point in our summer vacation, my brothers and I each got to stay with our grandparents for a blissful two weeks all by ourselves. From the time I could hold a spoon and stir, MaMa and I spent a part of every day of those two weeks in her little sun-filled kitchen, cooking together. So many things that I do in my own kitchen today stir up those memories and bring my grandmother close to me once again—making a big pot of vegetable soup, browning cubed round steak for a country steak in onion gravy, cooking poke sallet and green onions in rendered salt pork fat, stirring up a pound cake.

But for some reason, nothing does it quite so keenly as when I'm making pimento cheese. Maybe it's because my very small hands were just right for working part of the cheese to a paste with the mayonnaise before folding in the rest of it, but it was one of the first things I remember making with MaMa. She would talk me through it long after I no longer needed her guidance, mainly because she talked pretty much without stopping anyway. And to this day, as I begin to knead the cheese and mayonnaise together, I hear her prompting, "Uh-huh, that looks good . . . here, let me put in just a little bit more mayonnaise . . . there!"

Probably everyone thinks his or her grandmother made the best pimento cheese, but MaMa's really had no equal. It was nothing more than a judicious balance of good grated cheese, diced pimentos, and just enough mayonnaise to bind it. She didn't hold with pinches of mustard, grated onion, garlic, Worcestershire, or even hot pepper, because it didn't need any of those things: it was already nearer perfection than most of us see in this life.

Part of that perfection was the cheese, which is where my grandfather came into the picture. He ran a real country store, the kind with dry goods and groceries in the front and aged beef, poultry, pork, and house-made sausage in a sawdust-strewn butcher's shop at the back. He would buy the sharpest cheddar he could lay his hands on, in great cloth-bound wheels packed in wooden crates, and age it in the meat locker for at least another year—two, if he could manage it. Dense, slightly crumbly, and flecked with white protein crystals like a well-aged Parmesan, it was so sharp that it would take the roof off one's mouth. To this day it remains my standard against which all hard cheeses are measured.

It would've been hard for my grandmother to go wrong with cheese like that.

—Damon Lee Fowler

MaMa's Pimento Cheese

Unhappily, I have a hard time finding anything close to my grandfather's cheese, so nowadays I use the sharpest aged Vermont cheddar that I can get my hands on (dyed orange because, I'm sorry: pimento cheese that isn't orange just looks sickly), I add in a little Parmigiano-Reggiano to give it body, a pinch of dry mustard, which reinforces the cheese's flavor, and a touch of cayenne to give it the bite that my grandfather's cheese had. But that's all I add. —DLF

INGREDIENTS

8 ounces (1 small block, about 2 generous cups grated) extra-sharp cheddar

2 ounces (½ cup grated) Parmigiano-Reggiano cheese

5-6 tablespoons mayonnaise, preferably homemade

1, 4-ounce jar diced pimentos (drained but liquid reserved) roughly chopped

Dry mustard powder

Ground cayenne pepper

INSTRUCTIONS

1. Coarsely grate the cheddar through the large holes of a box grater and finely grate the Parmigiano through the finest holes. Set aside a big handful of the cheddar and mix the remainder of the two cheeses together.

2. Put the reserved cheddar in a mixing bowl and gradually knead 4 tablespoons mayonnaise into it until the mixture is creamy and smooth. This can be done in a food processor fitted with a steel blade, but it's not nearly as much fun, and you'll need to be careful not to over-process it or the mayonnaise could break and make the pimento cheese oily.

3. Work the remaining cheese, pimentos, a pinch of dry mustard, a dash of cayenne, and a tablespoon of reserved pimento liquid into the mixture until it is almost smooth but still a bit lumpy. Add mayonnaise by tablespoons until it is just spreadable (it should be very thick and taste of cheese, not mayonnaise). Taste and adjust the mustard and cayenne. Neither one of them should be noticeable, but the cheese flavor should be bright and forward.

4. To make the perfect summer sandwich, spread pimento cheese generously on thick-sliced white, wheat, or rye bread and dig in. When the weather cools, brush a heated grill with butter and grill the sandwich until the bread is toasted golden-brown and the cheese is melted. To dress them up for afternoon tea or reception finger sandwiches, use any thin-sliced bread, trim off the crusts, and cut them on the diagonal into small triangles.

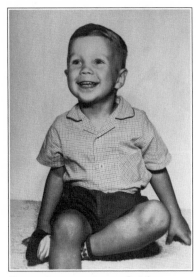

Damon Lee at an age perfect for making pimento cheese

That said, you don't need two slices of bread to enjoy pimento cheese. Put it in a pastry bag fitted with an open star tip and pipe it into 3-inch lengths of washed, dried, and strung celery (or just spoon it in and rake the top with a fork). You could also let it soften to room temperature and serve it as a cocktail or tea spread with crackers or sturdy pita chips. Or simply wait until no one is looking and eat it straight out of the bowl with a spoon.

Makes enough for 5-6 sandwiches or 12 hors' d'oeuvres

CHAPTER 34

(SOME) ACCOUNTANTS JUST WANT TO HAVE FUN

by Carol Cordray

Accountants bear the stereotype of being rather dull, impersonal people who have pen protectors in their pockets and wear ill-fitting suits bought at S&K. They usually aren't the office's first pick, either, to throw the annual Christmas shindig. I know from experience: I'm a CPA. But occasionally some of us go out of our way to prove the universe wrong, and that is the case with my dear buddy, Carol Cordray.

Carol is a native Elberton, Georgia, "The Granite Capital of the World." (More likely than not, the headstone sitting atop your dear sweet Granny's final resting place was quarried near this Northeast Georgia town.) This Elbertonian began her collegiate studies as a Romance Language major at Emory University, a degree befitting a talented cook and elegant hostess. But the Fates sometimes have a peculiar sense of humor, and for whatever reason—and I'm not sure Carol even knows—she ended up as a corporate comptroller instead of an editor at Doubleday.

By day she crunches numbers, pushes pencils, balances multi-company consolidated financial statements, and often terrorizes the millennial staff with threats due to missed deadlines, but in her spare time she is an incomparable cook. One of her favorite standards is Julia Child's classic, *Mastering the Art of French Cooking*—maybe some of that Romance Language training surfaces here? And to be part of one of the spectacular parties she throws in her spacious, 1920s Craftsman-style home in Atlan-

Our friend Carol (right), the accountant who loves to cook and entertain, with friend Gloria Garrett Seymour

ta's Virginia Highlands is a magnificent treat for all the senses. Libations flow freely, laughter and piano music abound, and the buffet is nothing short of extraordinary. One of Carol's close friends gives us this insight: "Carol is the hub and all of her friends are the spokes. The wheel of friendship goes round and round, picking up new friends along the way, making new memories . . . and a lot of those memories are centered on gathering around a table with good friends, good food, and good drink."

We became fast friends many years ago when we began working together at Junior Achievement. Like hers, my personality is rather an anomaly when compared to other CPAs. I have a bawdy sense of humor, love a good whiskey (or two or three), enjoy a fine cigar, and am much more comfortable at a dinner party with a group of interesting souls than sitting behind the semi-permanent walls of a cubicle. Maybe it's because we can run rows of figures on a ten-key adder with the speed of a Tasmanian devil, while not spilling any of our martini on the spreadsheets, that Carol and I get along so tremendously.

Here Ms. Cordray tells a funny story about her first job as an assistant comptroller at a paper mill in a small Alabama town—and her friendship over a cake with one memorable coworker. I know you'll enjoy reading it, and let me tell you, the pound cake recipe is the best you'll ever come across. My mama made the same one, and it turns out dense, moist, sweet, and with a crust that rises up and cracks to look like a layer of golden-brown bark.

It was 1977; I was just out of graduate school when I landed a job as assistant controller in a paper mill in Brewton, Alabama. Brewton was a pretty little town where, as in most small Southern towns, everyone knew everyone, perhaps too well. They followed the whereabouts of each other by where their cars were parked, since everyone knew the make and model of every car in town. There was one fellow, John Paul David, who had four cars, so it was impossible to determine his whereabouts. What single person with three names has four cars? I was not the only one who was curious about that and suspected something nefarious.

The mill was located on the outskirts of the town. At that time, when they were cooking pulpwood and if it was a cloudy day, something we called "snow" would rain down, and if you did not wash your car afterwards, it would eat a hole in the paint of your car. There were some serious chemicals going to work on that wood. The offices were laid out in such a way that the officers had private space along the side of what we called the fish bowl. Everyone who did not work in the mill worked in this huge room with desks crammed together in rows that were eight desks wide, and there must have been about six rows of them. Eunice Morgan sat behind me, and I was crazy about her. She wore glasses that made her eyes seem about five times the size they really were, and she smoked Virginia Slim menthols and wore them as much as she smoked them. A cigarette was always mysteriously attached to her mouth, and it bobbed up and

down as she spewed forth her advice of the day to me: "If you cain't git here on time, come when you can!" Eunice is no longer with us, but I think of her often. Here is the recipe she gave me all those many years ago for the best pound cake ever.
—Carol Cordray

Eunice's Cream Cheese Pound Cake

INGREDIENTS

2 sticks butter, at room temperature

2 sticks margarine, at room temperature

3 cups sugar

8 ounces cream cheese, at room temperature

6 large eggs

3 cups cake flour

1 teaspoon vanilla

INSTRUCTIONS

1. Preheat oven to 325 degrees.
2. With a mixer, cream the butter, margarine, and sugar in a large mixing bowl until well blended.
3. Add the cream cheese and mix until all of it is combined.
4. Add the eggs one at a time, beating after each egg until incorporated.
5. Add the flour in ½ cup batches and mix after each batch until it is incorporated.
6. Add vanilla and mix.
7. Place in a well-greased and floured tube pan and bake for 1½ hours or until a toothpick inserted comes out clean.

Serves 12-16

*　*　*　*　*

With me talking about what a spectacular cook Carol is, I wanted to include a couple of her personal favorite recipes so that you, too, could sample some of her magic. As I mentioned, she creates a number of dishes from Julia's first cookbook. She gave me a vintage copy several years ago, and in it wrote, "Johnathon, I have marked the recipes I know are exceptional for you. Enjoy! Carol!" One of those highlighted in the volume is a dish she has prepared for me in the past: *Supremes de Volaille a Blanc* (Breast of Chicken with Cream). It is one of the most elegant and flavorful chicken dishes you'll ever taste. Serve it over a bed of aromatic rice and alongside some young, sautéed haricots verts or asparagus. You should also have a baguette on the side to finish up any of the velvety smooth cream sauce that might be left on your plate.

Breasts of Chicken with Cream

Note from JSB: When Julia created this recipe, chickens were not grown to the mammoth proportions they are today. So if you compare her original recipe to the one I've adapted here, you'll see that the baking time of the breasts has been increased from a mere 8 minutes to 12 or more. My suggestion is to choose the smallest breast halves you can find, preferably no more than ⅓ pound each.

INGREDIENTS

4 skinless, boneless chicken breasts, about ¼ pound or ⅓ pound each

½ teaspoon lemon juice

½ teaspoon kosher salt, divided

¼ teaspoon ground white pepper

10 tablespoons unsalted butter, divided

2 tablespoons minced shallot

¼ pound sliced fresh mushrooms

¼ teaspoon fresh tarragon, chopped (or ⅛ teaspoon dried)

A round of waxed paper, cut in the diameter of your casserole dish, buttered on one side

¼ cup chicken or beef stock

¼ cup port, Madeira, or dry vermouth

1 cup heavy whipping cream

Kosher salt and black pepper to taste

2 tablespoons fresh minced parsley

INSTRUCTIONS

1. Preheat oven to 400 degrees.

2. Rub the chicken breasts with the lemon juice and sprinkle with ¼ teaspoon of the kosher salt and the white pepper. Set aside.

3. Heat 5 tablespoons of the butter in a large, heavy casserole dish, over medium high, and melt until foaming.

4. Stir in the minced shallots and sauté for a moment; do not brown.

5. Add the mushrooms, stir, and cook lightly for a minute or two. Sprinkle with the remaining salt and the tarragon; stir.

6. Add the chicken breasts to the pan one at a time, turning a couple of times to coat with the butter.

7. Lay the buttered wax paper—butter side down—over the chicken, place the lid on the casserole dish, and place in the preheated oven. After about 12 minutes, remove the pan and press the tops of the chicken to check for doneness. If they are still soft, return them to the oven for another few minutes, or until done—they will be springy to the touch.

8. Remove the chicken from the casserole dish and set aside. Make sure to leave all the mushrooms and sauce in the pan.

9. Place the casserole dish back onto the stove over high to medium-high heat and add the chicken or beef stock, and the port, Madeira, or dry vermouth. Stir, and allow the liquid to cook down until a syrupy consistency.

10. Stir in the cream, and allow to thicken slightly, 2-3 minutes. Taste the sauce, and add any salt or pepper as you feel needed.

11. Place the breasts back in the pan, coat with the sauce, and serve immediately.

12. To serve, place each breast over a helping of rice, cover with the mushroom sauce, and sprinkle with the fresh minced parsley.

Serves 4

* * * * *

This next recipe comes through Carol's sister, Nancy Reynolds. Nancy makes these treats for Carol's famous Christmas party each year, and nary a nut is ever left in the bowls. These spiced nuts are great as a hostess gift as well—make a batch, place them in a decorative container, and get a big hug in return. Trust me, they are divine.

Sweet Curried Cocktail Pecans

INGREDIENTS

1½ teaspoons onion powder
1½ teaspoons garlic powder
1¼ teaspoons kosher salt, divided
¾ teaspoon curry powder
¼ teaspoon cayenne pepper
2 tablespoons unsalted butter
2 tablespoons honey
3 cups pecan halves

INSTRUCTIONS

1. Preheat oven to 250 degrees.

2. Line a baking sheet with aluminum foil (I prefer nonstick varieties).

3. Mix the onion powder, garlic powder, 1 teaspoon of the kosher salt, curry, and cayenne in a small bowl.

4. In a saucepan, melt the butter, honey, and remaining ¼ teaspoon kosher salt over medium-high heat. Add in the pecans, stir to coat, and remove from heat.

5. Add the spices to the pan, and stir gently with a spatula so that all the halves are covered in the honey glaze and spices.

6. Spread the pecans on the lined cookie sheet in one layer.

7. Bake until the nuts are a toasted golden brown, about 40 minutes. Stir once or twice while cooking.

8. Remove from the oven, and allow to completely cool. Gently break apart any pecans that may be stuck together. Store in a covered, airtight container until ready to serve.

Makes approximately 3-plus cups

CHAPTER 35

MY DADDY, MAHLON COOPER GARRETT, SR.

(AND THE ROAST THAT MADE HIS NAME POPULAR)

by Gloria Garrett Seymour

I n the previous chapter you met Carol, the accounting hostess extraordi-
naire. Through her wheels of friendship I've had the pleasure of meeting
Gloria Seymour, who tells her story and provides the recipe for this
chapter.

Though now living in Atlanta, Gloria describes herself as a small-town
girl. She confesses to having had a fleeting ambition to be a singer and stage
personality, but instead led a thirty-year career at corporate AT&T. On the
side, she was able to follow her love of music by directing church choirs—
she is currently in the soprano section of Christ the King, Atlanta—and
singing with the Atlanta Symphony Orchestra.

She learned to cook at the feet of her mama and daddy, whom you'll
read about below. When she was in the sixth grade, she started an enter-
prise of baking and selling pecan pies (her family owned a pecan orchard),
and sold the pies for $1 each. She used the money to buy a new bicycle! She
was also active in 4-H, and says her greatest achievement at Rock Eagle was
winning the state biscuit-making competition. While she can still create a
luscious pecan pie and bake a feather-light, golden-crusted biscuit, she has
ventured into other food cultures as an adult. She particularly enjoys what
she calls American French, a la Barefoot Contessa.

In her warm account below, Gloria takes you back decades to her parents' home in Loganville, Georgia, where her father, the first yoga enthusiast in their small town, taught his daughter how to make one of *the* best beef roasts ever imagined. This dish is so simple but so very, very good. I've made it several times myself, and have actually even substituted a Boston butt for the beef roast. Read on, and prepare to be totally charmed.

Daddy was born in 1903 in the metropolis of Between, Georgia, in Walton County. That's right between Loganville and Monroe on US Route 78. Though he grew up in an agrarian society with his father being a cotton and chicken farmer, Daddy somehow broke out of that mold to become a college graduate from UGA and, after several business attempts, a schoolteacher.

During the Great Depression, Daddy ventured to Miami to find a teaching job. There he met and married Jennie Hortense Whitworth, whom he brought back to Georgia to settle in Loganville and raise a family of three children, me being the last. Hortense (perhaps Mahlon was attracted to the woman with a name as unique as his own) became the sole piano teacher in Loganville and the organist/choir director of the Methodist church. Our little white two-story clapboard house became the studio of budding pianists who later grew to be the church musicians of the community.

Mahlon was always there to support his Hortense in her endeavor of making a musician of every child who walked through the door. By default, Daddy became the family chef since he prepared many suppers as Mama was finishing up piano lessons at 7 p.m. Daddy was a progressive thinker for his time. As an example, he embraced the idea of yoga for exercise. One can imagine the shock a country kid would have as he came to a piano lesson and found a man standing on his head!

During the summer, as in most of the South of the 1950s, Daddy had a summer garden that put mostly okra, tomatoes, corn, cucumbers, and butterbeans on the dinner table (dinner was the middle and biggest meal of the day in my childhood of the fifties). Since my grandfather was a chicken farmer, there was never a Sunday dinner that didn't include fried chicken. Then came the day when Daddy decided to experiment with a recipe from one of the lunchroom ladies at his school. It was a slow-cooked chuck roast. Instead of the quintessential fried chicken on Sunday, the main course became a dish tagged in our family as "Mahlon's Roast." Daddy would put the roast on before Sunday school, and I, who became very popular because of this delicacy, would bring my friends home to devour this melt-in-your mouth beef with an addictive gravy that is spooned over mashed potatoes.

Today I love to share this recipe as well as stories of the unique and much-loved man, my Daddy, Mahlon Cooper Garrett, Sr.

Friends have a hard time remembering how to pronounce "Mahlon," so I remind them to say it with a long "A."

—Gloria Garrett Seymour

Mahlon Cooper Garrett, Sr., with his nephew, Larry King, 1966

Mahlon's Beef Roast

INGREDIENTS

4+ pound boneless chuck roast

½ teaspoon salt

½ teaspoon black pepper

¼ cup A.1. Steak Sauce

One packet dried Lipton's onion soup

One can cream of mushroom soup

½ soup can of water

INSTRUCTIONS

1. Preheat oven to 300 degrees.

2. Salt and pepper the roast on all sides.

3. Smear the A.1. Steak Sauce on all sides of the roast and place it in a large casserole dish.

4. Empty the dried onion soup on top of the meat.

5. Smear the undiluted cream of mushroom soup over the dried soup and meat.

6. Pour the water around the beef in the casserole dish. Cover with a lid.

7. Bake for three hours. The meat should fall apart. Serve the gravy separately to spoon over mashed potatoes. *You can also cook this dish in a crock pot or slow cooker for 6-7 hours or overnight.*

Serves 6-8

CHAPTER 36

THE HIDDEN CAKE

by Lilli Ann Barrett

Some of the blessings in my life include a number of incredible cousins, including the lovely Lilli Ann. She is one of the prettiest and sweetest ladies you'll ever encounter, and if you don't believe me, ask just about anybody who lives in Perry, Georgia; they would readily agree with my assessment. (Now, technically speaking, she is a cousin-in-law, having been married to my late first cousin, Billy. But you know in the South we like to claim kinship in close quarters, so I've always just referred to her as my "cousin.")

Lilli Ann and Billy's sister, my cousin Hellen—another gem in my crown of kin—were close friends growing up together in the tiny hamlet of Clinchfield, Georgia. After Billy and Lilli Ann married in 1956, the bond between the two ladies (now sisters-in-law) continued and grew even stronger over the decades. At any family gathering you can find them talking and laughing together in the corner, thoroughly enjoying each other's friendship and company.

Lilli Ann has written here an episode that gives insight to their close relationship, one that brought a chuckle at a family wake and is still talked about today. It even ended up giving a name to a cake.

Cheers, Lilli Ann and Hellen! I always love being around you, and just love you both, period.

Hellen "the cake hider" (left) with Lilli Ann "the trickster" at a birthday celebration, 1989

I've known my friend and sister-in-law, Hellen, since we were young girls. My mother and father were good friends with Hellen's parents, and we were all so close that I called them "Uncle" Roy and "Aunt" Margaret even though we weren't related. As time moved on, Bill and I fell in love and married, giving me my one of my best friends as a sister.

Over the years we've remained extremely close and spent as much time together as possible. We both had places up in the North Georgia mountains where we would spend summers and the glorious days of fall on Nottely Lake. And one of our favorite pastimes has been antiquing, or "picking" as they call it. You could find us at estate sales all across Georgia, from Blue Ridge down to Savannah. I think the only time we fussed was when we both wanted the same antique and one of us got to it first! We have lots of fun.

And while we are close, we do enjoy "pulling one another's leg" and joking together. One instance was after my mother-in-law (Hellen's mother) passed away in 1994. Everyone came back to our house to celebrate Mrs. Barrett's life and have a meal—as it is the Southern custom to break bread together after a funeral. And as with any wake in our small town, friends and family had brought in a beautiful spread of all kinds of dishes, including one particularly delicious cake. After the cake was about half gone, Hellen made an "executive decision" and told me she was going to hide the remainder so we could eat it after everyone left. (A side note here from JSB: Hellen is lovely but at the same time formidable and strong-willed, and I mean that in the dearest of terms.)

Well, I saw where she put the cake so I decided to play a trick on her. While she wasn't looking, I took the cake from its hiding place and removed it all to another plate except for one tiny sliver.

When Hellen went to retrieve her treasure, you should have seen the look on her face!

"What in the world happened to this cake? Where did it all go?!" She was incredulous. We of course had been waiting for her reaction, and when she saw us all laughing, she knew she'd "been had." And it didn't take her too long to figure out who was the culprit.

And hence the name given since to this favorite, "The Hidden Cake."

As I said, my sister-in-law and I have a very good relationship.

—Lilli Ann Barrett

The Hidden Cake

INGREDIENTS

1 box yellow cake mix

1 stick of butter or margarine, melted

4 large eggs

½ cup chopped pecans

8 ounces cream cheese

1 box powdered sugar

1 teaspoon vanilla

INSTRUCTIONS

1. Preheat oven to 350 degrees.

2. In a large bowl, mix together well the cake mix, melted butter, two eggs, and chopped pecans.

3. Press the mixture into the bottom of a buttered 9"x12" baking dish.

4. In another bowl, beat together the cream cheese, remaining two eggs, powdered sugar, and vanilla.

5. Spread the mixture over the top of the pressed crust in the baking dish.

6. Bake until done, 35-40 minutes. To serve, allow to come to room temperature; slice with a knife, and remove with a cake server or spatula.

Should serve 8 people, but if you have a relative who wants it reserved, or hidden, it will only serve those "in the know."

CHAPTER 37

THE DUCHESS'S REQUEST

by Nancy and Charlie Golson

One of the best and well-known restaurants in the South Carolina and Georgia Low Country is Charlie's L'Etoile Verte, or Charlie's Green Star. Located on Hilton Head Island, this elegant establishment has been helmed by Charlie Golson and his family since 1984. With a French-style country theme, the café brings together classical Continental dishes with some of the area's finest seafood: on the menu you'll find a pâté de maison offered next to a pan of roasted oyster stew, as well as breast of duck with a raspberry demi-glace listed alongside an entrée of grilled cobia that was harvested in the Atlantic that morning. It is one of my favorite dining destinations.

I've had the good fortune to get to know Charlie and his charming wife, Nancy, through our church. Though they live in Bluffton—which many of you know is "a state of mind"—they drive across the Savannah River each Sunday for Mass at St. Paul's Episcopal. And while Monsieur Golson operates a famous restaurant, Madame G owns one of the most interesting and unique stores you'll ever step into. Fittingly named "Eggs 'n' Tricities," the boutique is described by Nancy "brocante rustique and filled with funky junk and other good stuff." People stop by not only to shop and find a must-have treasure but also to gather, chat, and gossip a bit in Old Towne Bluffton.

In the following narrative, Nancy tells us the interesting way L'Etoile Verte came about, and Charlie adds a wonderful culinary tidbit on how he acquired one of his most sought-after recipes.

My husband, Charlie, has had a love of good food his entire life. After graduating from high school in his hometown of Savannah, Georgia, he lived in France for a year and became interested in small family-owned and operated bistros. L'Etoile Verte was one of his favorites of those spots in Paris; the cafe had an enormous menu and he ate there all the time. Following that venture he was able to take yet another year abroad by joining the Peace Corps, where he taught English to French-speaking students in Dakar, Senegal.

After returning to the States and graduating from the University of South Carolina, Charlie became chef at a restaurant called Washington House in Greenville. I was working as an interior designer at a firm next door; well, we met, fell in love, and got married! From there, he was chef at McCready's Club in Charleston and sous chef at the Arlington Hyatt at Key Bridge in Washington.

In the early 1980s, one of Charlie's former bosses told him that he needed to open his own restaurant, and we started to seriously consider the idea. We finally bought a small restaurant just outside Palmetto Dunes in Hilton Head called Bon Vivant, which had been in operation for ten years. Everything clicked and we took over January 1, 1984. Riding in the car one day, trying to think of a new name for the spot, Charlie mentioned his old favorite restaurant, L'Etoile Verte, in Paris. I said, "Let's call it Charlie's L'Etoile Verte," which we both thought was perfect. I then designed our original logo, a copper sauté pan with green stars spilling out, and the rest is history.

Chef Golson presenting desserts at Charlie's L'Etoile Verte.

It was a lot of hard work at first. Our children each learned to work every position in the restaurant, whether it was the kitchen or the front of the house, before they were in high school. Now our daughter Margaret is sommelier and manager—and makes most of our desserts—while son Palmer is in charge of the kitchen. He orders most of the groceries, cleans and butchers the fish, and then cooks them. So Charlie, who so loved those intimate, family-run restaurants in France, has now had his own for over thirty-two years in the South Carolina Low Country.

One of his most popular dishes over the years, one that gets frequent requests from diners, is his Quiche Lorraine. It is an interesting story to hear how he acquired the recipe, as he tells here:

In the early 1970s, Duilio Bigatin came to Savannah and assumed the position of Chef de Cuisine at the Chatham Club. Chef Duilio had grown up in Alsace-Lorraine and was of Italian descent. Before moving to the States, he had worked as a chef in the kitchen of the Grand Duchy of Luxembourg. Fresh out of college, I was delighted and thrilled to serve under a chef who cooked everything out of my personal cookbooks—but without using the books! His first job in our country was in Chicago. During his time there, he would occasionally receive a call from the Duchess when she was visiting the city. Her request was always the same: could he please make a Quiche Lorraine and send it to her hotel? I still make the quiche that he made for her. And my customers just love it.

—Nancy and Charlie Golson

*   *   *   *   *

Charlie has graciously shared with us this classic recipe; it is perfect for brunch, a special luncheon, or a light supper with a salad. I recently made the dish, and I can honestly say it is truly outstanding. So from Luxembourg to Charlie's L'Etoile Verte to your own kitchen, enjoy!

Quiche Lorraine

Note that the pâte brisée needs to chill an hour before using, so you'll need to make this part of the recipe in advance. If you don't care to make your own pastry, purchase a 10-inch deep-dish pie shell instead.

PÂTE BRISÉE

INGREDIENTS

1½ cups all-purpose flour
1 stick of butter cut into ½-inch pieces
3 tablespoons white vegetable shortening such as Crisco
Pinch of salt

INSTRUCTIONS

1. Mix the flour and salt in a bowl.

2. Cut the butter and shortening into the flour with your hands
or pastry tool.

3. Bring the crumbling ingredients together with ⅓ cup of cold ice
water.

4. Mix the ingredients into a ball and chill for one hour.

5. When ready to use, roll the dough out on a floured surface to fit a
10-inch pie pan.

QUICHE LORRAINE FILLING

INGREDIENTS

1 tablespoon butter
1 cup diced onions
1 cup diced leeks, both green and white parts (cleaned and washed first)
1 cup diced lean, raw bacon
1 cup diced cooked ham
1½ cups half and half
4 large eggs, lightly beaten
A pinch of salt and white pepper to taste
2 cups of hand-shredded Swiss cheese, loosely packed

INSTRUCTIONS

1. Preheat the oven to 375 degrees.
2. Melt the butter in a large skillet, and add the onions, leeks, and bacon. Sauté over medium heat for 5-8 minutes or until transparent.
3. Add the ham to the pan, stir, and set aside to cool.
4. In a large bowl, mix together the half and half, eggs, salt, pepper, and cheese.
5. Stir the sautéed vegetables and meat into the egg mixture.
6. Pour the filling into a 10-inch pie pan lined with pâte brisée or your favorite pie crust. Bake in preheated oven for 45 minutes or until golden and firm.

Serves 4–6 for a main course, or 8 for an appetizer portion

* * * * *

One of the most meaningful compliments my cooking ever received came from Charlie. I mean, even if he just smiled when he took a bite of one of my dishes, I would've been proud. But one Sunday at a church dinner, I brought in a salad—one of my favorites with a light but flavorful lemon-infused dressing. A few minutes into the meal, I overheard Charlie, who was sitting at another table, ask someone, "Who made this salad? It's delicious."

And, since this quiche needs a salad, and Charlie has sampled my recipe, I figured it would be appropriate to include in this chapter.

Mixed Greens with a Lemon Herb Dressing

INGREDIENTS

2 teaspoons very fine lemon zest

2 tablespoons fresh lemon juice

1 teaspoon finely minced fresh thyme

1 teaspoon finely minced shallots

½ teaspoon Dijon mustard

¼ teaspoon sugar

½ cup good, light oil (I don't recommend EVOO here—too strong)

12 cups lightly packed fresh greens, such as watercress, baby arugula, and Boston, green leaf, and butter lettuces

¼ teaspoon salt

Dash or two of black pepper

INSTRUCTIONS

1. Mix zest, juice, thyme, shallot, mustard, and sugar very well together.

2. Slowly whisk in the oil.

3. Sprinkle the greens with the salt and black pepper, and toss to coat.

4. Drizzle dressing over the seasoned greens and toss. Serve immediately.

Serves 8

CHAPTER 38

BISCUITS STRAIGHT FROM HEAVEN

by Meredith Bishop Stiff

W hen you hear the family name "Fincher" in the state of Georgia, one thing comes to mind: barbeque. Some of my fondest food memories from childhood come from their curbside service, where metal trays loaded with smoked meat, Brunswick stew, and sweet tea were attached to the windowsill of your car. Fincher's Barbeque has been in business in Macon since 1935, and was started by the grandmother of my friend Meredith Bishop Stiff, who shares with us some of her heartfelt memories of "Grammy" in the following story.

Meredith is a native of Macon and a graduate of Stratford Academy. On a tangent, I have to mention that two other writers in *Cook & Tell* are Stratford grads: Debra Brook and Nancy Fullbright. It seems that the academy has graduated some wonderful writers and excellent cooks! Meredith now lives in Augusta and is known throughout the region for her work as a nonprofit executive and community champion. She has served on numerous boards of directors and lent her time and talent to a long list of notable causes.

This loving granddaughter is also a prolific writer, and one who fully realizes the many gifts she has received in life from her family and loved ones, as you'll read here shortly.

This morning, just before 8:00 am, the doorbell rang. A very special friend delivered a surprise package that I will never forget. My morning was transformed from ordinary to extraordinary.

Still in my mismatched PJs and disheveled hair, I was greeted by my immaculately dressed and groomed friend with her radiant smile. (Don't you wonder how other women pull that off?) Linda gave me a hug and handed me a package before dashing off to start her day.

A friend's hug lasts longer than the hug itself. Linda's love lifted me in the morning and carried me through the day as I grieved the one-year anniversary of Grammy's death. I opened the bright green-colored bag to find a dozen perfectly round and delectable homemade biscuits she had baked for me that morning.

Linda has gotten to know my Grammy (Mary Lou Hulett Fincher) through my writing. While she never met my grandmother in person, she knows her all the same. Writing about people we love keeps them with us and introduces them to others. Grammy lived to be nearly ninety-six years old; she went to heaven on February 21 last year. A part of me went with her.

The biscuits were delicious. They were divine. They came straight from heaven through Linda's kitchen. They marked the first anniversary of Grammy's arrival into heaven. Linda remembered.

When a grandmother goes to heaven, she leaves wisdom behind. Those biscuits reminded me of one dose of wisdom Grammy gave me a couple of weeks before she died. On that particular morning, when I served her breakfast, she remarked, "These biscuits are delicious. Almost as good as my Aunt Suzie's. Did you make 'em?" I said, "No. I am not proficient at biscuit making. Got them at WifeSavers." Grammy said, "Well I swanny. Poor ole Jim. Every good wife needs to be able to make good biscuits. Remember the way to a man's heart is through his stomach."

Grammy warmed thousands of stomachs and hearts in her decades of cooking. In fact, she worked at her restaurant, Fincher's Barbecue, until she was eighty-three. I wonder what it was like to close that door and turn the key for the last time. I can still taste her barbecue and Brunswick stew. Proceeds from the sale of those two delicacies sent my mama, Grammy's only child, and me, Grammy's only grandchild, to college at Emory University. Mama was the first to attend college in the Fincher family.

Grammy standing at the front window of Fincher's, retiring after 58 years of serving some of the South's best BBQ.

Now that you know I am the only child of an only child, you can add my husband to your prayer list. He's a Yankee, yet he has delivered quite well on the occasions of my hissy fits. I bet I could really cash in my heart's desire on a silver platter if I mastered biscuit making. Jim says Yankee girls do not throw hissy fits. I'd say that puts them at quite a disadvantage. Bless their hearts. Grammy said we are all created equal, but special skills indigenous to the South, like hissy fits (and biscuit making), pay off. Grammy often remarked that my Jim is the nicest Yankee she ever met. She also thought Jim to be the nicest Catholic too, just like the one other Catholic family she knew that lived next door to me growing up. The Morans.

One night Grammy said she was hungry at 11:30 p.m., just after the hospice nurse left. We were sitting hand in hand in the side-by-side recliners. I bought them just before Grammy came home to live with us from the hospital. Grammy said, "Sure would love some grits with a scrambled egg mixed in, and a biscuit with some syrup and sausage." I said, "I am glad to cook that, but that's breakfast food, and it's almost midnight." (Grammy had been getting her days and nights mixed up.) Grammy said, "Meredith, breakfast is the most important meal. Important things should be enjoyed at any hour." I cooked and fed my wise and sweet Grammy her special-order breakfast at midnight. I will try to remember that the important things in life don't need confining to a specific hour or day.

Goodwill Industries proudly chose to honor my Grammy by posting this quote in its Helms Culinary College, the first in the history of Goodwills worldwide: "Over 90 years of cooking, I learned that one can reach a person's heart through his stomach." She was proud of that new college. A few months before she died, Grammy toured the campus with Goodwill's president, my husband Jim.

My little girl, Mary Margaret, is named after Grammy. She turns three at the end of March. She clearly remembers eating biscuits with Grammy. I cried this morning when she asked, "Mama, will you pour a little syrup on my 'Grammy biscuits'?" I didn't have to tell her that our biscuits came from heaven through Linda's kitchen. She just knew.

My Grammy's love lives on. Love is eternal like that. Today it came through a friend who has mastered the art of making biscuits. And love is the primary ingredient in that recipe.

Mama says my Papa, Grammy's husband, made them best without a roller or a cutter. She says Papa just rolled them right up in the palm of his hand, and they melted in your mouth. Mama says I called them "baskets" when I was young. Maybe because I couldn't speak clearly yet or because they were served in a special brown basket that Grammy gave me before she died.

I put the leftover biscuits in that basket when Mary Margaret and I finished breakfast. We saved some for Jim. Grammy would have wanted him to have some too. "Every good wife needs to be able to make good biscuits." Grammy is right. My husband deserves that.

I am going to learn to make biscuits. —Meredith Bishop Stiff

* * * * *

Here is my friend Linda's recipe for her incredible biscuits. She tells me that she never uses a fork or pasty knife to mix the dough but rather uses her hands with a light touch. Linda also provided an additional instruction (or confession, whichever way you choose to read it): "The secret is the baker needs to make these with love in her heart. I'm not joking—the one and only time I begrudgingly made biscuits, they turned out hard as rocks." —MBS

Linda's Buttermilk Biscuits

INGREDIENTS

2 cups self-rising flour

¼ cup Crisco shortening

¾ cup whole milk buttermilk (the colder the better)

INSTRUCTIONS

1. Preheat oven to 400 degrees.

2. Lightly grease a baking sheet or cast-iron skillet.

3. In a large mixing bowl, sift in the flour.

4. Add the Crisco to the flour, and mix in the shortening until the flour looks like coarse cornmeal (very small pellets).

5. Pour into the bowl ½ cup of the buttermilk and gently mix until it becomes a thick dough; gradually add the remaining buttermilk. The dough will be sticky, but that is okay.

6. Turn out onto a floured work surface and knead lightly about three times.

7. Form into a round disc and either flatten with a rolling pin or your hands to a thickness of about 1½ inches.

8. Using a floured 2-inch or 3-inch biscuit cutter, cut biscuits. Place on pan with biscuits slightly touching (very important). Lightly pat the tops with additional buttermilk.

9. Bake until lightly brown on top, 12-15 minutes.

10. Serve immediately.

Makes about 12 medium-sized biscuits

* * * * *

Speaking of biscuits and grandmothers, my mom left to me her mother's cast-iron flat griddle, one with a handle. It is more than 100 years old, and so seasoned it shines like a piece of black marble. If I had a dime for every biscuit made on that griddle I'd be rich enough to "have cotton in Augusta," as the saying goes.

And while I love a hot buttered biscuit slathered with cane syrup, or split and filled with a big helping of pear preserves, one of my favorite accompaniments is Mama's sawmill gravy, which was rich and luscious. Her secret? A dose of strong coffee added into the mix.

According to lore, this Southern specialty gets its name from logging camps in Appalachia. The specks of black pepper and bits of sausage supposedly looked like the sawdust that resulted from cutting the logs. The gravy was served to the workers as an inexpensive way to give them a filling and hearty meal. When preparing the dish below, note that you may have to add some butter to the pan to get the full 4 tablespoons of fat needed to make the gravy properly. The sausage you buy today, particularly from really good sources, contains much less fat than what was common in years past.

Sawmill Gravy

The gravy can be made a day ahead if needed—just cover tightly in a container and refrigerate. Reheat over low flame until hot.

INGREDIENTS

¼ pound good-quality breakfast sausage, made into 4 thin patties

4 tablespoons sausage fat renderings, and butter if needed

4 tablespoons flour

2 cups whole milk

¼ cup very strong coffee or espresso

¼ teaspoon finely ground black pepper

Dash of salt, or to taste

INSTRUCTIONS

1. Heat an iron skillet or other pan with deep sides over medium-high heat; add sausages.

2. Cook sausages through, browning well on both sides. When done, remove pan from heat.

3. Transfer sausages to a bowl, and coarsely chop or crumble into small, gravel-sized pieces.

4. Place your skillet back on stove over medium heat; if you do not have 4 tablespoons of fat in the pan, add some butter to make up the difference.

5. Add flour and make a roux, whisking; cook for 2-3 minutes until the flour starts to brown.

6. Add the crumbled sausage to the pan and stir to mix.

7. Whisk in milk, making certain the flour does not stick to the bottom of the pan. Allow to simmer and thicken several minutes, stirring often.

8. Stir in the coffee, add black pepper, and salt to taste. Serve hot

Makes about 2½ cups

CHAPTER 39

MY FIRST LOVE
AND OYSTER STEW

by JSB

Hands down, the briny taste of an oyster is one of my favorite delicacies. I've sampled these jewels of the sea sitting along the cold, frigid waters of the Damariscotta River in Maine and while in the opulent dining palaces of Old New Orleans. And living in the Low Country—where oyster roasts are a form of social and cultural artwork—I've eaten so many there should be enough shells left behind to pave a road from my home in Savannah up to Charleston.

But when oysters are mentioned, it is neither memories of faraway trips nor entertaining hours spent at landmark, seasonal gatherings that come to mind. Rather, visions from decades ago arise: a skinny, tow-headed boy and his first love—a stray puppy named Hobo.

The time was early fall 1968, and I was about to turn five years old. With frost on the ground each morning, it was unseasonably cold for that part of October. My father had been on a hunting trip in rural Middle Georgia on one of those chilly days, and when his truck pulled into the drive as he returned home, I rushed to meet him at the back door.

In his arms were two hunting bags. One held a dozen or so plump, gray-feathered doves that my mom would later cook in a cast-iron skillet. Inside the other was a ball of black and white fur with a pink tongue, its paws hanging outside the flaps.

"Look what I found for you, Buddy," he said as he came through the back porch screen door. He carefully lifted the pup out of the camouflage and placed him at my feet. I was thrilled to the point of being speechless.

Mama had joined us, and I heard Daddy explain that he was down by the old Bailey place on his way home and spotted the little dog on the side of the dirt road. He could tell, even from the truck, that it was shivering. What other choice did he have but to stop and pick it up? And, after all, Buddy needed a dog.

By then the dog was cuddled up on my lap as I sat on the porch floor. One of her eyes—one that she would soon lose—was closed shut with an infection. But other than that ailment, and being a bit tired and underfed, she seemed to be in good shape as she ducked her head and snuggled closer.

While Daddy left for the store to buy some dog food, Mama decided that the pup needed to eat sooner rather than later. It was a Sunday night, and on the family menu were a pot of oyster stew and a platter of freshly made hoecakes. My mom's parents had, at one time, owned a seafood market in the tiny town of Ochlocknee, Georgia, just north of the Florida border. She inherited from them a love of things from the sea, and whenever available, some salt-water dish was on the Barrett table.

She took a small slice of her flour hoecake, which is a skillet-fried version of a biscuit, and crumbled it into an old crockery dish. She then ladled up some of the stew from the stove and poured the warm milk, butter, and oyster juice on top.

Hobo—a name we later bestowed on her because of her wandering alone in the country—ate every last bit and was gifted with another small helping. And as the years progressed, whenever we had oyster stew at home, it was a tradition to put out a bowl for our smallest family member.

The two of us were inseparable until I left for college. She was with us for almost seventeen years, and never have I encountered a sweeter dog, or one with such a loving disposition, or, for that matter, one who so enjoyed a bowl of oyster stew. It seems her first meal with us was always her favorite.

How I loved that dog, and I cherish those sweet memories of her, and of oyster stew.

So of course I have to include for you my mom's oyster stew recipe and the one for her hoecakes. Mama was not one to complicate dishes; in her

JSB, Hobo, and a neighborhood friend, summer 1969

stew you will taste the brine of the oysters and the sweetness of the butter, milk, and cream. Some folks start their stew with a white roux, but Mama did not use one and neither do I—roux makes the liquid so thick it takes away from the delicate texture of the oysters.

We enjoy this dish often during the holidays served with a glass of a dry champagne. It is excellent as a light supper after Midnight Mass or as a starter course for a New Year's Eve celebration. But then again, it is also perfect for any cold winter's night, maybe a specially cooked pot for just you and your dog to share.

Joyce's Oyster Stew

INGREDIENTS

1 stick (8 tablespoons) butter, divided

¼ cup very finely diced celery

¼ cup plus 1 tablespoon (5 tablespoons) finely chopped green onion, white parts only

1 quart of oysters, drained, with the liquid reserved

1 quart whole milk

2 cups heavy cream

¼ teaspoon kosher or sea salt (or to taste)

¼ teaspoon white or black pepper

½ teaspoon Texas Pete hot sauce

Paprika and chopped parsley for garnish

INSTRUCTIONS

1. In a large pot, melt 4 tablespoons (half the stick) of butter over medium heat.

2. Add the celery and cook for 1 to 2 minutes, stirring constantly. Be careful not to let the butter brown.

3. Stir in the onions and cook another 2 minutes or so, until the celery is soft.

4. Add the remaining butter and pour in 1½ cups to 2 cups of the reserved oyster juice. Stir to mix, continuing on medium heat.

5. Add the milk and cream. Stir or whisk to mix well, and allow the liquid and vegetables to come just under a slight simmer. Reduce the heat to medium low. Allow the stew to cook for about 12-15 minutes—the tastes will marry and the liquid will thicken. Stir often.

6. Taste the stew at this point to see how much salt it will need. Because different oysters and their juices are brinier than others, you may not need ¼ teaspoon of salt, or you may need more. Adjust to your taste.

7. Add the black or white pepper and the Texas Pete. Stir.

8. Finally, add the oysters, and stir to mix. The oysters will cook quickly and, depending on size, the smaller varieties, like the Bluffton oyster, will be done much more quickly than the larger ones you find from New England or Washington State. For the small oysters the cooking

time will be only 2 minutes or so. The larger ones may take up to 4 minutes. The oysters are done when their outside edges begin to curl and "wave." Important note here: Do not let the delicate oysters overcook. Once overdone, they lose their wonderful, soft consistency and become rubbery. And remember, the oysters will continue to cook even as you ladle them into your bowls.

9. Serve immediately. Garnish each bowl with a sprinkle of paprika and freshly minced parsley.

Serves 6 to 8 as a main course.

* * * * *

These hoecakes are not the sweet, fried varieties you find at some "Southern" restaurants. Our family's recipe is basically a stovetop version of homemade biscuits. They are delicious at breakfast with a dollop of honey, cane syrup, or jelly. And they are a perfect accompaniment for oyster stew or fried fish. And with country ham. Well, the list could just go on and on!

Note again that these are not fried and do not call for any butter or oil during cooking. So make sure the griddle or skillet you use is either very well seasoned or a nonstick variety.

Ninnie's Hoecakes

INGREDIENTS

2 cups self-rising flour, sifted with a pinch of salt

2 tablespoons butter, sliced into ½-inch pieces

3 tablespoons Crisco or shortening

⅔ cup whole buttermilk

Additional butter for topping

INSTRUCTIONS

1. Place the flour and salt in a mixing bowl with the butter and shortening. With your hands, or a fork, mix the ingredients together until thoroughly incorporated. The mixture should now be in sizes of pea gravel.

2. Drizzle the buttermilk over the bowl, and stir together with a large fork until just mixed.

3. With a spatula, scrape out the dough onto a well-floured flat surface. Knead two or three times, and then form into a ball.

4. To make the hoecakes, you can either roll the dough out to about ½-inch thickness and cut with a biscuit cutter, or, as Ninnie and Mama would do, pinch off a scant ¼ cup of the dough and flatten it in the palm of your hand to the size of a small disc. Set these aside.

5. Heat your seasoned griddle, pan, or skillet (or nonstick cookware) over medium heat. When it's good and hot, set the hoecakes on top. Don't allow them to touch one another. Cook on each side 3 to 4 minutes until a dark golden brown, turning once. Depending on the size of your pan, you may need to cook these in two batches.

6. Remove them from the pan to a platter, and place a teaspoon or so of butter on top of each hoecake. Serve immediately.

Makes 8 to 12 hoecakes

CHAPTER 40

MAKING MERRY
WITH MARY KAY ANDREWS

by JSB

From my mom and her baby sister, my Aunt Beatrice, I inherited a love of books; both of these ladies could read a novel in a day with time to spare. Since childhood, I've had a special fondness for stories set in the South and have always liked mysteries as well. So when discovering Mary Kay Andrews and her Callahan Garrity series in the 1990s, I became besotted with her novels, particularly Callahan's feisty Southern mama, Miss Edna (who reminded me of my own spirited mother), the nearly blind and close-to-deaf duo Baby and Sister, and the mobile-home livin' Neva Jean. With titles to enchant audiences, such as *To Live and Die in Dixie, Every Crooked Nannie*, and, one of my favorites, *Strange Brew* (part of which took place in my old stomping ground of Middle Georgia), I eagerly awaited each new addition. So imagine my absolute delight and excitement to find out that we had a mutual friend, one who belonged to my small Savannah Supper Club, and Mary Kay was coming to dinner!

Mary Kay joined our group and fit right in with our pack of food-loving, cocktail-consuming, novel-reading, and opinionated politicos as if she'd known us from kindergarten days. Contacts made that night flourished, but we would have never guessed that our dinner group would be prominently featured in her next book, *Savannah Blues*. My fifteen minutes of fame came as a main character: the handsome (ahem), Kennedy-esque

Mary Kay Andrews, front center, at a dinner given by Ardsley Park Supper Club. Right, going up the stairs include Barbara Hubbard, Tom White, Carter Hubbard, Cathy Belford, Anne Rockwell, Brooks Stillwell, JSB, and Carolyn Stillwell. The event took place in the Stillwell home.

assistant DA was named in my honor, and a particular scene in the book—a dinner with our very own Ardsley Park Supper Club—took center stage in one of the chapters. I refer you to page 147 of the novel for your reading pleasure, as the house description was, well, mine.

Mary Kay has gone on to pen several *New York Times* best sellers besides *Savannah Blues,* and introduced audiences to even more funny, engaging, and adventurous characters that have you turning page after enjoyable page, such as in *Beach Town, Summer Rental,* and *Itty Bitty Lies.*

Besides being a phenomenal writer and storyteller, MKA is also a fabulous cook, and I've asked her to share one of her recipes with us. Her husband, Tom, also very much knows his way around the kitchen, and an invitation to one of their stellar parties is highly coveted. She and Tom were even so gracious as to throw the Atlanta launch party for my first book. Their historic Avondale Estates home in Atlanta was decked out to the nines, complete with open bar and a buffet that they cooked themselves, and all with recipes that came from *Rise & Shine!*

I also have to share that Mary Kay has a heart the size of Atlanta and is one of the most thoughtful people I've ever met. Over the years, she had signed many books for my mother, who was a big fan and owned copies of all MKA's works. When Mama passed away, Mary Kay was writing a new novel, *Ladies Night*, and, unbeknownst to me, she added a character in the book named Joyce Barrett. A friend called me one afternoon soon after the book's publication and said, "Your mom sure is entertaining in Mary Kay Andrews's new book!" (Which, by the way, was true to form.) I was totally taken by surprise. It also made me a little teary-eyed. What a truly lovely and oh-so-wonderful gesture. To know Mary Kay is to love her. That gift was one of the most special I've ever received, and it speaks volumes about this fantastic lady. (And I have to thank her, too, for the lovely foreword for this book!)

Here is one of her favorite go-to recipes, a luscious and rich macaroni and cheese dish that is perfect as a side for a meatloaf or platter of fried chicken. I've used this recipe several times now, and it is always a hit.

Old School Mac N' Cheese

Note from Mary Kay: This is the one dish of mine that everybody in the family asks for. It's what I send to a new mom, a grieving friend, or a neighbor too busy to cook. Buy good, extra-sharp cheddar cheese, what my ninety-one-year-old friend Nanny calls rat cheese. And shred it yourself. Make a double batch and freeze one in a disposable aluminum pan. Or, while you're grating all that cheese, go ahead and whip up a bowl of pimento cheese—another great make 'n' take.

INGREDIENTS

1 pound macaroni or pasta of your choice

1 pound extra sharp hand-grated cheddar cheese, divided

5 tablespoons butter, divided

3 tablespoons flour

1½ cups whole milk, heated until just hot

½ teaspoon salt

½ teaspoon ground mustard

½ teaspoon ground black pepper

1 cup bread crumbs or cracker crumbs

INSTRUCTIONS

1. Preheat oven to 350 degrees.

2. Cook macaroni in salted water according to package directions. Drain well and set aside.

3. Over medium heat, melt 3 tablespoons of the butter in heavy-bottom pot.

4. Whisk in the flour and mix thoroughly.

5. Pour in the heated milk, stirring constantly until you have a medium-thick white sauce. You can add more milk if the sauce gets too thick, but remember to stir it in well.

6. Add the salt, pepper, and dry mustard. Stir to mix.

7. Set half a cup of the cheese aside for topping, but add the remaining cheese to white sauce and stir over medium heat until melted.

8. Add the cooked and drained pasta to the cheese sauce, and mix well.

9. Pour the pasta and cheese sauce into greased casserole dish.

10. In a separate bowl or plastic bag, mix the crumbs and the remaining 2 tablespoons of melted butter until thoroughly incorporated. Spread the buttered crumbs over the macaroni, and scatter the remaining ½ cup cheese on top.

11. Bake until top is golden brown—about 30 minutes.

Serves 6-8

Cook & Tell took a year to compile, and when finished, I thought to myself, "Really, this could just be a beginning." For the 40-plus stories and almost 100 recipes in the book, there are thousands more out there waiting to be shared.

And it is hard to describe the immense contentment and joy I received from this project. It was wonderful to awaken the memories and hear the stories from all the folks I've encountered. Inevitably, too, one story would lead to another, and to another, and before long what started as a brief chat turned into a two-hour visit, complete with an offer of a glass of iced tea or a libation from the bar. People freely shared with me some of their most cherished memories of food, family, and friends, and it was a true honor to be so entrusted.

As the book comes to a close, I hope you'll be inspired to take pen to paper and capture some of your best recollections that come to mind. Write what you feel, what you remember, and why that recipe, or those dishes, meant something special to you and your family. I think every person who contributed to Cook & Tell would relate that by doing so, you will create a great gift not only for yourself but for your loved ones as well.

With warmest of regards,
JSB

Appetizers and First Courses

Breads

Desserts

Entrees & Main Courses

Jams, Jellies, Pickles, & Relishes

Salads & Dressings

Sauces & Gravies

Vegetables & Side Dishes

ACKNOWLEDGMENTS

First, my utmost appreciation to Gayle Morris for coming up with the title of *Cook & Tell*. It works perfectly. (And I'll always, always remember that chicken pot pie!)

Thanks to my partner of twenty-eight years, Tom, for his patience as I scattered the house from room to room with papers, photographs, and clippings for the last year. He ignored the piles I made, smiled, and kept encouraging me along. Too, I need to thank him for serving as chief taste-tester, pot-washer, and sous chef. Much love, TEW!

An enormous amount of gratitude to my best friend, Alphus (Chris) Spears, who "pre-edited" each of my narratives and the stories in *Cook & Tell*. Your help, like your friendship, is invaluable.

Additional thanks to my mentors, Janis Owens and Joyce Dixon, who gave me the guidance and support so that my first book, *Rise & Shine!* came to fruition—and so planted the seeds for this publication at hand. If it weren't for the two of you, I doubt I would have ever made it to press. Love to you both.

For Mercer University Press: you humble me with this opportunity to again write under your name. I've never worked with a finer group of people. Thank you.

And finally, to all of the folks who contributed to *Cook & Tell*: thank you a million times over for sharing your personal stories, recollections, and recipes. I have had an incredible time working with each of you, and am honored that you entrusted me in such a way. And I know, through your generosity, that you'll be encouraging readers near and far to sit down and put their own stories into the written word. I hope that makes you smile.